THE LITTLE BOOK OF
SHAKESPEARE

CONTRIBUTORS

STANLEY WELLS, CONSULTANT EDITOR

Stanley Wells, CBE, FRSL, Honorary President of The
Shakespeare Birthplace Trust, is Professor Emeritus
of Shakespeare Studies of the University of Birmingham,
Honorary Governor Emeritus of the Royal Shakespeare
Company, and an Honorary Fellow of Balliol College Oxford.
He is general editor of the Oxford and Penguin editions
of Shakespeare and co-editor of *The Oxford Companion
to Shakespeare*. His books include *Shakespeare for All
Time*, *Shakespeare, Sex, and Love*, and *Great
Shakespeare Actors*.

ANJNA CHOUHAN

Anjna Chouhan is Lecturer in Shakespeare Studies at
the Shakespeare Birthplace Trust. She has published
articles on Victorian theatre, farce, and religious stage
props, and edited a sourcebook on the Victorian actor-
manager Henry Irving. She spoke on the BBC programme
Great British Rail Journeys about Shakespeare in the 19th
century. She contributes to the Cambridge School
Shakespeare digital resource.

GILLIAN DAY

Dr Gillian Day lectures at the Shakespeare Birthplace
Trust and York University. She has taught English and
Drama in Britain, North America, and Scandinavia, and
held visiting lectureships at the universities of Helsinki
and Düsseldorf. Her publications include *King Richard III*
in the Arden *Shakespeare at Stratford* series (as editor),
and the introduction to *Henry VI Part III* and the
performance history of *Richard III* in editions of the plays
for Penguin Shakespeare.

JOHN FARNDON

John Farndon is a Royal Literary Fellow at Anglia Ruskin
University in Cambridge and an author, playwright,
composer, and poet. He has written many international
bestsellers such as *Do You Think You're Clever?* and
translated into English verse the plays of Lope de Vega
and the poetry of Alexander Pushkin. He taught the history
of drama at the Actor's Studio, studied playwriting at
Central School of Speech and Drama, and is now Assessor
for new plays for London's OffWestEnd Theatre Awards.

JANE KINGSLEY-SMITH

Jane Kingsley-Smith is a Reader at Roehampton University,
London. She has written two monographs – *Shakespeare's
Drama of Exile* and *Cupid in Early Modern Literature and
Culture* – and most recently edited for Penguin John
Webster's *The Duchess of Malfi* and *The White Devil*, and
John Ford's *The Broken Heart* and *'Tis Pity She's a Whore*.
She is a regular lecturer at Shakespeare's Globe, London.

NICK WALTON

Nick Walton is Shakespeare Courses Development
Manager at the Shakespeare Birthplace Trust in Stratford-
upon-Avon, and serves as Executive Secretary to the
International Shakespeare Association. He has written
introductory material for the Penguin editions of *Timon
of Athens* and *Love's Labour's Lost*, and is co-author of
The Shakespeare Wallbook. He has worked closely with
professional theatre companies at home and abroad, and
has been a guest speaker at the British Museum and the
National Theatre.

CONTENTS

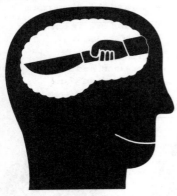
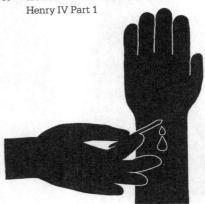

THE KING'S MAN
1603–1613

INTRODU

Born more than four and a half centuries ago, William Shakespeare (1564–1616) is generally acknowledged to be the greatest imaginative writer in the English language. He was a major poet, writing two narrative poems, 154 sonnets, and other verses. But above all, he was a poetic dramatist, the author or part-author of almost 40 plays, which range from the most delicate of romantic comedies, such as *A Midsummer Night's Dream, As You Like It, and Twelfth Night*, through a series of plays about English and Roman history, to the most profound tragedies, including *Hamlet, Macbeth, and King Lear*.

Far from dwindling with the passage of time, Shakespeare's reputation and influence have grown from year to year. His works, in their original texts, in translation into most of the world's languages, and in an enormous range of adaptations, are read, taught, and performed all over the globe. They have influenced countless other works of art, and nobody with a claim to a liberal education can afford to be ignorant of them. This book offers a comprehensive guide to his plays and poems, concentrating on their content and form, while also considering their reception and influence.

Shakespeare and Stratford

William Shakespeare was baptized in Holy Trinity Church in the town of Stratford-upon-Avon, England, on Wednesday 26 April 1564. His exact date of birth is not known, but since the 18th century his birthday has been celebrated on 23 April.

Shakespeare's father, John, came from farming stock and worked in Stratford as a "whitawer" – a tanner of white leather – and glover (glove maker). John's wife, Mary, whose maiden name was Arden, came from a more prosperous background. They lived in the house in Henley Street, Stratford, now known as Shakespeare's Birthplace, a place of pilgrimage for hundreds of thousands of visitors from all parts of the world every year. They had two daughters who died in infancy before William came along, and went on to have two more daughters and three more sons. The youngest, Edmund, was 16 years younger than William. Like his older brother, Edmund became an actor in London. Very little is known about him except that he died, aged only 27, a few months after the death in infancy of his illegitimate son.

John Shakespeare was a businessman who played a major part in civic life, becoming an alderman and rising to the rank of bailiff or mayor in 1568. At this time, churchgoing was required by law. Both at church and at home, Shakespeare would have gained the familiarity with the Bible, the Book of Common Prayer, and the Books of Homilies (sermons) that is apparent from his writings.

Stratford was a market town with a splendid church, a well-established grammar school where education for boys (only) was free, fine houses, and townsmen who were educated and wealthy. The records for the school are lost, but Shakespeare's writings show that he had a typical grammar-school education of the period. Such schools

...CTION

provided a rigorous training in oratory, rhetoric, and classical literature comparable to that of university graduates studying Classics today. From an early age, the boys were required to write and speak in Latin. In a scene (4.1) in *The Merry Wives of Windsor*, a boy called William is put through his paces in Latin grammar, and quotes from a textbook prescribed for use in every such school. It is surely the most autobiographical scene in all Shakespeare's plays.

Marriage and children

As a boy, Shakespeare would have been able to attend and act in plays in Stratford. Touring professional companies regularly visited the town during his boyhood and youth, playing in the guildhall, while local amateurs put on entertainments, especially at Whitsuntide.

Shakespeare probably left school when he was about 15. We don't know what he did for a living at first, but he may have helped in his father's workshop. When he was only 18, towards the end of 1582, he married Anne Hathaway. She was 26. A daughter, Susanna, was baptized six months later. Twins, Hamnet and Judith, followed in late January or early February 1585. Hamnet died and was buried in Stratford on 11 August 1596. The location of his grave is unknown.

William and Anne had no more children. Except for a passing mention in a law case of 1587, there is a gap in the record of Shakespeare's life from the birth of the twins to 1592 (when he is first credited as a writer). The best guess is that at some point

> 66 Articles are borrowed
> of the pronoun, and
> be thus declined.
> *Singulariter nominativo:*
> *'hic, haec, hoc'.*
> **William**
> **The Merry Wives**
> **of Windsor** 99

he joined a theatre company – perhaps even one of those that visited Stratford – as actor or writer or both. His wife and children appear to have stayed in Stratford.

In 1596, the College of Heralds granted Shakespeare a coat of arms, bestowing on him and his descendants the status of gentleman and the right to be termed "Master". His father died in 1601, presumably at more than 70 years old, and was buried in Stratford. In 1602, Shakespeare spent the great sum of £320 for the purchase of 107 acres of land in Old Stratford. In 1605, he was wealthy enough to pay £440 for an interest in the Stratford tithes, entitling him to a share in the area's farming income, which would have brought him an annual income of around £40. In London, he lived only in modest lodgings. His daughter Susanna married the physician John Hall in 1607; their only child, Elizabeth, was born nine months later. Judith married a vintner named Thomas Quiney, with whom she had »

three children, all of whom died young. Elizabeth Hall died in 1670, and was Shakespeare's last descendant.

Shakespeare's first texts

The first reference to Shakespeare as a writer comes from 1592, by which time he was well established on the London theatrical scene. In 1593, his name appears in print for the first time, not as a dramatist but as the author of the narrative poem *Venus and Adonis*. His second narrative poem, *The Rape of Lucrece*, appeared in the following year. These poems were exceptionally successful, and were reprinted more frequently than any of Shakespeare's plays. In part, this is because plays were written primarily to be acted, so many never reached print. In 1594, *Titus Andronicus* was the first of Shakespeare's plays to be printed, but it seems certain that he must have written a number of other plays before then.

In 1595, he is named along with two actors – Richard Burbage and Will Kemp – as having been paid for performances during the previous Christmas season at the court of Queen Elizabeth I by a company of players formed late the previous year under

the patronage of the Lord Chamberlain, Lord Hunsdon. From now on, he was the resident playwright of the most important theatre company in the land. No other playwright of the period had so long and stable a relationship with a single company. Shakespeare was also an actor and a "sharer" – a businessman with a financial interest in the company's success. Plays were normally the property of the acting company for which they were written, rather than of their author. There was, however, a reading public for dramatic texts, and about half of Shakespeare's plays were printed in his lifetime. These, along with the missing texts, were assembled by his colleagues after he died and published as the *First Folio* in 1623.

The theatrical scene

Shakespeare grew up during a period of increasing stability and prosperity in England. Queen Elizabeth I was unifying the nation, and patriotic sentiment was growing. The arts of music, painting, architecture, and literature were flourishing. Great works of classical and continental, especially Italian, literature were appearing in translation and finding a wide readership. Many of these were to provide Shakespeare with inspiration and with plot material for his plays.

Both English dramatic literature and the theatrical profession developed greatly during the early years of Shakespeare's working life. A major development came in 1576 with the construction of the first successful professional playhouse, called simply the Theatre, in London. A new

 What win I if I gain the thing I seek? A dream, a breath, a froth of fleeting joy. **The Rape of Lucrece**

> 66 Can this cock-pit hold
> The vasty fields of France?
> Or may we cram Within this
> wooden O the very casques That
> did affright the air at Agincourt?
> **Chorus**
> Henry V 99

generation of dramatic writers emerged, including playwrights such as John Lyly and George Peele, with whom Shakespeare was to collaborate on *Titus Andronicus*. Figures from the later 1580s, such as Thomas Kyd, Robert Greene, and above all Christopher Marlowe, author of plays including the two-part drama *Tamburlaine*, *Dr Faustus*, *The Jew of Malta*, and *Edward II*, were all to influence Shakespeare. Growth in the size of acting companies and in the popularity of theatrical entertainment encouraged the writing of longer and more ambitious plays, interweaving plot with subplot, tragedy with comedy, and diversifying with songs, dances, masques, and spectacular effects made possible by the increasing sophistication of theatrical design.

Theatrical performances

Theatres of the time were three-storeyed buildings with open roofs and uncurtained platform stages that thrust forwards into the auditorium. Performances were given during daylight hours. At the back of the stage were doors from which the actors entered, and behind them the tiring house, or dressing room. There was an upper acting level that could represent a balcony or the walls of a city. A canopy over the stage held machinery to allow the descent of gods. There was no scenery. Musicians had their own space. The audience stood at ground level, or occupied the tiers of seating built into the walls. In London today, at Shakespeare's Globe on Bankside, there is a reconstruction of the Globe Theatre, originally built in 1599, for which many of Shakespeare's plays were written. In 1609, the company started to use a more exclusive indoor theatre, the Blackfriars, which had more elaborate stage machinery. These new possibilities are reflected in the stage effects required by, for instance, *Cymbeline* and *The Tempest*. Indoor theatres were lit by candles, and as the candles required frequent trimming to keep them alight, playwrights began to divide their plays more clearly into five acts. The Sam Wanamaker Playhouse at Shakespeare's Globe is an indoor stage that gives an impression of this kind of theatre. The actors who first performed Shakespeare's plays were skilled professionals, required by law to be organized into companies under the patronage of a high-ranking person – such as a nobleman, or even the Queen herself. A typical company was made up of 12 or 14 men, who could be supplemented by extras, known as hired men. Some of Shakespeare's plays require no more than the standard number of actors, but in »

others the same actor would have had to play two or even three roles in the same performance. All female roles were played by boys – no professional female actors appeared on the English stage before 1660. This explains the relatively small number of female parts in each play: for instance, only two in *Julius Caesar* – Portia and Calpurnia – and the same number in *Hamlet* – Ophelia and Gertrude.

Music and special effects

Music played an important part in performances, as is evident from the number of songs and dances in the plays. Actors would sometimes have accompanied their songs on lutes, and a band of playhouse musicians supplied incidental music. Ceremonial entries of royal persons and great warriors would be heralded by fanfares and drum rolls. Thunder could be imitated by the use of a thunder run – cannon balls rolled down a wooden trough – and it was even possible to imitate lightning by the use of special stage effects.

Theatres were closed during the 40-day religious observance of Lent, and companies frequently went on tour in the English provinces. As there were no custom-built playhouses outside London, they had to play in improvized settings such as inn yards, the halls of great houses, guildhalls, and even occasionally in churches. Facilities would be limited, so play texts were adapted to suit the constraints of the new venues.

A wealth of plays

Shakespeare was an extremely versatile playwright, constantly experimenting with new styles of drama and developing his range of subject matter and the depth of understanding of character throughout his career. His first plays include the light comedies *The Two Gentlemen of Verona* and *The Taming of the Shrew*, the bloody tragedy of *Titus Andronicus,* and four plays, also more or less tragic in form, based on English history – three on the reign of Henry VI and a follow-up about Richard III. All these were written before the founding of the Lord Chamberlain's Men, in 1594. The end of that year saw a performance of his brilliantly plotted Comedy of Errors, in which he interweaves a tale of mistaken identity derived from Roman comedy with the romantic tale of a family parted but eventually reunited.

A successful playwright

As a shareholder in the Lord Chamberlain's Men from 1594, and no longer needing to work in collaboration with other playwrights, Shakespeare had more independence to write what he wanted, but clearly felt he had to provide his colleagues with plays written in a variety of styles, keeping up an average of roughly two a year.

During the next five years or so, he wrote a dazzling series of romantic comedies – *Love's Labour's Lost, A Midsummer Night's Dream, The Merchant of Venice, Much Ado About Nothing*, and *As You Like It*, along with more plays about English history –

> 66 Life's but a walking
> shadow, a poor player
> That struts and frets his hour upon the
> stage, And then is heard no more.
> **Macbeth**
> Macbeth 99

Richard II and *King John*, both in tragic form, the two parts of *Henry IV*, which feature his greatest comic character, Sir John Falstaff, and their triumphant sequel *Henry V*, as well as the romantic tragedy of *Romeo and Juliet*, the somewhat unromantic comedy *The Merry Wives of Windsor*, which also has Falstaff at its centre, and the Roman tragedy *Julius Caesar*.

His company acquired a new theatre, the Globe, in 1599. For this playhouse, he wrote the last two of his romantic comedies, *As You Like It* and *Twelfth Night*. This is the period, too, of his greatest success to date, the tragedy of *Hamlet*. After this, his plays become darker in tone. They include the highly original, bitter tragicomedy *Troilus and Cressida*, and two other plays – *Measure for Measure* and *All's Well that Ends Well* – which, though comic in form raise serious moral concerns. In this period, he also wrote the profound tragedies *Othello*, *Macbeth*, and *King Lear*. On the death of the Queen, in 1603, his company became the King's Men.

Collaborators and rivals

Around 1606, for reasons unknown, Shakespeare returned to his former practice of collaborating with other playwrights. Thomas Middleton who, along with Ben Jonson, had emerged as his most serious rival, worked with him on *Timon of Athens*, but the only text of this play that has come down to us is incomplete. A new departure in dramatic style comes with *Pericles*, written with the minor playwright George Wilkins, a tragicomic narrative that foreshadows the later, singly authored *Cymbeline*, *The Winter's Tale, and The Tempest*.

During this phase of his career, he wrote two highly contrasting tragedies of ancient Rome, the austere *Coriolanus* and the flamboyant *Antony and Cleopatra*, and, with John Fletcher, some fifteen years his junior, a now lost play, *Cardenio*, *The Two Noble Kinsmen*, and the play known in its time as *All is True* but printed in the First Folio as *Henry VIII*. During an early performance of *All is True* in 1613, the firing of a stage cannon set the thatch of the Globe playhouse on fire, burning it to the ground. Shakespeare's career as a playwright ended with the destruction of the playhouse that had seen some of his greatest successes.

In the last three years of his life, Shakespeare wrote little or nothing. He died in April 1616, leaving most of his property to Susanna, and £150 to his younger daughter Judith. Among other bequests he left 26s and 8d »

each to three colleagues in his acting company, the King's Men – Richard Burbage, Henry Condell, and John Heminges – to buy mourning rings, a common practice of the time.

What makes him great?

Why is it that Shakespeare, a long-dead author of plays conceived for playhouses very different from those of the present day, written in an increasingly archaic language, employing unrealistic dramatic conventions, and telling stories that are often remote from the daily experience of his audiences, should be celebrated both in English-speaking countries and elsewhere as an author of enduring significance?

Part of the answer is that he was a master of both prose and verse. He could construct powerful pieces of rhetoric, such as Mark Antony's speech to the Roman citizens in the Forum in *Julius Caesar*, and the king's address to his troops before the battle of Agincourt in *Henry V*. He could write beautiful passages of lyrical verse, such as the love scenes of *Romeo and Juliet* and the exquisite speeches of Oberon and Titania in *A Midsummer Night's Dream*. He could write speeches that are both witty and comic, such as those that Lance addresses to his dog Crab, in *The Two Gentlemen of Verona*, or those of Bottom and his colleagues in *A Midsummer Night's Dream*.

He could write with powerful simplicity, piercing our hearts with simple statements such as Leontes's "O, she's warm!" in *The*

Winter's Tale, or Prospero's "Tis new to thee" in response to Miranda's "O brave new world, / That has such people in it" in *The Tempest*, or the largely monosyllabic reunion of King Lear and Cordelia.

Memorable characters

Shakespeare could also tell gripping stories. The overall design of the plays drives the plots forwards – and sometimes there are complex stories with more than one plot, as in *Hamlet* or *King Lear*. He builds tension in individual scenes, such as the trial scene in *The Merchant of Venice* and the banquet scene in *Macbeth*, with great dramatic effectiveness.

He gives us a strong sense of individual character, making us believe in the reality of the people in his plays, often by making them speak in individual ways – such as the Nurse in *Romeo and*

> 66 This is the excellent foppery of the world: that, when we are sick in fortune – often the surfeits of own behaviour – we make guilty of our disasters the sun, the moon, and the stars
> **Edmond**
> **King Lear** 99

Juliet, or Shylock in *The Merchant of Venice* – sometimes by making them behave in a manner that is at once unexpected but credible.

Crucially, he is not judgmental or moralistic. Even the characters who behave badly, such as Paroles in *All's Well That Ends Well*, (perhaps above all) Falstaff in the *Henry IV* plays, or a villainous murderer such as Macbeth, can make us feel what they feel rather than pass judgment on their sins.

His plays provide a wealth of complex and theatrically effective roles, which offer rich and demanding opportunities to actors. Tragic roles such as Hamlet and King Lear, Lady Macbeth and Cleopatra, heroic ones such as Henry V and Coriolanus, wittily comic roles such as Benedict and Beatrice in *Much Ado About Nothing*, and broadly comic ones such as Bottom in *A Midsummer Night's Dream*, all provide actors with exceptional opportunities to demonstrate their skills.

Stories for all times

Many of the stories that he tells, such as in *King Lear* or *The Tempest*, have a quality of myth or legend that enables people of later ages to relate to them easily. Some plays, such as the history plays and *Julius Caesar*, also have a political dimension that can easily seem relevant to issues of modern times.

To speak of Shakespeare as the world's greatest dramatist is inadequate. It would be closer to the mark to speak of him as a philosopher, a psychologist, or a poet possessed of the artistry that enables him to express his perceptions in dramatic form, and in so doing render them with unique subtlety and communicative power.

Structure of this book

This book offers a section on each of Shakespeare's plays, giving information about their major themes, a concise description of their principal characters, a breakdown of the action arranged by act and scene, and a full synopsis of their plots. This is followed by information about each play's reputation and impact over the ages. There are also informative sections on Shakespeare's narrative poems, *Venus and Adonis* and *The Rape of Lucrece*, on his sonnets, and on his other two poems, *A Lover's Complaint* and *The Phoenix and the Turtle*. The exact order in which Shakespeare wrote his works is uncertain. In this book, we follow both the text and the chronology of the *Complete Oxford Shakespeare*, General Editors Stanley Wells and Gary Taylor, first published in 1986. It was reissued in 2005 with the addition of *Edward III*, which by that time was generally agreed to have been written at least partly by Shakespeare, and the full text of *Sir Thomas More*, a play that survives only in manuscript, and to which Shakespeare appears to have contributed at least one fine scene. ■

THE FREEL
WRITER
1589–1594

The young William Shakespeare probably arrived in London in the late 1580s. We do not know exactly when, however. After the birth of his twins in early 1585, no more is heard of him for seven years.

Some believe he spent these years as a school teacher; others that he travelled to Italy, although there is no real evidence for this. One theory is that he lived with a Catholic family in Lancashire, where he developed Catholic sympathies that he had to keep secret ever after to avoid running foul of England's Protestant regime.

Provincial upstart

All we can really be sure of is that he was living in London and writing plays by 1590 or so. We know this because he was clearly ruffling feathers among the university-educated literary dramatists used to ruling the roost in the capital until he came along. One of these dramatists was Robert Greene (1558–92), who, in 1592, as he lay dying in poverty, wrote bitterly in a pamphlet: "for there is an upstart Crow, beautified with our feathers, that with his Tyger's hart wrapt in a Players hyde, supposes he is as well able to bombast out a blanke verse

as the best of you: and…is in his owne conceit the onely Shake-scene in a countrey." The phrase "Tyger's hart wrapt in a Player's hyde" is a parody of a line from *Henry VI Part 3*. So it would seem that by this point Shakespeare was already well known, yet still sufficiently new on the scene for Greene to call him an "upstart".

Exciting times

London in the late 1580s was an exciting time to be a playwright. It was the fastest-growing city in Europe, a bustling metropolis rivalled in size only by Paris and Naples. It was a young city – most of the population was under the age of 30 – and the theatre scene was booming. Beyond the city walls, in the lively, squalid city fringes, new theatres were beginning to attract large audiences. James Burbage had opened the Theatre in Shoreditch in 1576, and his rival Philip Henslowe had opened the Curtain Theatre nearby in 1577.

It is speculated that Shakespeare may have started his career with one of these companies as an actor, and he may have started writing plays soon after. His earliest surviving works, *The Two Gentleman of Verona* and *The Taming of* the Shrew, date from about 1590. He may even have written for several companies at the same time.

The Armada effect

These were dangerous times, too. The wounds caused by Henry VIII's break from Catholic Church were still raw, and Catholic sympathizers everywhere were constantly watched by government spies.

In 1587, the long-imprisoned Catholic Mary Queen of Scots was executed after being implicated in a plot to kill her cousin, Queen Elizabeth I. In response, Philip II of Spain sent the 140-ship Armada, the "greatest fleet that ever swam upon the sea". Philip, who had been married to Elizabeth's Catholic sister, Mary I, aimed to invade England, depose the "heretic" Elizabeth, and restore the Catholic faith. Remarkably, the smaller, more manoeuvrable English fleet, with the aid of tides and storms, routed the vast Armada. And though this was a crushing blow for Catholic hopes, there was probably hardly anyone in England, Protestant or Catholic, who did not feel a glow of pride at this unlikely triumph. It secured Elizabeth's reign and sent a wave of patriotic feeling

through the country, which Shakespeare rode, writing so successfully about England's history over the following years with his raft of history plays.

He made his mark quickly, and by 1592 already had half a dozen popular successes, including his first series of plays about the Wars of the Roses: the Henry VI plays and Richard III, and Titus Andronicus.

Plague and poetry

Then, disaster struck. A major outbreak of plague ravaged London. To impede the spread of the epidemic, the theatres were closed from June 1592 to May 1594, and theatre companies banished from the city. Some went on tour, but it is not known what Shakespeare did. He probably used this time to turn his hand to poetry: in April 1593, his great poem Venus and Adonis was published. It proved to be the biggest literary success of his life, far outselling any of his plays and going through many reprints. A second poem, The Rape of Lucrece, came out the following year. He may also have been writing plays. Perhaps anticipating a hunger for entertainment with the reopening of the theatres, his next two works were comedies. ■

IN LOVE WHO RESPECTS FRIEND?

THE TWO GENTLEMEN OF VERONA (1589–1591)

Valentine prepares to leave for the Duke of Milan's court to complete his education as a gentleman. Proteus refuses to go with him because of his love for Julia. Valentine deplores the effects of love upon his friend.

Julia discusses her suitors with her maid, Lucetta. Lucetta singles out Proteus for admiration, but Julia observes that he has made no suit to her. When Speed delivers a letter from Proteus, Julia pretends that she doesn't want to read it, and tears it up. In private, she pieces the letter together and admits her love.

Proteus is celebrating Julia's confession of love in a further letter, when his father announces that he must join Valentine. Proteus says goodbye to Julia. They exchange rings, and he vows to be faithful to her. Lance gives a comic account of his leave-taking in which only the dog, Crab, remained dry-eyed.

At the court of Milan, Valentine has changed his attitude to love, having become infatuated with Silvia, the Duke's daughter, who is intended for the wealthy Thurio. Proteus arrives at court and is instantly enamoured of Silvia, too. Valentine reveals he and Silvia are betrothed and plan to elope. Proteus betrays this plot to Silvia's father, who tricks Valentine into revealing the rope ladder and letter, hidden in his cloak. The Duke banishes Valentine from Milan.

Proteus offers to help Thurio by praising him in front of Silvia and slandering Valentine. As he sings beneath her window, he is overheard by Julia, who has come in search of her lover, disguised as the page boy Sebastian. Proteus takes her into his employment and sends her to woo Silvia, giving her a letter and a ring (the one Julia gave him). Silvia sends Proteus a portrait of herself, but refuses to read his letter and tears it up. Julia's account of Proteus's betrayal of his first love makes Silvia cry.

Silvia enlists the help of Eglamour, a knight who has taken a vow of chastity after his true love died. They meet at Friar Patrick's cell after confession and make their way towards Mantua, where Silvia believes Valentine to be living.

In the forest, Proteus rescues Silvia from the outlaws who have captured her. Silvia still refuses Proteus's love, and he is about to rape her, but Valentine intervenes. Proteus is immediately contrite. Valentine pities him and renounces all his affection for Silvia. Julia returns to Proteus the ring she had forgotten to deliver. Proteus recognizes it as one he gave Julia and becomes suspicious. Julia reveals who she is, and Proteus remembers his love for her. Thurio relinquishes his claim to Silvia and the Duke agrees that Valentine shall marry her. The outlaws are repealed from exile and the couples prepare for a double wedding. ∎

IN CONTEXT

THEMES
Friendship, love, lust, ambition, change, betrayal, sacrifice

SETTING
Verona, the court of Milan, a forest near Mantua

SOURCES
1531 The Proteus–Valentine plot echoes the story of *Titus and Gisippus* from Boccaccio's *Decameron*. Shakespeare may have read this in Sir Thomas Elyot's *The Governor* (1531).

1542 Jorge de Montemayor's prose romance *Diana* (1542, translated into English in 1598) may have provided the plot for Julia in male disguise sent to woo her lover's new mistress. (This could also have come from a lost play *Felix and Felismena* (1585).

For a romantic comedy, *The Two Gentlemen of Verona* is surprisingly negative about the experience of love. Passion is seen to inhibit the development of young men, who should be fighting in wars, studying at university, or travelling abroad. Not only does it stall their intellectual development, it is imagined as being physically destructive: "As the most forward bud / Is eaten by the canker ere it blow, / Even so by love the young and tender wit / Is turned to folly, blasting in the bud" (1.1.45–48).

Valentine may well be reliant on "writers" for this opinion – having never experienced love himself – but when he does fall for Silvia, his behaviour only reinforces the point. His wit is so enfeebled that he does not realize that Silvia is declaring her affections for him when she asks him to write love poetry on her behalf.

Throughout the play, characters describe themselves as being "metamorphosed" by love. Julia puts on male attire and makes a dangerous journey to follow her beloved Proteus. Valentine changes his clothing and behaviour for those of the stereotypical lover. Although Speed's account of this is largely comic, his acknowledgement that "when I look on you I can hardly think you my master" »

A 2012 Shona production related the play's themes of exile and deception to life in contemporary Zimbabwe. All 15 characters were played by one pair of actors.

> What should it be that
> he respects in her
> But I can make
> respective in myself,
> If this fond love were
> not a blinded god?
> **Julia**
> Act 4, Scene 4

(2.1.29–30) reflects the deeper anxieties that surrounded male erotic desire in Shakespeare's time, where to love was to be rendered effeminate. But Proteus's transformation is the most serious. In classical mythology, Proteus was a sea god who could change his shape at will. However, Shakespeare's character has little control over his shape-shifting, which causes him to betray his vows to Julia, and destroy his friendship with Valentine.

Friendship versus love

Shakespeare's times placed great value on male-male friendship, imagining it a pure and ennobling love, without the turbulence of lust. It was thought to enable friends to perfect themselves through the mirror they provided to one another: "true friends should be two in body, but one in minde, / As it were one transformed into another", said Richard Edwardes in his 1564 play *Damon and Pythias*. Given that friends were meant to share the same judgment, taste, and appetite, and to hold all things in common, it is no surprise that Proteus should desire Valentine's beloved. One theory that *The Two Gentlemen of Verona* has been used to illustrate is that we are taught what to admire by other people – encouraged to see with their eyes. It is what Proteus does next that is a breach against the friendship code, when he betrays Valentine in order to steal his mistress, insisting that "I to myself am dearer than a friend" (2.6.23).

Furthermore, in Shakespeare's most notorious addition to the drama, Proteus threatens to rape Silvia. His immediate confession and penitence when interrupted by Valentine can hardly atone for the crime he was about to perpetrate, or the betrayals that have brought him to this point. And yet, Valentine immediately forgives him and, renouncing all ties to Silvia, offers her to Proteus. Proteus seems invigorated by lust, and his betrayal of their friendship might imply that he has escaped the confines of the friendship narrative, even if Valentine has not.

The place of women

Shakespeare's rape threat has also proven controversial because of the way in which it undermines the play's women. The male characters insist that women say "no" when they mean yes; their characters are soft, as if moulded out of wax. Yet it is the men who are fickle, while Julia and Silvia remain attached to their first loves. As Proteus asserts: "O heaven, were man / But constant, he were perfect" (5.4.109–110). Silvia's fate is finally decided by Valentine, Thurio, and her father, without her uttering a word, and the likelihood of Julia's happiness with the ever-changing, would-be rapist Proteus is not meant to trouble us. The friendship theme gains the upper hand, with Valentine's anticipation of "One feast, one house, one mutual happiness" (5.4.171) invoking less the terms of the marriage service (man and wife becoming "one flesh") than the image of male friends as "one in mind".

While Shakespeare would return to many of the themes and motifs of this play, he would never again risk subordinating romantic love to friendship in this way. ∎

> It is the lesser blot,
> modesty finds,
> Women to change
> their shapes than men
> their minds.
> **Julia**
> Act 5, Scene 4

I KNOW NOW HOW TO TAME A SHREW

THE TAMING OF THE SHREW (1590–1594)

A drunken tinker called Christopher Sly argues with the hostess of an alehouse and is thrown out. A passing Lord and his servants trick him into believing that he is a lord, and invite him to watch a play. The play is set in Italy and begins with Lucentio and his servant Tranio arriving in Padua. They overhear Baptista Minola explaining to Hortensio and Gremio, suitors to his daughter Bianca, that they cannot marry her until a husband is found for Katherine, his eldest daughter. Lucentio also falls in love with Bianca, and plans to beat the other suitors for her hand in marriage. He decides to don a disguise and offer his services as her tutor, and instructs his servant, Tranio, to impersonate him.

Hortensio's friend Petruccio arrives in Padua and declares his intention to marry a woman with a large dowry. Hortensio suggests Katherine Minola and Petruccio determines to woo, win, and wed her, despite her shrewish reputation.

Petruccio comes to woo Katherine and presents Licio (Hortensio in disguise) as a music master for the sisters; Hortensio will attempt to woo Bianca, while Petruccio secures his marriage to her sister. Gremio enlists Lucentio (disguised as Cambio) to woo on his behalf, while Tranio, already disguised as Lucentio, continues to woo Bianca for his master.

After a lively exchange of words with Katherine, Petruccio confirms his intention to marry her, and a date is set for the wedding. The wedding party is kept waiting due to Petruccio's late arrival, but when he appears, his clothing does not befit the occasion. Petruccio then declares that he and his wife will not attend the wedding dinner, but return to his home immediately. Petruccio denies his wife food and sleep in an attempt to tame her shrewish behaviour.

Having revealed his true identity, Lucentio wins Bianca's heart, leaving Hortensio to marry a widow. Lacking funds, Lucentio and Tranio convince a merchant to imitate Lucentio's father, Vincentio. All is well until Lucentio's real father arrives, and is bemused to meet the impostor. The confusion is explained by Lucentio. As Katherine and Petruccio return to Padua for a banquet, Katherine obeys Petruccio's commands.

Petruccio wagers that his wife will prove more obedient than both Lucentio and Hortensio's wives. When the men call for their wives to attend them, only Katherine appears; Petruccio wins the wager. Katherine speaks forcefully to the other women about what is expected of a good wife, and about the nature of the relationship between husband and wife. The guests are left surprised by Katherine's transformation. ∎

IN CONTEXT

THEMES
Love, marriage, power, fathers, daughters, money, status, men, women

SETTING
Warwickshire, England, Padua, Italy

SOURCES
10th century Christopher Sly's story shares similarities with a tale from *The Arabian Nights*, while the tale of the shrewish woman takes its inspiration from ballads and folk stories of the period.

1566 The plot involving Bianca, Lucentio, Hortensio, and Gremio is based on George Gascoigne's comedy *Supposes*.

Some critics may wish that Shakespeare had never written *The Taming of the Shrew*. There are actresses today who would not want to be cast as Katherine, and theatre reviewers who would prefer to see the play disappear from the stage. Others, however, would include the play in their list of favourite Shakespearean comedies, and identify Katherine as one of the playwright's most memorable early creations.

In his presentation of the "taming" of a "shrew" Shakespeare gave voice to a variety of attitudes towards women and marriage that were common to his times. Such attitudes are more likely to offend than entertain contemporary audiences, but they reflect the playwright's engagement with the period in which he was living. At this time a woman could be described as "shrewish" if she openly disagreed with a man or seemed bad tempered. The very title of Shakespeare's play promised drama and extreme behaviour. It also promised a battle of the sexes.

The property of men
Women are often spoken about in this play as commodities, owned by men. Katherine's first utterance is one of disgust at hearing the way in which her father speaks of her to Gremio and Hortensio, underlining her father's financial interest in her marital status. Financial gain is the first thing that occurs to Petruccio when he accepts the challenge of wooing Katherine: "I come to

Sexual tension or brutal bullying? Productions have reflected the sexual politics of their time. Franco Zeffirelli's film of 1967 starred husband and wife Elizabeth Taylor and Richard Burton.

wive it wealthily in Padua; / If wealthily, then happily in Padua." (1.2.74–75). Love does not enter his thoughts, though he clearly has sex in mind: "For I will board her though she chide as loud / As thunder when the clouds in autumn crack." (1.2.94–95). It is clear that Katherine, who is thought of by the men as a "fiend of hell" (1.1.88) will be turned into a "gentler, milder mould" (1.1.60). The question remains whether the transformation will be consensual.

Taming tactics

Shakespeare has Petruccio rehearse his "taming" strategy through soliloquy before meeting Katherine: "Say that she rail, why then I'll tell her plain / She sings as sweetly as a nightingale. / Say that she frown, I'll say she looks as clear / As morning roses newly washed with dew. / Say she be mute and will not speak a word, / Then I'll commend her volubility, / And say she uttereth piercing eloquence." (2.1.170–176). Without recourse to this soliloquy, Petruccio's behaviour would seem eccentric and insensitive. While this soliloquy does not excuse his conduct (including withholding food and denying sleep), it serves to emphasize that he is donning a role to achieve a desired result.

As the couple make their way to the banquet at the close, Petruccio's "reign" (4.1.174) over Katherine is apparent. He has essentially talked her (or in some productions, beaten her) into submission. He treats her, in his own words, like a falcon (4.1.176), shaping her appetites to suit his will. Petruccio's treatment of Katherine is ruthless. It contrasts strongly with the farcical romantic sub-plot in which Bianca is besieged by starry-eyed suitors. Petruccio does not seem interested in having the love as well as the obedience of his wife. Katherine is bewildered by his behaviour and angered that "He does it under name of perfect love" (4.3.12).

At the close of the play Katherine performs the role of Petruccio's "perfect wife", appearing at his command and echoing his words in her final speech to the women at the banquet: "Thy husband is thy lord, thy life, thy keeper, / Thy head, thy sovereign, one that cares for thee, / And for thy maintenance commits his body / To painful labour both by sea and land, / … / And craves no other tribute at thy hands / But love, fair looks, and true obedience, / Too little payment for so great a debt." (5.2.151–159).

Whether or not the play ends in joy is open to interpretation. There have been productions where Kates and Petruccios have left the stage arm in arm into a happy future together; but there have also been those left staring at one another in stony silence. ∎

Shrewish women

In the 16th century a woman had to do little more than challenge a man's opinion to be termed a "shrew". She might be labelled "shrewish" if she spoke too much, or appeared mean spirited or sexually promiscuous.

There were many ballads and folk tales about unruly wives that Shakespeare could have based his presentation of Katherine around. Here is a verse of a ballad called *The Cruel Shrew*: "She never lins her brawling, / Her tongue it is so loud; / But always she'll be railing, / And will not be controlled. / For she the breeches still will wear, / Although it breeds my strife. / If I were now a bachelor, / I'd never have a wife."

Punishments in the 16th century for being thought "shrewish" were brutal. Women could be forced to wear a horrific metal device called a scold's bridle. This fit over the woman's head and pushed a metal plate into her mouth to hold down her tongue. Having silenced his wife, a husband could tie a rope around her neck and parade her in front of his neighbours.

THE COMMONS, LIKE AN ANGRY HIVE OF BEES THAT WANT THEIR LEADER, SCATTER UP AND DOWN
HENRY VI PART 2 (1590–1591)

Young King Henry VI is overjoyed as Suffolk hands the beautiful Margaret of Anjou to him to be his queen. Lord Protector Gloucester, and Warwick, are appalled at the political cost – the return of Anjou and Maine to France. York reveals that he aims to take the crown himself. Gloucester's wife Eleanor dreams that he should be king. Margaret and her lover Suffolk determine to bring down Gloucester by setting a trap for his wife. Eleanor is seen consulting with witches who prophesy the king's overthrow. She is arrested.

While he is out hawking with the queen at St Albans, Henry receives news of the arrest of Gloucester's wife. Gloucester resigns as Protector. York reveals his claim to the throne to Salisbury and his son Warwick who pledge allegiance. Gloucester is distressed when Eleanor is banished.

In Parliament, Margaret and Suffolk denounce Gloucester, but Henry defends him feebly. England's territories in France have been lost, while York and Suffolk order the arrest of Gloucester. Henry is upset, but Margaret, York, and the Cardinal agree that Suffolk should have Gloucester murdered. York is sent to Ireland to quell a rebellion and, given an army, he sees his chance. When Henry hears of Gloucester's death, he is distraught and turns against Suffolk. Warwick shows Gloucester's body to prove he was murdered and accuses Suffolk. Despite Margaret's pleas, Henry banishes Suffolk. Margaret and Suffolk part sadly.

> **❝** Can we outrun the heavens?
> **King Henry**
> Act 5, Scene 4 **❞**

After a sea battle, Suffolk is beheaded and his head sent to Margaret. Jack Cade, encouraged by York, begins a peasant's rebellion, killing Stafford and others. The rebels head to London, where Margaret cradles Suffolk's head. The rebels are persuaded to disperse. Cade hides but is killed. York has landed in England in force, demanding the arrest of Somerset.

York reaches London intent on claiming the throne. Buckingham and the King assure him that Somerset is in the Tower, but Margaret arrives with Somerset. York explodes and tells Henry that his rule is over. As Salisbury and Warwick switch allegiance to York, war begins. At St Albans, York kills Clifford and his son Richard kills Somerset. Margaret drags Henry away to London. The Yorkists march on London to proclaim their victory. ∎

IN CONTEXT

THEMES
**Ambition, weakness,
social order, kingship**

SETTING
**London, Kent, Blackheath,
St Albans**

SOURCES
1548 One source for the play
is Edward Hall's *The Union
of the Two Noble and Illustre
Families of Lancaster and York.*

1587 As for many of his History plays,
Shakespeare also drew on Raphael
Holinshed's *Chronicles of England,
Scotland, and Ireland.*

Henry VI Part 2 is often considered
the strongest of Shakespeare's
three plays about Henry VI, who,
historically, was the king of England from
the age of nine months in 1422 until 1461
and again from 1470 until 1471. The play
focuses on the dark period in English
history leading up to a Yorkist challenge
to the Lancastrian monarchy that spiralled
into the civil and dynastic war known as
the Wars of the Roses.

This first of Shakespeare's great plays
about English history – written before
Henry VI Part 1 – may have first been
performed in 1591. It was printed as
early as 1594 in a quarto version under
an extraordinarily lengthy title, which
was presumably the publisher's publicity
blurb rather than Shakespeare's own title.
Most people refer to it as *The Second Part
of Henry VI* (as it is entitled in the 1623
Folio edition) or *Henry VI Part 2.*

Making history

Although the rawness of the verse shows
the young Shakespeare still developing
his craft, its attraction lies in the way it
brings a panoply of shadowy historical
figures and events vividly to life and
shapes them into a gripping narrative.
Characters from history, from the brutally
ambitious Richard of York to the strong-
willed Margaret of Anjou, attain such
intensity each time the play is performed
that it is difficult for historians to escape
Shakespeare's re-creation of them.

Using the poetic style and stage
techniques of his contemporaries,
Shakespeare creates a heightened,
emotionally charged drama, and he reshapes
the material in his historical sources to
create a pattern to the events, drawing out
themes of kingship and ambition.

Recasting Cade

One of the most vivid characters in the play
is Jack Cade, the lively rabble-rouser who,
egged on by York, stirs up the common-folk
of Kent to rebellion and leads them on a
terrifying assault on London. But the Cade
in *Henry VI Part 2* is not the well-educated
young man described in Holinshed's
Chronicles; he is a conflation of the
historical Jack Cade who led a rebellion
in 1450, and an earlier rebel, Wat Tyler,
who led the Peasant's Revolt of 1381.

In the play, Cade instructs the rebels to
hang a clerk because he can write, and Dick
the Butcher calls, "let's kill all the lawyers"
(4.2.78). But it was Tyler's rebellion, according
to Holinshed, that condemned literacy and
lawyers for being socially divisive, not
Cade's. Shakespeare mixes the two, emphasizing the
chaos that ensues when proper social and
political relationships are cast aside: "like
an angry hive of bees / That want their
leader" (3.2.125–126). However, Cade is no
egalitarian – change will happen when Cade
is king himself, "as king I will be" (4.2.71–
72), an echo of York's claims to kingship.
However, it would be wrong to assume
that Shakespeare is out of sympathy with
the plight of the poor, whose suffering in
such unhinged times is made very clear. »

 It is great sin to
swear unto a sin,
But greater sin to
keep a sinful oath.
Salisbury
Act 5, Scene 1

Henry VI (depicted with his wife Margaret of Anjou in this 15th-century manuscript) gave away territories to Margaret's father. Shakespeare portrays Henry as easily influenced by his wife.

The empty centre

At the heart of this breakdown in relationships is King Henry himself. He wants to be a peacemaker. But York and Queen Margaret condemn his "church-like humours" (1.1.247) as unfit for the crown, and describe his obsession with prayer as unmanly. Ultimately, his piety becomes simply vacillation, and his indecision makes him increasingly irrelevant. "What are you made of?" Margaret cries desperately when they are caught in the Battle of St Albans at the end, "You'll nor fight nor fly" (5.4.3).

The emptiness at the centre creates a power vacuum that sucks in and destroys all but the strongest – from Eleanor, the "good" Duke of Gloucester's wife, who is caught conspiring with witches, to the queen's unfortunate lover, Suffolk, who is beheaded at sea. Suffolk's departure is one of the most touching scenes in the play. He is a brutal schemer, responsible for entrapping Eleanor and arranging the murder of Gloucester. Yet their parting is poignant: "To France, sweet Suffolk. Let me hear from thee. / For wheresoe'er thou art in this world's Globe, / I'll have an Iris that shall find thee out." (3.2.409–412). When Margaret cradles Suffolk's decapitated head in her lap, it is a moment of true anguish.

Henry's weakness has unleashed the demons, and at the end of the play, the ruthless ambition of York and his sons chillingly takes control. ∎

Performance history

Despite the weakness of the character of King Henry, who vacillates and hesitates, the powerful parts of Richard of York and Queen Margaret provide challenging roles that dominate and drive the play.

Many directors have presented the *Henry VI* trilogy along with *Richard III*, creating a tetralogy on the Wars of the Roses. Often the same actor plays the same character across the plays, as Chuck Iwuji (pictured) did in 2008, playing Henry VI for the RSC.

Well-regarded theatrical performances include the 1963 John Barton and Peter Hall adaptation at the RSC titled *The Wars of the Roses* with Peggy Ashcroft as Margaret and Donald Sinden as York. These productions highlighted the political and social unrest prevalent in the plays, which reflected the civil upheaval of the 1960s – a period of momentous events such as the erection of the Berlin Wall and the assassination of John F Kennedy.

Acclaimed television productions include a 1981 BBC version of all four plays directed by Jane Howell, which stayed very close to the play.

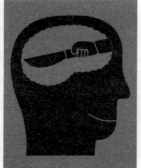

I CAN SMILE, AND MURDER WHILES I SMILE

HENRY VI PART 3 (1591)

After the Yorkists' victory at St Albans, Henry VI is forced to make a pledge: he will remain king, but Richard of York will become king after his death. York agrees to this, but his son Richard Plantagenet persuades him to break the oath. War breaks out and Clifford murders York's son Rutland. After the Battle of Wakefield, York is cornered and Queen Margaret and Clifford taunt him with Rutland's blood before killing him.

York's sons Edward, Richard, and George plan their revenge and are joined, crucially, by Warwick. Margaret and Clifford, confronted by the rampant York brothers, try to rouse Henry to fight. In the Battle of Towton, Warwick saves Richard from Clifford. Henry laments the tragedy of civil war. Clifford is killed, the Yorkists are victorious, and Edward is crowned King Edward IV.

Henry is captured. In London, Edward IV blackmails Lady Gray into a marriage. Richard (now Duke of Gloucester), railing against his deformities, reveals his ambition to be king. Meanwhile, Henry has been sent to the Tower of London. Margaret appeals for help to the French king Louis and learns that Warwick is arranging a wedding between Edward and Louis' sister, Lady Bona. Just as Louis agrees to the wedding, news arrives of Edward's marriage to Lady Gray. Warwick disavows Edward and joins with Margaret.

 Why, what is pomp, rule, reign, but earth and dust? And, live we how we can, yet die we must.
Earl of Warwick
Act 5, Scene 2

In England, Edward learns that his brother George, now Duke of Clarence, has joined Warwick and the Lancastrian forces. Warwick raids Edward's camp, takes the crown from Edward, and makes him a prisoner. Henry VI, restored to power, makes Warwick and Clarence his Protectors. But Edward, with the help of Gloucester, escapes. At the head of his foreign army, Edward is victorious and reclaims the throne, imprisoning Henry in the Tower.

The Yorkists capture Coventry, and Clarence rejoins his brothers. Warwick flees but is killed. Queen Margaret leads an army against the Yorkists but is defeated and taken prisoner. Edward IV, Gloucester, and Clarence kill her young son, Edward, but refuse to kill Margaret. In the Tower, Henry taunts the deformed Gloucester, who kills him and vows to kill his brothers. Edward IV and his queen have a new baby, but Gloucester is already plotting. ■

IN CONTEXT

THEMES
Kingship, revenge, betrayal, civil war, battles

SETTING
London, Yorkshire, Warwickshire, and various towns around England

SOURCES
1513 Thomas More's *History of King Richard III*.

1545 Edward Halle's *Union of the Two Noble and Illustrious Families of Lancaster and York*, a biased, Tudor-friendly account of the events covered in the play.

1587 Raphael Holinshed's *Chronicles of England, Scotland, and Ireland*.

Henry VI Part 3 is the last of Shakespeare's three plays about the reign of Henry VI (1422–61 and 1470–71). It covers the bloodiest period of the Wars of the Roses, in which the Yorkist faction gained ascendancy over Henry's Lancastrians in the battle for the throne, and the eldest of the Duke of York's sons snatched the crown from Henry to become Edward IV. It ends with the murder of Henry in the Tower of London in 1471 by another son of York, Richard of Gloucester, later Richard III.

Henry VI Part 3 was performed first in about 1591. England was wracked by the violent aftermath of Henry VIII's break from Rome and Elizabeth I's hold on the throne was still under threat. The depiction of leaders cynically playing for power would have struck a chord with audiences. The Yorkists Edward and Richard are portrayed in a very poor light, while the Earl of Richmond, later Henry VII, and Elizabeth's grandfather, is praised.

A molehill for a kingdom

In this vicious world, the weak but well-intentioned Henry is entirely lost. When he is banned from the Battle of Towton, he meekly agrees, admitting with unwitting irony: "They prosper best of all when I am thence" (2.5.18). But his abdication of responsibility turns him, like the audience, into an appalled spectator watching the tragedy unfold. As he sits away from the battle on the molehill to which his kingdom has shrunk, he witnesses

Henry VI meditates on the brutality of civil war, watching son kill father and father kill son, in this amalgam of Shakespeare's works titled Forests, by Catalan director Calixto Bieito.

the real horror of civil war in the affecting tableau of a soldier who has killed his son and another who has killed his father. He laments, "And let our hearts and eyes, like civil war, / Be blind with tears, and break, o'ercharged with grief" (2.5.77–78). But there is self-indulgence too when he sighs, "Here sits a king more woeful than you are" (2.5.124).

Henry's absence allows two characters to dominate the action – Richard, Duke of Gloucester, and Queen Margaret. Both are seen as "monstrous", freaks of nature that have thrived in the absence of normal moral values – Richard physically deformed at birth with his "crookback" and shrivelled arm, and Margaret unnaturally manly.

A tiger's heart

As Margaret stands exultant over Richard of York, handing him a handkerchief soaked in his son's blood, he describes her famously as the "She-wolf of France" (1.4.112) – a "tiger's heart wrapped in a woman's hide" (1.4.138). She is an "amazon" who does not behave as women should – "soft, mild, pitiful, and flexible" (1.4.142). In Shakespeare's play, she seems to represent a world turned upside down. While enemies describe Margaret in disparaging terms, her strength inspires great loyalty among her supporters. However, when her own son is

killed, she responds with tender, motherly outrage: "O Ned, sweet Ned – speak to thy mother, boy. / …No, no, my heart will burst an if I speak; / And I will speak that so my heart may burst…You have no children, butchers; if you had, / The thought of them would have stirred up remorse." (5.5.50, 58–59, 62–63). In her exasperation at her husband's weakness, Margaret bans him from the battle, although she could also be seen as a strong woman who is protecting a childlike man.

The shape-shifter

Richard, Duke of Gloucester, will have his own play in *Richard III*, but his personality emerges here. In a soliloquy in Act 3, Scene 2, he explains that his character has been shaped by his physical deformity. Deprived from birth of normal love by his misshapen body, he has turned himself into a Machiavel, a political player who sets himself apart from common humanity. He is interested only in the tactics that bring the highest prize, the crown, and becomes the consummate actor: "Why, I can smile, and murder whiles I smile" (3.2.182).

By means of this soliloquy and other asides, Shakespeare allowed audiences to join the characters on their psychological journeys. This was a new form of stage drama. ∎

Revenge in the play

Revenge drives much of the action in this energetic piece – which features no fewer than four battles (Wakefield, Towton, Barnet, and

Tewkesbury), more than any other of Shakespeare's plays. Both the Lancastrians and the Yorkists are hungry to wreak vengeance on the other side to right various wrongs that have been committed. Clifford, in particular, is eaten up with the desire to revenge the death of his father. Margaret exults in the murder of Rutland (Richard's son) by Clifford, only to have to suffer in retaliation the murder of her son before her eyes.

Richard's sons, Edward, Gloucester, and Clarence

seek to avenge his death, along with the previously loyal Warwick, who after suffering a humiliation at the French court, turns against Henry and joins his enemies.

Even Gloucester's ambitions for the crown appear to be an urge to even the score for the unkind treatment he received as a boy. Near the end of the play, when he kisses King Edward's baby, he whispers the ominous "so Judas kissed his master" (5.7.33), promising more betrayal and vengeance to come.

THIS BRAWL TODAY... SHALL SEND, BETWEEN THE RED ROSE AND THE WHITE, A THOUSAND SOULS TO DEATH AND DEADLY NIGHT

HENRY VI PART 1 (1591)

At the funeral of Henry V, a row breaks out between the young King Henry VI's uncles, Gloucester and Winchester. Messengers arrive from France. Town after town has fallen to the French, and England's hero Talbot has been captured. Outside besieged Orléans, the Dauphin Charles meets the maid Joan la Pucelle, whose visions promise victory for France. Talbot is freed in a prisoner exchange. The French triumph over the English. Joan beats Talbot in a duel but spares his life. Talbot retakes Orléans.

In the garden of the Temple in London's lawyers' quarter, a quarrel between Richard Plantagenet and Somerset ends in them plucking red and white roses to signify their opposing loyalties. Richard's uncle Mortimer tells him how the king's grandfather, Henry IV, deposed the rightful Richard II, and says that Richard has a claim to the throne.

In Parliament, a fight breaks out between the men of Gloucester and Winchester. As King Henry tries to calm them, he agrees to make Richard Duke of York. In France, Joan takes Rouen from the English, but Talbot retakes it. Joan persuades Henry's uncle Burgundy to switch sides. Talbot travels to Paris where Henry is to be crowned. There, Henry learns of Burgundy's treachery. He urges York and Somerset to put aside their quarrel but unwittingly insults York by donning a red rose. To repair the damage, Henry makes York Regent of France and orders Somerset to back him. Meanwhile, outside Bordeaux, Talbot and his son are

> ❝ Break thou in pieces, and consume to ashes, Thou foul accursèd minister of hell. ❞
> **Richard, Duke of York**
> Act 5, Scene 6

fatally wounded in a battle; Talbot dies with his son's body in his arms.

Gloucester tells the king that the French Earl of Armagnac wishes to arrange a peace. Henry agrees, and is persuaded to marry Armagnac's daughter to seal the deal. The people of Paris revolt and Charles and Joan march on Paris. Joan conjures spirits to help her cause, but the English triumph and Joan is captured. Suffolk is bewitched by the beauty of Margaret of Anjou, and promises to make her Henry's wife. York condemns Joan to burn as a witch, and rails against the "effeminate" peace Henry is making with France. Suffolk excites Henry with his account of Margaret's beauty and he agrees to marry her. ■

IN CONTEXT

THEMES
Battle, kingship, family ties, civil war

SETTING
London, Paris, Orleans, Auvergne, and Angiers

SOURCES
1516 Some scenes were inspired by Robert Fabyan's *New Chronicle of England and France*.

1545 Edward Halle's *Union of the Two Noble and Illustrious Families of Lancaster and York*.

1577 Raphael Holinshed's *Chronicles of England, Scotland, and Ireland*.

After defeating him in hand-to-hand combat, Joan la Pucelle (Katy Stephens) spares the life of Lord Talbot (Keith Bartlett) in a 2006 production at the Courtyard Theatre, London.

E vidence suggests that *Henry VI Part 1* was written after the second two parts of the *Henry VI* trilogy, and staged, to great acclaim, for the first time in 1592. So it is essentially a prequel, setting the events of the later two plays in context. It is grand in scale, encompassing England and France with sweeping battle scenes and thrilling hand-to-hand duels, while the other two parts are more narrowly focused.

The death of the heroic Henry V leaves English rule in France in chaos, as the new king, Henry VI, still little more than a child, finds himself unable to quell the quarrels at home. At first, the strife is between his uncles Gloucester and Winchester over who should be his protector. But conflict soon erupts between the supporters of the Lancastrian faction led by Somerset and the Yorkists led by Richard Plantagenet (who secretly believes the throne is rightfully his). Each faction chooses a rose for its emblem: white for York; red for Lancaster. The play presents this choice in a scene in the Inner Temple garden in London, in which Richard Plantagenet asks the assembled lords to pluck a rose. The lawyer picks a white rose, suggesting that he thinks Richard's case is strong in law. Challenged to make his case, Somerset replies that his argument is his sword. The scene is set for the Wars of the Roses.

Against this civil conflict, the maid of Orléans, Joan la Pucelle, known today as Joan of Arc, emerges to lead the French with her divine visions. She is pitted against a worthy English hero in Talbot, who at the end is failed by his quarrelling countrymen.

Dubious authorship

Because of the variable quality of the verse, critics have long questioned the play's authorship. The poet Samuel Taylor Coleridge was certain Shakespeare could not have written it, or at least not all of it. Many critics now think it was a collaborative work with writers such as Thomas Nashe, who perhaps wrote Act 1. Computer analysis of language patterns suggest that, while Shakespeare probably wrote *Henry VI Part 2* and most of *Part 3*, he was the author of only some of *Part 1* – the Temple garden scene, and the scene in Act 4 between Talbot and his son.

Early commentators, such as the English playwright Ben Jonson, *criticized Henry VI Part 1* for its crowd-pleasing battle scenes. Jonson insisted that, in a proper literary play, such battles would have been created in the imagination with skilful use of words, not crude stage techniques. However, over the last half century, critics have » rediscovered in the play some of the excitement and political sharpness that would have engaged audiences in 1592.

Family crisis

At the heart of the play lies the importance of family as the glue that binds society together. After all, claims to be the rightful king – claims that foment the terrible strife to come between the Yorkists and Lancastrians – hinge on proper family relationships. But it goes further than that. Familial bonds, such as the deep bond between Talbot and his son, are fundamental – and when these are lost, society is set adrift. Legitimacy is crucial. Gloucester emphasizes that Winchester is the "bastard of my grandfather", while Talbot inveighs against the "bastard Orléans" who killed his trueborn son. The play omits Talbot's real-life illegitimate son, Henry, who also died in the same battle. Political crisis emerges from a crisis in the family. Some critics argue that this is why the women in *Henry VI* are so negatively portrayed – Joan la Pucelle, Margaret, and the Countess of Auvergne are all presented as dangerous women who cause chaos by their effect on men and on proper relationships.In the first four acts, Joan is mostly portrayed as a holy visionary, but in Act 5, she morphs into the witch, conjuring up demons. She engages with

York to beg for her life with hysterical ferocity and wild curses (understandable, perhaps, when she is about to be burned alive).

Some directors have noticed that the very moment one *femme fatale*, Joan, leaves the centre of the action, another, Margaret of Anjou, makes her entrance. When the *Henry VI* plays are performed together, the same actress sometimes plays both Joan and Margaret to underscore the point that they are part of the same danger, although Margaret, Henry's future queen, is very different. While Joan dresses as a man to win her battles, Margaret remains womanly on the outside and her power comes from her sexual allure. Suffolk, the earl who enticed Henry with Margaret's charms, closes the play with the promise that: "Margaret shall now be queen and rule the King; / But I will rule both her, the King, and realm" (5.7.107–108).

But Suffolk is deluded. He likens himself to Paris, who elopes with the beautiful Helen to Troy. But it is a telling choice. Like Helen, Margaret will only bring strife, and Suffolk is banished and gruesomely beheaded. ∎

An illustration from a 15th-century French manuscript shows Joan of Arc leading the siege of Paris in 1429. It suited the play's anti-French politics to portray Joan as a demon-invoking witch.

WHY, THERE THEY ARE, BOTH BAKED IN THIS PIE
TITUS ANDRONICUS (1591–1592)

Saturninus and Bassianus quarrel over who should become Emperor of Rome. Marcus tells them that the hero, Titus Andronicus, is also a candidate, but Titus uses his influence with the people to name Saturninus emperor. Saturninus offers to marry Titus's daughter Lavinia as a reward, but Bassianus insists that he is betrothed to her. Saturninus is angry and decides to marry Tamora instead. She makes peace between the new emperor and Titus, but secretly vows to take revenge upon the whole family.

The weddings of Saturninus and Tamora and Lavinia and Bassianus are celebrated with a hunt. Aaron finds Chiron and Demetrius arguing over their love for Lavinia, and tells them to use the occasion of the hunt to rape Lavinia and murder Bassianus. He plots to pin the crime on Titus's sons, Martius and Quintus. Chiron and Demetrius kill Bassianus and throw his body into a pit. They rape Lavinia. Aaron leads Martius and Quintus to the pit, into which they fall. Saturninus discovers his brother's body and has Quintus and Martius arrested. Titus's son Lucius reveals that he has been banished, and sees the mutilated Lavinia. Aaron tells Titus that if he, Marcus, or Lucius will cut off his hand and send it to the emperor, his sons' lives will be spared. Titus sends his own hand, which is returned to him, with the heads of Martius and Quintus.

Lavinia writes the names of her attackers in the sand. Marcus, Titus, Young Lucius, and Lavinia swear an oath of vengeance. The Nurse brings to Aaron an infant – his child with Tamora – and tells him that because the child is black, Tamora wishes it killed. Aaron plots to swap it for a white infant, and to have the latter's parents bring up his child.

When news arrives that Lucius is returning with Goth troops, Tamora promises to persuade Titus to call off the attack. In disguise as Revenge, with Demetrius and Chiron as Murder and Rape, she visits Titus whom she thinks does not recognize them. She asks him to invite Lucius to a banquet, where she will bring Saturninus and the Empress. Tamora leaves her sons with Titus, who kills them. Titus, dressed as a cook, presides over the banquet at his house. He kills Lavinia in front of his guests, saying that she had been raped by Chiron and Demetrius, both of whom have been baked in the pie the guests have been eating. He stabs Tamora, and Saturninus kills Titus. Lucius then kills Saturninus. Marcus and Lucius tell the Roman people what has happened and Lucius is named emperor. Aaron is sentenced to death. Saturninus, Titus, and Lavinia are interred in their family tombs, but Tamora is denied any funeral rites. ∎

IN CONTEXT

THEMES
**Revenge, fatherhood,
motherhood, lust, madness**

SETTING
Late Imperial Rome

SOURCES
No direct sources are known, but
Shakespeare may have drawn on
the following:

8 CE Ovid's *Metamorphoses*. A copy
of the poem is used on stage in
the play.

1st century CE Thyestes, a
gory revenge story by Roman
playwright Seneca.

13th century *Gesta Romanorum*, an
anonymous collection of fictionalized
Roman legends and myths.

itus Andronicus is perhaps best
known for its extreme violence.
It features at least five stabbings,
two throat slittings, and one hand
amputation – and this is only the violence
that happens onstage. It does not include
the rape and mutilation of Lavinia.

The play was probably written in
collaboration with George Peele, who is
thought to be responsible mainly for the
first act. It was undoubtedly influenced by
theatrical fashion, and may have recalled
Peele's *The Battle of Alcazar* (c.1591), in
which severed heads appear in a banquet,
or the hand-chopping scene in *Selimus*
(*c*.1592), by Robert Greene and Thomas
Lodge. The play's violence has been called
gratuitous – to the extent that critics
used to deny that Shakespeare could
have written it. However, the violence
has deeper political and cultural meanings.

Escalating violence

Perhaps most horrifying is the moment when
Tamora realizes that she has consumed the
flesh of her own children, but cannibalism is
an idea that resonates throughout the play.
One of the challenges of revenge tragedy is
how to exceed the initial crime. Titus's main
act of revenge against Tamora for destroying
his family will be murder. Why should he
also require that she devour her sons?

One explanation is his need to punish
her sexual appetite by turning it into a
kind of monstrous feeding, "bid[ding] that

Demetrius and Chiron are soon to be
baked into pie in this 2006 production of
Titus Andronicus at the Globe Theatre,
London, with Douglas Hodge in the lead role.

strumpet, your unhallowed dam, / Like to the earth swallow her own increase" (5.2.190–191). But the play is also pervaded by a kind of maternal dread, where the mother is an all-consuming figure, against whom the male child must struggle to define himself. This fear emerges in some unlikely places. For example, the pit into which Martius and Quintus fall (with dead Bassianus at the bottom) is hailed: "What subtle hole is this, / Whose mouth is covered with rude-growing briers / Upon whose leaves are drops of new-shed blood / …A very fatal place it seems to me" (2.3.198–200, 202). In this way, the play anticipates the literal feeding that the female mouth will perform at the end.

Roman values

A mother figure is absent among the Andronici clan. The mother of Titus's 26 children is dead, and there is no mention of a wife for Lucius. Nevertheless, disturbing parallels emerge between father and mother, Roman and Goth, which complicate the roles of both Titus and Tamora. Titus has buried 20 sons before the play begins, all killed in wars, and his first action in the play is to place a coffin in the family tomb. In the original staging, the trapdoor would probably have been used to signify the tomb, and also the pit in Act 2 – thereby creating a sinister likeness between these spaces. At the start of the play we discover that Titus is "surnamèd *Pius*" (1.1.23). This was a title associated with Aeneas, one of the founders of Rome. It signified the best Roman values of honour, piety, and familial loyalty.

By contrast, Tamora is described as all that is un-Roman: promiscuous, treacherous, and bestial. And yet, Titus himself shapes what Tamora becomes by making her first-born son, Alarbus, a sacrifice. Tamora's accusation, "O cruel, irreligious piety!" (1.1.130), is hard to argue with. Titus and Tamora are both driven to violence through their sense of shame: Titus kills his son, Mutius, in a rage at being defied in front of the Emperor; Tamora vows revenge against Andronicus for making a queen kneel to him. Both characters represent a challenge to the core Roman values Titus is supposed to embody, implying that there are dangerous tensions between them, not least between personal honour and family loyalty.

Rome itself fulfils its reputation for ingratitude when it banishes one of Titus's sons and condemns two others to death, ignoring his pleas for mercy. By making Tamora devour her sons, Titus could be seen as forcing her to act like the ungrateful city. But although Tamora's body may be cast beyond the walls at the end, the anxieties and tensions she represents will remain at the very heart of Rome. ∎

Aaron

Aaron is an early villain in Shakespeare, the forefather of Don John in *Much Ado About Nothing* (pp.154–61), and Iago in *Othello* (pp.240–49).

The monstrous glee he shows at his own villainy links him to the comic Vice of the medieval morality play, but he has become a much more troubling figure in modern times because of the connection that he makes between his evil and his ethnicity. In particular, his wish to "have his soul black like his face" (3.1.204) might seem to justify long-held associations of blackness with devil-worship, treachery, and lust. The ease with which Aaron assimilates himself into Rome suggests that he can convincingly assume Roman values – he can read Latin texts better than Chiron and Demetrius, and he is more paternal than Titus. But he remains a difficult figure for modern productions. Julie Taymor's 1999 film *Titus* was accused by critics of simply updating its racial stereotypes by identifying Aaron with the contemporary "supercool hipster", "sexual athlete", and "nihilistic gangster".

34

MADE GLORIOUS SUMMER BY THIS SON OF YORK

RICHARD III (1592)

The long and bloody civil war between the houses of York and Lancaster has ended with the murder, in prison, of the Lancastrian King Henry VI. Edward IV of York now reigns, and England can rejoice in peace. This is what Edward's brother Richard tells us at the opening of the play. He then invites us to watch as, with devious skill, he takes the throne for himself.

Initially, we are intrigued by Richard's daring. He woos and wins Lady Anne as she escorts the funeral cortège of her father-in-law, Henry VI. Then Richard plots against family and friends. He engineers the imprisonment and death of his brother Clarence, news of which sends his eldest brother, King Edward IV, to an early grave.

Helped by the Duke of Buckingham, Richard sends Edward's sons – the young Edward V and Richard, Duke of York – to the Tower of London. When their mother's family objects, he has her male relatives executed. All of this is predicted by Henry VI's widow, old Queen Margaret who, filled with grief, haunts the palace and in vain warns everyone against Richard.

Richard now seeks the support of London's citizens in making himself king. Their silence shows public unease at Richard's ambition but Buckingham stage-manages this into approval and Richard takes the crown. Denied access to her sons, Queen Elizabeth fears the worst. Once he's on the throne, Richard tells Buckingham he wants his nephews dead. When Buckingham hesitates, Richard orders Tyrrel to kill them.

 Are you drawn forth among a world of men To slay the innocent?
Clarence
Act 1, Scene 4

Clouds gather for Richard as his surviving friends and enemies join forces. Buckingham deserts him to assist an invasion force from France led by the Earl of Richmond. As Richard moves from London to challenge Richmond, his progress is interrupted by his mother, the Duchess of York, and Queen Elizabeth who condemn him. He tries to turn this to his advantage by persuading the Queen to let him marry Princess Elizabeth, now that Anne, too, is dead. Their encounter is a powerful one and Richard believes he has won. But the Queen won't change sides. On the eve of the Battle of Bosworth, both Richard and Richmond dream of the ghosts of Richard's victims, who promise Richmond fortune and curse Richard as a traitor, murderer, and villain. Richard wakes sweating and tries to dismiss their words. But the voice of his conscience declares him guilty. When they meet in battle Richmond kills the unhorsed Richard. Finally, Richmond promises that he and Elizabeth will bring England the peace and prosperity that Richard described at the start. ∎

IN CONTEXT

THEMES
Murderous villainy, ambition, loss, retribution

SETTING
15th-century London and Leicestershire

SOURCES
1st century The tragedies of Roman playwright Seneca.

14th–15th centuries The figure of Vice in morality plays; the cyclical pattern and biblical parallels of the mystery plays.

c.1520 Thomas More's *History of King Richard III*.

Richard's opening speech sets the stage by moving us from the wintry horrors of the battlefield to the summer holiday that peace has brought, "Now is the winter of our discontent / Made glorious summer by this son of York" (1.1.1–2). Only Richard's discontent remains. Mocking the idle courtly life in a tone that is increasingly ironic, he resolves to let his dissatisfaction darken Edward IV's sun-filled reign.

Politics and the past

Richard is a more subtle operator in this fourth play of Shakespeare's Henry VI tetralogy than he was in part 3. Where once he would have used violence, now he manipulates court in-fighting and the self-interest of ambitious men. Shakespeare gives him the cunning of a Machiavel, and reinforces this by moving most of the bloodletting off-stage – although not every modern director keeps it there.

Queen Elizabeth was a widow who married Edward IV after refusing to be his mistress, much to his family's disgust. Richard plays on class consciousness, setting up her brother and two young sons by her former marriage as social climbers – "silken, sly, insinuating jacks" (1.3.53). He then blames them for his plots – the imprisonment of his brother Clarence and

Lord Hastings – and accuses them of having ambitious designs on the new young king. This allows him to play the kindly uncle and lodge the two boys in the Tower of London. Shortly afterwards he has Rivers, Dorset, and Gray executed.

Such a swift rise to power relies on the collusion of others. Buckingham, Catesby, Hastings, the Bishop of Ely, even Richmond's stepfather, Stanley, may not be duped by Richard but they all stay silent about what they know.

Settling history's account

To a degree, Richard's plotting brings down those figures who were disloyal to the House of York during the civil war. Most of this is predicted by old Queen Margaret, the widow of Henry VI, who appears anachronistically at court to call down vengeance on those who for so long set brother against brother. She conveniently forgets her own role in the fighting, as Richard observes, but she sets out a pattern of retributive vengeance that echoes history's script; one that we watch Richard go on to fulfil.

Apart from Margaret, no one at court speaks out against Richard's acts. But in the London streets the citizens do. The first half of the play is confined to a London that Richard clearly regards as his domain. But the commoners represent a wider audience whose judgement Richard's clever performance can't control. Another part of this audience comprises the women – Anne, Queen Margaret, the Duchess of York, and Queen Elizabeth. They watch and remember. As Richard's mother points out, women are often the sole surviving keepers of accounts.

The landscape widens

Dreams, nightmares, curses, prophecies, and premonitions present a metaphysical dynamic in the play beyond Richard's control. As soon as he murders the innocent princes in the Tower his fortunes begin to fail. He becomes prey to doubts and fears, and Anne reveals that he's long had "timorous dreams" (4.1.84). With his first careful words as king he tries to share responsibility for the coup with »

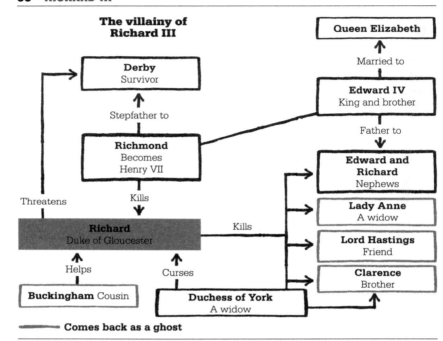

The villainy of Richard III

Buckingham: "Thus high by thy advice / And thy assistance is King Richard seated" (4.2.4–5). But Buckingham grows suspicious and this puts their double-act under strain. Just when Richard needs help from his self-interested friends, confined as he now is at the centre of the action, he finds himself increasingly isolated and dependent on strangers such as Tyrrel to complete his plots.

Buckingham's departure from the court heralds the waning of Richard's sole command of the action. It also prompts Richmond's arrival on the scene. We learn of his planned invasion from France, secretly supported by Lord Stanley and Queen Elizabeth. Now the action of the play opens up and moves from London's square mile to rural Leicestershire, the heart of England, and to Bosworth Field.

As the seasons turn from Richard's busy sunshine to his autumnal fall, Margaret returns. In a counterpart to Richard's prologue she ushers in the inevitable conclusion: "So now prosperity begins to mellow / And drop into the rotten mouth of death" (4.4.1–2).

The shape of villainy

Richard's physical shape is a gift to any dramatist and Shakespeare makes much of it. Many in the audience would have enjoyed the hugely successful Henry VI plays and also known the crookback figure as he is portrayed in Tudor history – a monstrous creature of bloody civil war and a future demon king.

Shakespeare capitalizes on Richard's physical non-conformity by making it his motivating force. In the preceding play, he severs all links to family and faction and sets himself against the principle of blood bond that took York and Lancaster to war. Given his deformity he feels that family bonds and natural inheritance have let him down. He decides, therefore, to be self-sufficient – "I am myself alone" – and, like an actor, turn his shape to advantage by playing his way to the throne. This is the performance he introduces us to at the opening of the play. There he lets us in on his plots and simplifies history into fiction with its heroes, lovers, and villains.

The disruptive force of Richard's villainous nonconformity is clear in his first five appearances in the play. Upsetting the smooth running of Edward IV's new state, he interrupts a series of courtly ceremonies and meetings and redirects them all. Some productions show him appearing through a different entrance from that used by the other characters as if, like the morality play figure Vice, he comes to create chaos from quite another place.

Wit and wordplay

Richard shows us he's the master of improvised duplicity, especially with language, and is equally at home in street speech and witty repartee. His versatility takes him from mock anger to mock modesty. The wit and smooth rhetoric that let him catch his opponents off-guard often take us in the same way.

His verbal skills are to the fore when he persuades Lady Anne to be his wife (1.2), and Queen Elizabeth to let him marry her daughter (4.4). Strategically placed at each end of the play, these parallel scenes chart the rise and fall of Richard's fortunes. He approaches Queen Elizabeth with the same bravado but she turns his tactics back on him. This time the woman leads the debate. Her put-downs are delivered with such feeling that they stifle Richard's efforts to defend his evil actions.

At the end, Richard stops the performance and no longer draws us into his confidence. When he tries not to despair on the night before Bosworth his soliloquy addresses a fresh audience: his conscience. The debate is a judicial examination, devoid of witty self-deceptions, with Richard both the prosecution and defence. Finally his conscience tells him that he is the villain he promised to be: "My conscience hath a thousand several tongues… / And every tale condemns me for a villain" (5.5.147, 149).

From sun to shade

Now we watch as Richard is disturbed by prophesies and curses. He can't sleep before his final battle and the sun fails to shine the day he dies. Ultimately he's defeated both by history in the form of Richmond, and by himself – "Myself, myself confound" (4.4.330). He admits that he has no pity even for himself. In performance, it's the strength of Richard's prowess in the battle that often determines our feelings about him at the end. Perhaps his cry "A horse! A horse! My kingdom for a horse!" (5.7.7) reminds us that he was always happiest in a fight. Richmond ends the play, but the final focus rests also on Richard. Behind Richmond's perfect picture of "smiling plenty, and fair prosperous days" (5.7.34) there lingers a shadow of Richard's sun-filled opening words. ■

Tudor propaganda?

John Rous, a historian writing during the reign of Richard III, described his king as a "good lord" with a "great heart" who enacted just laws. But by the reign of the first Tudor king, Henry VII, Rous had reversed his opinion. Richard, he wrote, was a freak: stunted and physically weak, he was responsible for killing Henry VI and for poisoning his own wife. Other historians, among them Sir Thomas More, joined in the vilification of Richard, citing his "crook-backed" deformity as evidence of inward corruption. It may be that More and others were seeking to legitimize Tudor rule with anti-Yorkist propaganda. But it is from their accounts that Shakespeare drew his material. More described Richard as being devious and flattering while he plotted, but also clever and courageous. Shakespeare retained all these features, and gave the king added depth by encumbering him with a formidable conscience. The character is so enduring that the historical Richard has been obliterated. Indeed, there is no surviving account by anyone who knew him in person.

TO DIE IS ALL AS COMMON AS TO LIVE

EDWARD III (1592–1593)

At the English court, King Edward III is discussing his claim to the French crown with the Comte d'Artois, who has joined the English side. When the Duc de Lorraine arrives from France to insist Edward swear allegiance to the French King John, Edward declares war. Meanwhile, the King of Scotland besieges the Countess of Salisbury in Roxburgh Castle. King Edward sends his son Prince Edward to France, and heads to Roxburgh himself. Enticed by the Countess's beauty, King Edward decides to stay.

As the king grows infatuated with the Countess, he asks his secretary Lodowick to write love letters to her. The king pressures her to yield to his desires, even though they are both married. She refuses, so he compels her father Warwick to intervene. Unable to deny the king, Warwick urges his daughter to comply. There is a distraction as young Prince Edward announces his readiness to lead the army for France, but the king soon resumes his amatory pursuit. The Countess reminds him that they are both married so the king promises to kill both their spouses. The Countess is horrified; the king finally sees sense and apologizes.

Off Sluys on the Belgian coast, the English rout the French navy, Prince Edward triumphs on land, and the French king, encamped at Crécy, tries to buy him off. When Prince Edward demands the crown instead, battle ensues. News reaches the king that his son is in danger. He refuses to send help, insisting that this is his son's chance to prove himself. Prince Edward returns triumphant and is

> 66 Tell him the crown that he usurps is mine, And where he sets his foot he ought to kneel.
> **King Edward**
> Scene 1 99

knighted by the king. The king besieges Calais while the Prince pursues King John. In Brittany, the Countess of Salisbury's husband offers the French prisoner Villiers freedom in exchange for a safe passage to Calais. A captain of Calais offers to surrender the town to the king, but the king insists he will only accept the surrender if six wealthy citizens are sent to him.

A prophecy that says John will appear in England seems favourable to the French. Faced with a large French army, Prince Edward turns down a French offer of mercy. Bad omens appear in the sky and the French panic. The captured Salisbury is spared on the intervention of Villiers. Prince Edward is victorious and captures King John.

The six wealthy men of Calais are brought to the king. The queen urges mercy and he spares their lives. Salisbury arrives with the news that Prince Edward has been killed at Crécy. The king comforts the distraught queen, but suddenly, Prince Edward arrives, with King John as his prisoner. The excited Prince Edward promises more foreign adventures. ■

IN CONTEXT

THEMES
Honour, kingship, valour, patriotism, brutality of war

SETTING
The royal court, London; Roxburgh Castle, Scottish borders; Flanders; Crécy, Poitiers, and Calais, France

SOURCES
1377 Jean Froissart's *Chronicles*, a French source for the early battles of the Hundred Years War.

1575 *The Palace of Pleasure*, by William Painter, features a story entitled "The Countesse of Salesberrie", on which the wooing scene is based.

1587 Raphael Holinshed's *Chronicles* is a source for the battles (although for dramatic reasons they have been compressed in time).

E dward III is the story of one of England's most formidable warrior kings, who ruled the country for half a century until his death in 1377.

The play was written in the early 1590s, around the same time as the *Henry VI* plays, but only in the last few decades has it been accepted among Shakespeare's works. Most editors now agree that Shakespeare did at least have a hand in some of the play but they generally believe that he was responsible for at most a few scenes, including Scenes 2 and 3, between Edward and the Countess of Salisbury, and Scene 12, in which Edward the Black Prince ruminates on death. Performances have been so few that, when the RSC staged it in 2002, they described it, rather inaccurately, as a "new" play by Shakespeare.

The story covers Edward III's defence of the kingdom against the Scottish King David II, and his wars in France, including the historical rout of the French navy at Sluys (1340), his victory over superior

French forces at Crécy (1346), and finally the battle of Poitiers (1356) at which his young son, Edward, the Black Prince, proved himself a hero. However, the portrait of Edward III presented in this play is very different from that of Shakespeare's other great warrior king, Henry V. While Henry V emerges as a dynamic young leader, inspiring his troops to victory with stirring speeches, Edward is anything but inspiring. No sooner has he, like Henry, sent the French ambassador packing with a declaration of war than we see him in Scotland in a far from heroic light.

Rough wooing
Arriving to lift the Scottish siege of Roxburgh Castle, Edward is entranced by the beautiful Countess of Salisbury, whose husband is fighting in France. He then embarks on a siege of his own to conquer her, and his tactics are not honourable. After his love letters, penned by his secretary Lodowick, are rejected, he resorts to power games, commanding her father to order her to submit to his desire. The strong-willed countess refuses, and desperately tells Edward that their spouses stand between them. Astoundingly, Edward offers to kill both of them, saying, as if he is judge on their lives: "Thy beauty makes them guilty of their death" (3.157). »

In the play, the Black Prince is a gung-ho adventurer, a portrayal that is probably close to the historical truth. His tomb in Canterbury Cathedral shows him resplendent in armour.

The Countess is mortified, exclaiming: "O, perjured beauty! More corrupted judge!" (3.160). She tells him that there is a higher court, above the king – "the great star chamber o'er our heads" (3.161) – that will judge such a crime.

After this disturbing but memorable interlude, the countess is all but forgotten, and the play settles into a far more conventional to-and-fro of battles. However, the countess's absent husband, Salisbury, becomes a key focus for the sense of justice that runs through the play, along with his French counterpart, Villiers. Against the run of events, they both insist on behaving honourably.

Unsentimental leader

It is surprising just how negative a portrait this is of one of England's most dynamic monarchs, a king whose military victories turned England into a major power. The reason may have been due to contemporary Tudor politics. Edward III was a Plantagenet king, whose line ultimately came to an end with the first of the Tudors, a dynasty still keen to bolster its legitimacy in Shakespeare's day. Besides the unsavoury incident with the countess, Edward is seen as a tough, uncaring father. When Prince Edward, known to history as the Black Prince, is beleaguered in battle, Edward refuses help, saying, "Then will he win a world of honour too / If he by valour can redeem him thence. / If not, what remedy? We have more sons / Than one to comfort our declining age." (8.21–24).

Late in the play, news comes through that the young prince has apparently perished and his mother weeps in distress, but Edward's brand of comfort is to promise pitiless revenge. Moreover, when the citizens of Calais send him six leaders of the town as a gesture of submission, only the queen's intervention dissuades him from slaughtering them. There is a foretaste here of Shakespeare's other warrior-king Henry V, who threatens Calais with even more savage brutality. Although there are heroes in this play – Salisbury, Villiers, and Prince Edward – it does not shy away from showing war as a very brutish business. A French mariner reports the sea battle of Sluys in gruesome terms: "Purple the sea whose channel filled as fast / With streaming gore that from the maimèd fell" (4.161–162).

Edward in *Edward III* is a far from attractive character, and yet the play ends, happily for him, with the young prince excited and eager for fresh challenges and Edward in calm control after a series of stunning military victories. With the French and Scottish kings his captives, and also the dauphin, he muses contentedly on their strange new unity:

"God willing, then for England we'll be shipped, / Where in a happy hour I trust we shall / Arrive: three kings, two princes, and a queen." (18.242–244). ∎

The Battle of Sluys is depicted in a French manuscript of 1400. The play omits the French king Philippe VI, who was defeated at Sluys. Instead, Philippe's son John loses the battle.

WHAT ERROR DRIVES OUR EYES AND EARS AMISS?

THE COMEDY OF ERRORS (1594)

The city of Ephesus is at war with Syracuse. Syracusans visiting Ephesus illegally must pay a fine or be executed. One such is Egeon, a merchant just arrived. He tells Duke Solinus that he, his wife Emilia, their young twin sons, and their twin servants, were separated by a storm at sea years before. Egeon and his remaining son and servant returned to Syracuse, where he named the boys after their respective siblings. Once grown, Antipholus and Dromio as they were called, set off to seek their brother twins, but never returned. Now Egeon has risked death by coming to Ephesus in search of both sons and their servants. Moved by the tale, Duke Solinus gives Egeon a reprieve until five in the afternoon to raise the fine.

Unknown to Egeon, those he seeks have also just arrived. Sending Dromio to the inn with their money for safekeeping, Antipholus of Syracuse sets off to explore. Little does he know that the subjects of his own search are nearby. Antipholus of Ephesus, a thriving merchant, lives with his wife, Adriana, and her sister, Luciana, both of whom resent the time he spends away from home visiting the tavern and a courtesan.

Furious that he's late again for dinner, Adriana spots Antipholus in the street and becomes angry with him. He responds surprisingly politely and seems unusually happy to eat with her. In fact, she has met her husband's twin, Antipholus of Syracuse, and he promptly falls in love with her sister. When her husband returns with friends, he finds the door to his home barred by someone claiming to be Dromio. He leaves, threatening revenge.

A series of mistaken encounters ensues. Antipholus of Ephesus sends Dromio of Ephesus for a rope to punish Adriana. But before the servant returns, a goldsmith arrests Antipholus of Ephesus for non-payment for a chain, which was delivered in error to his Syracusan brother. Dromio of Syracuse arrives and is sent to Adriana for the bail money. Dromio of Ephesus then returns with the rope.

Confused and frightened, Antipholus of Ephesus turns violent. Seeming mad, he's tied up with the rope, but escapes. Meanwhile, the Syracusan twins attempt to flee the town. But, pursued by almost everybody in Ephesus, they take refuge in the abbey. As the fateful hour of 5 o'clock arrives, Adriana and Antipholus of Ephesus petition the Duke to mediate. While he hears their conflicting accounts, the abbess enters with the Syracusan twins and all becomes clear. When the twins recognize Egeon, the Abbess, in a final twist, reveals she is Emilia, Egeon's long-lost wife. So the family is reunited and the tale complete. ∎

THEMES
Twinship, identity, marital and filial relationships, loss

SETTING
Port of Ephesus

SOURCES
1390 John Gower's English version of the Greek romance *Apollonius of Tyre* forms the basis of Egeon's and Emilia's frame narrative.

1595 Roman playwright Plautus's *Menaechmi* ("The Brothers Menaechmus") translated into English. A second play, *Amphitruo*, may have inspired Act 3, Scene 1.

The confusion at the heart of *The Comedy of Errors* is caused by a natural phenomenon, twinship, a subject that interested Shakespeare because he was the father of twins. Individuals like to think of themselves as unique, so identical twins are intriguing because they appear to duplicate identity. They suggest the possibility of one person being in two places at one time. And that can be both funny and frightening.

Shakespeare exploits both the comedy and the fear. He doubles the identical twins that he found in Plautus's *Menaechmi* by adding servant Dromios to the original twins. This nicely doubles the opportunity for farce as the play's mistimings gather pace. We're told that the servant twins have shared the lives of their masters since birth, which means that when the errors begin it's not just the master-servant relationship that comes under comic strain, clearly there are bonds of lifelong friendship and trust that are also tested.

Exploration of identity
Shakespeare's changes to his source material let him explore how far identity is influenced by others. We see the fear and isolation felt by each twin when even his servant-partner disputes his version of events. Each man appears to see and hear a slightly different world. Confusion over mistaken identity makes Antipholus of Syracuse want to leave town because the inconsistency he finds seems to confirm the place's reputation for witchcraft. It makes his twin brother so frustrated that he turns to violence, especially when his sanity is doubted. But this only convinces everyone that he is indeed mad. When identities and the bonds of trust between individuals are threatened in this way, it becomes apparent how swiftly family and social relationships can fall apart.

Dramatic structure
Egeon's tragic story frames the comic action, and the day's grace given to the old man to redeem himself fixes the length of the play. The completion of the tale with the revelation that the Abbess is his long-lost wife, Emilia, brings a sense of wonder; because no hint of this is given. Emilia's return also completes a change of mood from threatened death to festive re-birth. The family is whole again. And so is their story.

Within this framing narrative, time goes adrift. As events move out of sequence, only the audience holds the narrative threads together. The farce builds up through scenes that almost mirror one another. And within these, Shakespeare's use of rapid one-line repartee maintains the momentum, creating a comic double act between master and servant. Even when they're arguing, there's an obvious bond between them. The dialogue is so fast-paced and funny that there's little time to stop and think. For if anyone were to do that, the reason for the errors might come clear.

The love story between Luciana and Antipholus of Syracuse offers a brief respite from the chaos and a variation on the identity theme. In contrast to the anger all around, the gentle Antipholus woos the surprised Luciana with a lyricism that she clearly hasn't heard before.

The twins' relationships

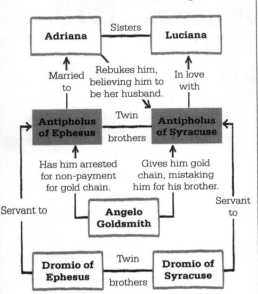

The Kyogen of Errors

In 2001, the Mansaku Company of Japan performed *The Kyogen of Errors*, a Japanese-language production of the play, to English-speaking audiences. *Kyogen*, meaning "mad words", is a form of traditional Japanese theatre known for its earthy, comic style, for which Shakespearean slapstick is particularly suited, with language proving no barrier to farce.

At key moments, the audience was encouraged to join the comedy by chanting "*Ya-ya-koshi-ya!*" ("How complicated!"). In keeping with the traditions of Japanese Noh theatre, with which Kyogen is closely associated, each set of Antipholuses and Dromios wore identical masks – props that aided the play's visual complexities.

The success of the production showed how the themes in the play – marital relationships, loss, and identity – are so powerful and universal that they transcend even the most challenging of linguistic and cultural differences.

Marriage bonds

Marriage, too, can be regarded as a type of twinship. Shakespeare draws attention to its responsibilities and strains by building up the role of Adriana, the Ephesian wife. His audience would know Saint Paul's "Letter to the Ephesians", which discusses the respective duties of husbands and wives, masters and servants; details that Luciana, Adriana's sister, is obviously versed in. Adriana, however, longs to lose herself in a fairer relationship, and says so at length, but to the wrong twin. Possibly her real husband wouldn't have listened to her so patiently. As the Abbess observes, if she criticizes too much she runs the risk of ruining everything about Antipholus that she loves.

The key props in the play – a gold chain and a rope – neatly symbolize its emphasis on bonds: of love and trust, and of punishment and control. The gold chain represents a husband's love, but is promised to the courtesan in an act of spite. When it's given to the wrong twin, his brother is arrested for debt. Finally, it finds the right Antipholus and, we hope, Adriana.

The last bond in the play is that of the Dromios who, reunited as brothers, leave as equals, hand-in-hand – to the audience's applause. ∎

HUNTING HE LOVED, BUT LOVE HE LAUGHED TO SCORN
VENUS AND ADONIS (1592–1593)

IN CONTEXT

THEMES
Erotic desire, youth, longing, temptation

SETTING
Ancient Greece

SOURCES
8 CE Book X of Roman poet Ovid's *Metamorphoses*, in its original Latin, was probably used by Shakespeare.

1565–67 An English translation of Ovid's *Metamorphoses* by Arthur Golding was also drawn on for the poem.

The poem *Venus and Adonis* retells the mythical tale of Venus, goddess of love, who woos and attempts to seduce the beautiful mortal youth, Adonis. Shakespeare announces the theme in the opening lines: "Even as the sun with purple-coloured face / Had ta'en his last leave of the weeping morn, / Rose-cheeked Adonis hied him to the chase. / Hunting he loved, but love he laughed to scorn."

Venus approaches Adonis, begs a kiss, drags him from his horse and tethers it to a tree, thrusts the boy to the ground, and smothers him with kisses. His bashfulness inflames her lust and, pinning him to the ground, she tells him at length how lucky he should feel to be desired by one who was wooed by so great a figure as the god Mars. But Adonis, complaining that he's getting burnt by the midday sun, with much difficulty shakes her off. "Away he springs, and hasteth to his horse." (l.258). Tempted by a passing mare, however, the horse breaks away and dashes into a wood with his mate. Venus renews her advances and takes Adonis by the hand, "A lily prisoned in a jail of snow" (l.362), saying that Adonis should take a lesson from his horse: "O, learn to love! The lesson is but plain, / And, once made perfect, never lost again." (ll.407–408).

Hunter hunted

She pretends to collapse before him. Guiltily he tries to bring her round and gives her a farewell kiss, which inflames her again, but he says he is unripe for love: "Before I know myself, seek not to know me." (l. 525). His unwise offer of a kiss inflames her again. He tells her that he plans to go boar hunting, which causes her such pain that: "She sinketh down, still hanging by his neck. / He on her belly falls, she on her back." (ll.593–594).

Horrified that he may be killed, she advises him to hunt harmless animals such as hares. Adonis rebukes her for succumbing to lust: "Love comforteth, like sunshine after rain, / But lust's effect is tempest after sun." (ll.799–800).

Some scholars have speculated that Shakespeare may have seen a copy of Titian's painting *Venus and Adonis* (1554), in which the young hero seems to spurn the over-eager Venus.

At last he escapes, leaving her to bemoan her fate. Next morning, hearing sounds of hunting, she dashes to see what is happening. She spies "the hunted boar" (l.900), sees Adonis's exhausted and wounded hounds, and bemoans his suspected fate.

Deluded into supposing that he is still alive she reproaches herself for being too fearful but, coming upon his body, speaks an elegy for him and prophesies that henceforward sorrow will always attend upon love. Adonis's body melts away and she vows to cherish the purple flower that springs up in its place. Finally, she returns to Cyprus in her dove-drawn chariot, planning to seclude herself away in perpetual mourning.

Publication and date

Venus and Adonis first appeared in print in 1593. London's theatres were closed that year and for much of the following year because of an outbreak of plague, and it seems likely that Shakespeare, who was already an established playwright, had time on his hands. The poem was published »

 With this she seizeth on his sweating palm, The precedent of pith and livelihood, And, trembling in her passion, calls it balm – Earth's sovereign salve to do a goddess good.
Venus and Adonis
ll.25–28

Ovid wrote his narrative poem *Metamorphoses* in the first decade CE. Running to 15 books and covering 250 myths, it would have given the schoolboy Shakespeare a thorough grounding in classical mythology.

by Richard Field, a well-known London printer. Field, who was also from Stratford-upon-Avon, went on to publish *The Rape of Lucrece. Venus and Adonis* was the first book to bear Shakespeare's name as author.

The first edition bore a Latin motto from the poems Amores ("The Loves") by the Roman poet Ovid: "Vilia miretur vulgus; mihi flavus Apollo pocula Castalia plena ministret aqua" – "let low-minded people admire vile things, but for me let Apollo supply goblets full of the water of the Muses".

Dedication

The poem bears a dedication to Henry Wriothesley, 3rd Earl of Southampton, a precocious and talented nobleman who was only 17 at the time. The formal dedication reads, "Right Honourable, I know not how I shall offend in dedicating my unpolished lines to your lordship, nor how the world will censure me for choosing so strong a prop to support so weak a burden. Only, if your honour

seem but pleased, I account myself highly praised, and vow to take advantage of all idle hours till I have honoured you with some graver labour. But if the first heir of my invention prove deformed, I shall be sorry it had so noble a godfather, and never after ear [till] so barren a land for fear it yield me still so bad a harvest. I leave it to your honourable survey, and your honour to your heart's content; which I wish may always answer your own wish and the world's hopeful expectation. Your honour's in all duty, William Shakespeare." Shakespeare also dedicated his other narrative poem, *The Rape of Lucrece*, published in the following year, to Southampton.

Source

Shakespeare based *Venus and Adonis* on an episode from one of his favourite books, the long poem *Metamorphoses* ("Changes") by Ovid, which he would have studied at school and which he refers to and quotes from many times in his plays. He even brings a copy of the poems on stage in his early tragedy *Titus Andronicus* and in his late romance *Cymbeline*. Shakespeare seems to have referred both to the original and to an English translation by Arthur Golding. But while Ovid tells the tale in only 75 lines, Shakespeare expands it to 1,194 lines of verse. He modifies both the characterization and the events of the original tale. In Ovid's version, the youthful Adonis returns Venus's love, but Shakespeare turns him into a bashful

> ❝ O, what a sight it was
> wistly to view
> How she came stealing
> to the wayward boy,
> To note the fighting conflict
> of her hue,
> How white and red each
> other did destroy!
> **Venus and Adonis**
> ll.343–346 ❞

adolescent who shies away from the goddess's lustful advances. He also expands the story; the most substantial addition is the episode (ll.259–324) in which Adonis's horse lusts after a mare and gallops after her into the forest, frustrating Adonis's attempts to escape from Venus's clutches.

Style and reception
The poem is written in six-line stanzas. Each line is an iambic pentameter, meaning that it has ten syllables and every other syllable is stressed: for example "She looks upon his lips, and they are pale" (l.1123). The lines are rhymed in this order: a b a b c c, resembling the last six lines of a Shakespearean sonnet. The style is witty, narrating events with knowing detachment while also achieving lyrical beauty in the descriptive passages.

The poem was to be more frequently reprinted than any other of Shakespeare's works during his lifetime: nine times by 1610. It was especially popular with adolescents. In about 1600, Cambridge scholar Gabriel Harvey wrote that, "the younger sort take much pleasure in Shakespeare's *Venus and Adonis*, but his *Lucrece*, and his tragedy of *Hamlet Prince of Denmark*, have it in them to please the wiser sort." Venus and Adonis acquired a reputation as soft porn due to lines such as these in which Venus tries to tempt Adonis with the delights of her body: "I'll be a park, and thou shalt be my deer. / Feed where thou wilt, on mountain or in dale; / Graze on my lips, and if those hills be dry, / Stray lower, where the pleasant fountains lie." (ll.231–234). In a play performed by Cambridge students early in the 17th century, a character boasts of how he woos his mistress with speeches larded with quotations from *Romeo and Juliet* and *Venus and Adonis*, and declares that he will "worship sweet master Shakespeare".

The poem's artificial style and digressive story line caused it to fall out of fashion until romantic poet and critic Samuel Taylor Coleridge's *Biographia Literaria* (1817) helped to restore its critical reputation. ∎

In 2007, the Royal Shakespeare Company, in association with the Little Angel Theatre of Islington, London, gave a performance in which the poem was recited aloud while the story was acted out with puppets.

WHO BUYS A MINUTE'S MIRTH TO WAIL A WEEK

THE RAPE OF LUCRECE (1593–1594)

IN CONTEXT

THEMES
Lust, betrayal, honour

SETTING
Rome, 509 BCE

SOURCES
27–25 BCE *History of Rome* by the Roman historian Livy.

8 CE *The Book of Days* by the Roman poet Ovid.

The Rape of Lucrece is a poem that tells the classical story of the Roman general Tarquin, who desires and rapes Lucrece, the wife of his fellow warrior Collatinus (called Collatine in the poem). Shakespeare jumps straight into the action in the opening lines: "Lust-breathèd Tarquin leaves the Roman host / And to Collatium bears the lightless fire / Which, in pale embers hid, lurks to aspire / And girdle with embracing flames the waist / Of Collatine's fair love, Lucrece the chaste."

The narrator explains that Tarquin has left the Roman camp for Collatium because, on the previous night, the warriors had been boasting of the beauty and chastity of their wives. This has filled him with desire for Lucrece.

When he reaches Collatium, Lucrece welcomes him. He finds her even more beautiful than he had expected, praises her husband's valour, and goes to bed aching with desire for her. In a long soliloquy, Tarquin meditates about his intention to seduce Lucrece, aware of the horror and danger of what he intends to do, but unable to resist his evil impulses: "Here pale with fear he doth premeditate / The dangers of his loathsome enterprise, / And in his inward mind he doth debate / What following sorrow may on this arise." (ll.183–186).

A passage of vivid narrative describes how he makes his fearful way to the chamber where Lucrece lies sleeping: "Her breasts like ivory globes circled with blue, / A pair of maiden worlds unconquerèd, / Save of their lord no bearing yoke they knew, / And him by oath they truly honourèd." (ll.407–410).

When Lucrece awakes, Tarquin says he will kill her and her attendant slave unless she yields to him. She pleads with him in vain, and he rapes her: "with the nightly linen that she wears / He pens her piteous clamours in her head, / Cooling his hot face in the chastest tears / That ever modest eyes with sorrow shed." (ll.680–683).

Having done the deed, Tarquin creeps away in shame. From this point onwards, the poem concentrates on Lucrece. She addresses night, time, and opportunity in a series of laments, and curses Tarquin before deciding to kill herself for shame and to tell her husband what has happened. She calls

A one-woman musical and dramatic performance based on the poem was given by Camille O'Sullivan in 2011. It toured Britain and Ireland under the auspices of the RSC.

her maid but does not confide in her. Lucrece writes to Collatine summoning him home and then meditates on a painting of the siege and fall of Troy, which is described at length. When Collatine arrives with her father and other lords, she tells them what has happened without at first naming Tarquin until all the men have vowed to avenge her. Then she suddenly stabs

> 66 She bears the load of lust he left behind, And he the burden of a guilty mind.
> **The Rape of Lucrece**
> ll.734–735 99

herself. "Even here she sheathèd in her harmless breast / A harmful knife, that thence her soul unsheathed. / That blow did bail it from the deep unrest / Of that polluted prison where it breathed." (ll.1723–1726).

Her father and Collatine grieve over her body and Tarquin and all his family are banished from Rome.

Publication
Shakespeare seems to have thought of *The Rape of Lucrece* as a tragic companion piece to the ironically comic *Venus and Adonis*. In dedicating the earlier poem to the Earl of Southampton, he had promised that, if the Earl liked it, he would "take advantage of all idle hours till I have honoured you with some graver labour." *The Rape of Lucrece*, also dedicated to the earl, followed a year later, in 1594. Like the earlier poem, it was printed by Shakespeare's fellow Stratfordian Richard Field. (The title page calls it simply *Lucrece*, but the pages are headed with the longer title.) »

Dedication

The dedication to this poem is written in much warmer terms than that to *Venus and Adonis*: "The love I dedicate to your lordship is without end, where of this pamphlet without beginning is but a superfluous moiety. The warrant I have of your honourable disposition, not the worth of my untutored lines, makes it assured of acceptance. What I have done is yours; what I have to do is yours, being part in all I have, devoted yours. Were my worth greater my duty would show greater; meantime, as it is, it is bound to your lordship, to whom I wish long life still lengthened with all happiness. Your lordship's in all duty, William Shakespeare." Dedications could be mere formalities, intended

Italian artist Palma Giovane depicted the rape of Lucrece in this painting in about 1570. Many artists would have portrayed this famous tale in paintings that Shakespeare would have seen.

 Even here she sheathèd
in her harmless breast
A harmful knife,
that thence her soul
unsheathed.
That blow did bail it
from the deep unrest
Of that polluted prison
where it breathed.
The Rape of Lucrece
ll.1723–1726

to indicate to potential purchasers that the author of a book had an eminent patron, and perhaps in the hope of a reward – two guineas (a little over £2) was a standard sum – from the dedicatee. But the warmth of affection – indeed, the "love… without end" – expressed here has

understandably given rise to the suggestion that Shakespeare had a genuinely close friendship with the young, precociously talented, and remarkably good-looking aristocrat.

After the dedication comes "The Argument", a prose summary of the poem's action. The story it tells differs somewhat from that of the poem itself, and it may not have been written by Shakespeare.

Style and reception

The poem is written in the seven-line stanza form known as rhyme royal, which Shakespeare also uses in "A Lover's Complaint". Each line is an iambic pentameter – ten syllables in which, normally (though with variations), every other syllable is stressed, as, for example, in line 6: "And girdle with embracing flames the waist". The lines rhyme a b a b b c c. The tone, unlike that of *Venus and Adonis*, is deadly serious throughout, and there are many digressions from the basic narrative.

The opening sequence, with its intense account of Tarquin's tormented state of mind as he approaches Lucrece's chamber, is the most vividly powerful. Shakespeare recalls the events and style of this poem in later writings, most memorably when Macbeth, on his way to murder King Duncan, speaks of "withered murder" which, "With Tarquin's ravishing strides, towards his design / Moves like a ghost." (*Macbeth* 2.1.52–56).

Like *Venus and Adonis*, the poem was popular right from its first publication. Six editions appeared in Shakespeare's lifetime, with another three by 1655. There are several admiring contemporary references to it. In 1818, the English poet Samuel Taylor Coleridge wrote of *The Rape of Lucrece* that the poem "gave ample proof of his possession of a most profound, energetic, and philosophical mind, without which he might have pleased, but could not have been a great dramatic poet".

The poem's rhetorical style fell out of fashion in later times, but more recently it has come to be admired for its profoundly dramatic quality and for its anticipations of Shakespeare's later work, especially in his plays based on Roman history and in *Macbeth*.

Britten's opera

In 1946, British composer Benjamin Britten wrote an opera based on Shakespeare's story. He was inspired on seeing a play adapted from the poem by French playwright André Obey. Britten's work is a "chamber opera" – an intimate work with 13 musicians and eight singers. ∎

Classical tale

Like *Venus and Adonis*, *The Rape of Lucrece* is an example of a literary genre that flourished in the 1590s: long, classically based narrative poems telling stories of romantic love, often inspired in both tone and subject matter by the Roman poet Ovid, whose writings were much studied in grammar schools such as that of Stratford-upon-Avon.

Unlike *Venus and Adonis*, this time the subject matter is historical, not mythical. The events took place in 509 BCE and were already legendary by the time of the first surviving account, by the Roman historian Livy in his history of Rome published between 27 and 25 BCE. Shakespeare seems mainly to have used the account given by Ovid in his poem *Fasti*, known in English as *The Book of Days*, or *Chronicles*, first published in 8 CE. He seems also to have drawn on the Roman historian Livy and other sources. Shakespeare concentrates on the private rather than the political aspects of the story, and makes a little narrative material go a long way.

THE LORD CHAMBERL

1594–1603

By the time the theatres reopened after the plague epidemic of 1592–94, the literary success Shakespeare had achieved with the publication of *Venus and Adonis* in 1594 helped him engineer a uniquely secure position in the theatre world.

With the theatres back in business, Lord Hunsdon, the Lord Chamberlain, reconstituted his theatre company as the Lord Chamberlain's Men. It brought together leading actors of the day, such as the tragedian Richard Burbage, who would launch some of Shakespeare's greatest roles; the clown William Kemp, who triumphed as the comic creation Falstaff; and Shakespeare himself. Crucially, the leading actors all owned shares in the company; Shakespeare had a 10 per cent stake.

That stake ensured Shakespeare had an income of between £200 and £700 a year – by no means a fortune, but far above any other playwright's earnings. Shakespeare chose to live frugally, renting various places to live in London, and by 1597, he had saved enough to buy his family a large house in Stratford – New Place. He went on to buy land nearby, and even a coat of arms.

Creative drive

Shakespeare's position in the company gave him a platform for his plays – and he made the most of it. In the two-year break caused by the plague, he had honed his poetic and dramatic skills, and over the next nine years, he wrote 17 plays, ranging from the romantic comedies *A Midsummer Night's Dream* and *Twelfth Night* to the stirring history of *Henry V* and the tragedy of *Hamlet*. Many thousands packed the theatre to watch them.

Evidence for the dating of the early plays is limited, but reference to several of Shakespeare's plays is made by the little-known writer Francis Meres in a book called *Palladis Tamia: Wit's Treasury* published in 1598. Meres asserts that "Shakespeare among the English is the most excellent for the stage; for comedy, witness his *Gentlemen of Verona*, his *Errors*, his *Love Labour's Lost*, his *Love Labour's Won*, his *Midsummer's Night Dream*, and his *Merchant of Venice*; for tragedy, his *Richard II, Richard III, Henry IV, King John, Titus Andronicus*, and his *Romeo and Juliet*." Thus scholars have been given a date by which all of these plays must have been written.

Theatre on the edge

Although the Lord Chamberlain's men often performed before the queen, theatre life was precarious. The company was always playing cat-and-mouse with authorities keen to control what they saw as salacious entertainment, and theatres stayed on marginal land beyond the city walls. In 1598, the landlord of a Shoreditch playhouse known as The Theatre demanded a huge rise in rent, then decided to tear down the building altogether. Shakespeare's company secretly dismantled it beam by beam and carried the timbers over the river to Southwark to erect a new theatre, The Globe, which was owned by the company. The Globe was an instant triumph. In its opening year, 1599, it saw performances of *Julius Caesar*, *As You Like It*, *Henry V*, and *Hamlet*. The company's worries, however, went beyond capricious landlords. Theatre at this time could be political dynamite, and actors faced a constant battle to get scripts past the Master of the Revels, who vetted every play.

Dangerous times

Just how far this censorship went is clear from the cuts made to the script of *Sir Thomas More*. This play, which Shakespeare had a hand in but which has several authors, portrays the Chancellor of King Henry VIII, who refused to grant the king a divorce, in a favourable light. Some have argued that Shakespeare was a Catholic rebel, who stuffed his plays with coded symbols designed to evade the censor but convey a powerful message to anyone who understood them. If this is true, he was playing a risky game. It is true that the Lord Chamberlain's Men were not afraid of political controversy. On 7 February 1601, Sir Gelly Meyrick, acting on behalf of the Earl of Essex, commissioned a special performance of *Richard II* at The Globe, including the scenes in which the monarch is deposed and murdered – scenes too incendiary to publish at the time. The performance went ahead, and the very next day the Earl of Essex led a small army towards Whitehall Palace to bring down the queen and replace her with James VI of Scotland. Essex's revolution ended in farce and the Earl was executed. It could all have turned out badly for Shakespeare and the Chamberlain's Men, but somehow they managed to escape punishment. ■

WHO CAN SEVER LOVE FROM CHARITY?

LOVE'S LABOUR'S LOST (1594–1595)

At the court of Navarre, King Ferdinand tells his lords that, to be successful, they must study and renounce women for three years. Dumaine and Longueville agree but Biron is reluctant. The king agrees that he must make an exception for the Princess of France who is soon to arrive. Biron, seeing that rules can be bent, agrees to the oath. The pompous Armado has Costard imprisoned, saying that he saw him with Jaquenetta, and then reveals that he is in love with Jaquenetta. The Princess of France arrives. Her ladies each praise one of the lords so warmly that the princess swears they must be in love. The princess plays at being offended by her cool reception from the king. Biron and Rosaline spar verbally and Dumaine and Longueville ask Katharine and Maria's names. Boyet insists that the king is in love with the princess, and the ladies tease him for being a "love-monger".

Armado asks the boy Mote to sing to Jaquenetta for him, but Mote and Costard make fun of him. Armado sets Costard free on condition he takes a letter to Jaquenetta. Biron also gives Costard a letter for Rosaline. Biron curses his foolishness in falling in love – and with a girl so deficient.

The princess and the ladies are hunting when Costard says he has a letter for Rosaline from Biron. The princess asks to see it and in his confusion, Costard gives Boyet Armado's letter. Boyet realizes it is meant for Jaquenetta, but the princess asks him to read it out loud. Boyet teases Rosaline bawdily about Biron and she responds in kind. Boyet indulges in an innuendo-laden exchange with Maria, joined by Costard who doesn't quite get it all. Holofernes discusses the hunt with Dull and Nathaniel. Jaquenetta arrives with Costard and asks them to read the letter from Armado. It is, of course, Biron's letter to Rosaline and after Holofernes analyses the poem's merit they take it to the king.

Biron overhears the king composing a love sonnet. Biron and the king hear Longueville doing the same. Longueville hears Dumaine composing a sonnet. Longueville accuses Dumaine of breaking their agreement. The king accuses Longueville. Biron criticizes all three. Costard arrives with Biron's letter to Rosaline. The quartet agrees to forget their pact and woo the ladies in earnest.

Armado, Holofernes, Nathaniel, Dull, and Mote are to entertain the party. They disguise themselves, but the ladies, forewarned, play them along. When the men return dressed as themselves, the ladies pretend not to recognize them. The lords decide to woo from now on only with honesty, but then news arrives that the princess's father has died. Her marriage is postponed, and the ladies prepare to depart. ∎

These are barren tasks, too hard to keep – Not to see ladies, study, fast, not sleep.
Biron
Act 1, Scene 1

Love's Labour's Lost is the most conspicuously poetic of all Shakespeare's plays, with nearly two-thirds of the play in rhyming verse. Its clever word-play must have delighted the intellectual elite at the Elizabethan court, who counted this among their favourite Shakespeare plays.

However, the play's contemporary in-jokes have often been lost on audiences since then, and in the 18th and 19th centuries, it was the least performed of all Shakespeare's plays. Audiences watching the play can all too easily feel like the constable Dull, who, when the schoolteacher Holofernes comments, "Thou hast spoken no word all this while," replies, "Nor understood none neither, sir." (5.1.142–144).

The poetic knot-garden

In recent years, directors have found ways to release the play's witty comedy and sweet romance and make the most of its ingenious structure, likened by some to the elaborate Elizabethan knot garden that the pretentious

British director Kenneth Branagh made his movie version of *Love's Labour's Lost* (2000) a romantic 1930s Hollywood musical. Here, the young lords anticipate the arrival of the ladies.

Spaniard Armado alludes to in his letter to the king. It is a play that may be clever, but it also has a heart that goes beyond mere verbal tricks, as the surprisingly nuanced and affecting ending bears out.

The set-up is very simple. With the country at peace, the King of Navarre calls upon his lords to do nothing but study for three years – to eat little, to sleep little, and to renounce the company of women. The joke is, of course, that they haven't a hope of succeeding, least of all the king. As Biron, the least convinced of his lords, points out: "'Item: If any man be seen to talk with a woman within the term of three years, he shall endure such public shame as the rest of the court can possibly devise.' / This article, my liege, yourself must break; For well you know here comes in embassy / The French king's daughter with yourself to speak" (1.1.128–133). So already the king must make exception for the French king's daughter and her ladies – and as soon as this first exception is made, the whole plan quickly breaks down.

Much of the humour hinges on how the lords and the king pretend to each other that they are not falling under the romantic spell of the ladies, while the ladies amuse themselves watching the men squirm. The plot could hardly be simpler. Yet Shakespeare uses this straightforward story to create a gloriously intricate game of words. There is ample scope for a clever and merciless spoof of the pretentious wordplay of the day, which in many places is also downright obscene.

Finding love and self

The thrust of the play is clear enough: that it is absurd for men to cut themselves off from women and from love in order to find » out about the world – women and love are the only true education. As Biron finally acknowledges: "From women's eyes this doctrine I derive. / They sparkle still the right Promethean fire. / They are the books, the arts, the academes / That show, contain, and nourish all the world" (4.3.326–329).

Shakespeare is keenly aware that love poetry is no substitute for real-life love, and, as later plays such as *Romeo and Juliet* and *As You Like It* show, young men who indulge in love poetry are often mistaking the idea of love for the real thing. This indulgence is the path taken by the King of Navarre, Biron, Dumaine, and Longueville, and so they are easily fooled by the ladies into paying court to the wrong girl when the ladies swap accessories.

The men are misguided enough, too, to think that they can disguise themselves to go wooing. The girls are not fooled – and only pretend not to know the lords when they come back as themselves. Finally, Biron realizes he must learn to be himself rather than act an image of love. In his succinct summary of the play, he says: "Let us once lose our oaths to find ourselves, / Or else we lose ourselves to keep our oaths." (4.3.337–338).

The final lesson

Unexpectedly, Shakespeare avoids giving us a neat happy ending. After Biron and the other men have been through this moment of self-discovery, they sit down to watch the pageant of the Nine Worthies presented by Holofernes, Nathaniel, Moth, Costard, and Armado. The women watch quietly, but in their performances, the men mock so mercilessly that even the pedant Holofernes is moved to a heartfelt criticism, "This is not generous, not gentle, not humble" (5.2.622).

In the middle of the pageant, news arrives that the princess's father, the King of France, has suddenly died. The normal round of weddings that might tie up a comedy do not happen. Instead, the ladies each ask their suitors to wait a year, and to use that year to learn more about people and the world. Rosaline instructs Biron to tend the sick, and when he protests that there are no jokes in a hospital full of death, Rosaline reminds him that: "A jest's prosperity lies in the ear / Of him that hears it" (5.2.847–848). The play ends poignantly with haunting songs of the seasons, first the cuckoo for spring then the owl for winter. ∎

This orderly Elizabethan knot garden at Nyewood House in East Sussex, echoes the careful grouping of actors and the mannered patterns of speech of *Love's Labour's Lost*.

DOWN, DOWN I COME LIKE GLIST'RING PHAETHON
RICHARD II (1595)

The play opens with an accusation of treason made by Bolingbroke against Mowbray. The latter stands accused of murdering the Duke of Gloucester, but John of Gaunt suspects that King Richard himself is implicated in the murder. Richard banishes Bolingbroke for 10 years, later commuted to six, but Mowbray is permanently exiled.

Bolingbroke wins popular sympathy as he leaves, while Richard alienates the people by levying high taxes. When Gaunt dies, Richard seizes all the land and wealth that by rights should pass to Gaunt's son, Bolingbroke. The nobles Ross, Willoughby, and Northumberland agree to meet Bolingbroke, who is to arrive back on English shores with an army.

While Richard is quelling a rebellion in Ireland the Queen is comforted by Bushy, Bagot, and Green. Then news is heard of Bolingbroke's return and the nobles' desertion. York, whom Richard left in charge, prepares for their attack.

At Berkeley Castle, York accuses Bolingbroke of treason. Bolingbroke insists that he was banished as Hereford, not as the Duke of Lancaster, and that he has a right to defend his inheritance. York allows them to enter the castle.

Richard lands on the Welsh coast and greets the land joyfully. However, he despairs at the news brought by messengers. At Flint Castle, Bolingbroke demands that Richard repeal his banishment and restore his inheritance. Richard appears on the battlements and grants his request. Bolingbroke kneels to Richard but the power has shifted. Richard submits to travel to London with him.

York's son Aumerle is accused by Bagot of plotting Gloucester's death and being disloyal to Bolingbroke. Multiple challenges to fight ensue. York announces that Richard has named Bolingbroke his heir and is ready to resign his throne to him.

Richard is forced publicly to renounce the throne. He takes off his crown and sceptre but refuses to read the charges against him. Looking at his face in a mirror, he comments that "A brittle glory shineth in this face. As brittle as the glory is the face." (4.1.277–278). Bolingbroke has him taken to the Tower. On the way, Richard meets his Queen and they say goodbye. York discovers that his son, Aumerle, is involved in a plot against Bolingbroke, now King Henry IV. He betrays him to the King, but the Duchess's eloquence manages to secure a pardon. Carlisle and the other conspirators will be executed.

Sir Piers Exton murders Richard at Pomfret Castle, and takes the body to Bolingbroke, expecting a reward, but the new King is deeply ashamed of the action. He has Exton banished, and sets off on a pilgrimage to the Holy Land. ∎

IN CONTEXT

THEMES
Kingship, betrayal, character flaws

SETTING
Locations in England and Wales during the reign of Richard II (1367–1400)

SOURCES
1587 Raphael Holinshed's *Chronicles of England, Scotland and Ireland*.

c.1592 Christopher Marlowe's play *Edward II*.

1595 Samuel Daniel's epic poem *The First Four Books of the Civil Wars*.

When Richard observes of himself "Down, down I come like glist'ring Phaethon" (3.3.177), he offers a complex image of his own tragic fate. Phaethon was the son of Phoebus/Apollo, the sun-god of Greek mythology. According to legend, the youth stole his father's fiery chariot and drove it through the sky, but he could not keep control of the horses and caused terrible destruction to Earth. Jove hurled a thunderbolt at the chariot, and Phaethon plunged to his death.

Often interpreted as signifying the dangers of ambition, the myth initially seems more appropriate to the usurping Bolingbroke than to Richard, the divinely-appointed king of England, whose inherent majesty is often described in terms of the sun. Yet the myth was also used to condemn a failure of government, which is how Richard uses it, describing himself as, like Phaethon, "Wanting the manage of unruly jades" (3.3.178). The gardener will later confirm that it was Richard's inability to control his nobles that brought about his downfall: "We at time of year / Do wound the bark, the skin of our fruit trees, / Lest, being over-proud in sap and blood, / With too much riches it confound itself. / Had he done so to great and growing men, / They might have lived to bear, and he to taste, / Their fruits of duty." (3.4.58–64)

Power struggle
Richard's difficulties reflect the reality of 14th-century England, which saw a struggle between the nobles and the monarchy. At the start of the play, Richard cannot quell the argument between Bolingbroke and Mowbray because their obedience to the king matters less to them than personal honour. Indeed, the play's extraordinary language of sacramental kingship is partly driven by an awareness that the king is but one among a number of competing nobles who all have a claim to the throne.

Contemporary parallels
When Shakespeare wrote the play, the story of Richard II was a controversial one because of perceived analogies between his reign and that of Elizabeth I. The latter famously said to William Lambarde in 1601, "I am Richard II. Know ye not that?"

Like Richard, Elizabeth was perceived to be unduly influenced by court favourites, most notably the earls of Leicester and Essex. Like Richard, she had to contend with rebellion in Ireland, although she sent Essex to deal with it, rather than making the mistake of leaving the kingdom. She was also in the difficult position of lacking an heir. One of the accusations against Bushy, Bagot, and Green in Shakespeare's play is that they have prevented Richard from ensuring the succession. This is attributed not only to dissension between Richard and his Queen, but to his being "corrupted" in a homosexual sense, in a possible echo of Marlowe's Edward II where the king's sexual preferences are more

 Ah, Richard! With the eyes of heavy mind I see thy glory, like a shooting star, Fall to the base earth from the firmament.
Earl of Salisbury
Act 2, Scene 4

explicitly divisive. Elizabeth did not have this particular charge to answer, but her failure to produce an heir – a consequence of her refusal to marry – encouraged ambitions among her powerful nobles, which would have been dissipated if the succession had been clearly determined. »

Richard compares himself to Phaethon, the youth of Greek myth who was struck from the skies. The fall is depicted here by Michelangelo, in an engraving Shakespeare may have seen.

Gaunt's speech

This royal throne of kings,
*   this sceptred isle,*
This earth of majesty,
*   this seat of Mars,*
This other Eden,
*   demi-paradise,*
This fortress built by
*   nature for herself*
Against infection and
*   the hand of war,*
This happy breed of men,
*   this little world,*
This precious stone set
*   in the silver sea,*
Which serves it in the
*   office of a wall,*
Or as a moat defensive
*   to a house*
Against the envy of less
*   happier lands;*
This blessèd plot, this earth,
*   this realm, this England*
(2.1.40–50)

John of Gaunt's speech is one of the most quoted in the Shakespearean canon, and was anthologized as early as 1600. Its imagery of England as walled in by the sea, protected by Nature, has been central to constructions of the nation, as has its imagery of England breeding warriors and kings. It provided titles for at least two British World War II films: David Lean's *This Happy Breed* (1944) and David MacDonald's *This England* (1941). That said, the speech's jingoism has also undergone some major reassessment, not least because "this England" subsumes within it the separate nations of Wales and Scotland. We should also remember that Gaunt's speech is uttered by a man on his death bed, who testifies to the ways in which "this England" has been ruined. It is an ideal that already does not exist.

Harry Bolingbroke v Richard II

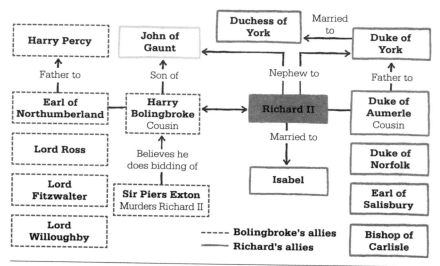

Harry Percy

Father to ↑

Earl of Northumberland

Lord Ross

Lord Fitzwalter

Lord Willoughby

John of Gaunt

Son of ↑

Harry Bolingbroke
Cousin

↑ *Believes he does bidding of*

Sir Piers Exton
Murders Richard II

Duchess of York — *Married to* → Duke of York

Father to ↑

Nephew to

Richard II

Married to

Isabel

Duke of Aumerle
Cousin

Duke of Norfolk

Earl of Salisbury

Bishop of Carlisle

- - - - Bolingbroke's allies
——— Richard's allies

Shakespeare's play was implicated in the problems of his Queen when it was performed on the eve of a rebellion by the Earl of Essex, who had fallen out of favour following failures in Ireland. Supporters of Essex commissioned the Lord Chamberlain's Men to perform the play at the Globe on 7 February 1601. Presumably the deposition scene of Act 4 Scene 1 was included. It had been thought too seditious to be printed, and was absent from the published text until 1608. The next day, the Globe audience tried to stir up rebellion. However, Essex was denounced as a traitor and support dwindled. Shakespeare's company was investigated but not punished.

Self-fulfilling prophecy

While *Richard II* is a history play, it is entitled *The Tragedy of King Richard the Second*. Richard's image of himself as "glist'ring Phaethon" brings to mind the myth of the young god's fall, which has a tragic beauty to it, as Phaethon falls from the sky like a star to earth.

The story reflects something similarly self-aggrandizing in Richard, whose fall inspires wonder and whose self-perception is echoed by other characters. Gaunt warns that "His rash, fierce blaze of riot cannot last" (2.1.33), while Salisbury laments: "Ah, Richard! With the eyes of heavy mind / I see thy glory, like a shooting star, / Fall to the base earth from the firmament" (2.4.18–20). Richard seems to be in love with this image of his own tragic fall and consciously tries to bring it about. Indeed, this is one of Shakespeare's few history plays with no battle scene, reflecting the ease with which Bolingbroke wins the crown. When he offers to "tell sad stories of the death of kings", Richard implicitly refers to the popular medieval definition of tragedy, the so-called de casibus tragedy, derived from Boccaccio's *De Casibus Virorum*

 I live with bread, like you; feel want, Taste grief, need friends. Subjected thus, How can you say to me I am a king?
King Richard II
Act 3, Scene 2

Illustrium (1355–74) (*Of the Fates of Famous Men*). The subjects all suffered a sudden descent from good fortune to adversity and death. When Richard calls for a mirror in which to read his downfall, he may have been alluding to a popular English collection of similar tales called *The Mirror for Magistrates*, which included Richard II.

A willing victim?

Clearly, Shakespeare's character imagines himself as a victim – of Bolingbroke, of the inherent nature of kingship, of fate, and perhaps of his own flaws. But more important than the cause of his tragic fall is the spectacle it makes, to the extent that Richard has been accused of "doom-eagerness", indulging in fantasies of his tragic abjection before they have become a political necessity. For example, Bolingbroke is ostensibly only pursuing repeal from banishment and restoration of inheritance, but Richard mentions deposition as early as Act 3 Scene 3, when he asks: "What must the King do now? Must he submit? / The King shall do it. Must he be deposed? / The King shall be contented. Must he lose / The name of King? A God's name, let it go" (3.3.142–145). Bolingbroke needs to do little more than stand there with an army looking menacing.

Playing the King

The king's pleasure in wordplay and his self-indulgent loquacity suggest Richard as an early forerunner for Hamlet. Along with Hamlet, this is one of the few Shakespearean tragic roles that has been played by women (most recently by Fiona Shaw and Cate Blanchett). Such casting can heighten the contrast between Richard's hyper-emotionalism, including a tendency to weep, and the pragmatism and self-control of Bolingbroke. Alternatively, casting a Richard and a Bolingbroke who look very like one another, or who share the roles between them, can also be effective, bringing out the play's exploration of what makes a king.

Some productions have had two actors play the roles of Richard and Bolingbroke on alternate nights, suggesting the arbitrariness of which man was king, and looking forwards to the Wars of the Roses, during which power would swing from the house of Lancaster to York, and back again. Shakespeare had already staged a series of plays on this theme: Henry VI Parts One, Two, and Three, and Richard III. In Richard II, he was returning to an action – the murder of a lawful king – that would change the perception of kingship. At the same time, however self-aggrandizing Richard appears, the play supports his argument that to be a king is inevitably to be the hero in a tragic cycle. ∎

A romantic engraving depicts Richard dying heroically at the hands of Piers Exton. The manner of Richard's murder is not known for certain. It is possible that he was starved to death.

A PAIR OF STAR-CROSSED LOVERS
ROMEO AND JULIET (1595)

The chorus sets the scene as Verona, where two families feud. The play will last two hours, Chorus says, and tell the story of two of their children whose doomed love will end in death, reconciling the families at last.

The play then erupts onto the streets of Verona, and a brawl between the rival families, the Montagues and Capulets, is halted only by the intervention of the Prince of Verona. To appease the Prince, old Capulet agrees to marry his 13-year-old daughter Juliet to the Prince's young kinsman, Paris, and arranges a masked ball to celebrate. Young Romeo Montague and his friends (including the wit Mercutio) sneak into the ball to get a glimpse of Rosaline Capulet, the object of Romeo's unrequited love – but Romeo is instead completely smitten by Rosaline's cousin Juliet.

Later that night, Romeo, lingering in the orchard below Juliet's balcony, overhears her declare that she loves him despite his family name, and he makes himself known to her. Ecstatic, the pair resolve to marry the following night. Friar Laurence and Juliet's nurse agree to help them, hoping the union will end the feud. Next day in the street, Mercutio taunts Tybalt Capulet and the two begin to fence. But although only Romeo knows it, Tybalt is now his cousin-in-law and Romeo tries to break up the fight. Tybalt fatally wounds Mercutio. Romeo kills Tybalt in revenge, and the Prince banishes Romeo from Verona to Mantua.

Seeing Juliet distraught, though not knowing why, old Capulet decides her wedding to Paris must go ahead right away. Desperate, Juliet asks Friar Laurence for help. The friar advises her to escape the wedding by taking a sleeping-draught, which will make her seem dead for 42 hours. The friar will send a message to Romeo in Mantua, who can then rescue her from the family tomb when she awakens. Juliet goes ahead with the plan, and is found apparently dead on the morning of the wedding.

The friar's message does not reach Romeo and he hears only of Juliet's death. Grief-stricken, Romeo rushes back to Verona and creeps into the Capulet tomb, where he meets Paris. The two fight and Paris is killed. Romeo lays down beside Juliet's apparently lifeless body, takes poison, and dies. Not long after, Juliet regains consciousness and finds Romeo dead. She tries to take the poison from his lips with a kiss, but death eludes her, so she takes Romeo's dagger, stabs herself, and dies.

As the bodies are discovered, Friar Laurence explains the sorry situation to the Prince, who lambasts the families whose feuding has brought this tragedy. The old men shake hands and agree to end their enmity. ■

IN CONTEXT

THEMES
Jealousy, loyalty, betrayal, romantic love, male friendship

SETTING
Verona, Italy

SOURCES
1562 Arthur Brooke's poem *The Tragical History of Romeus and Juliet.*

Romeo and Juliet is perhaps the most familiar of all Shakespeare's plays: a tale of two young lovers, doomed to be kept apart. There are many other stories of separated lovers, but the intensity of Romeo and Juliet's romance gives Shakespeare's drama an emotional charge that has resonated through the ages.

Romeo and Juliet fall in love instantly, marry the next day, and have one brief and precious night of love before they are forced asunder by their families' feud, and plunged into the spiral of events that brings them both to suicide. Few plays have ever captured so well the wild and heady energy of youthful emotion – not only its loves, but its rage, its vitality, and its volatility in a fractured world where elders fail to provide wise guidance.

No wonder this play often seems to speak to contemporary youth with such startling immediacy.

Shakespeare makes the fate that awaits the lovers clear right from the start. In the short 14-line opening verse, the Chorus reveals the entire plot, telling us that the play is about two "star-crossed" lovers – lovers whose sad and conjoined fate is written in the stars – and that they will die before their parents see sense: "The fearful passage of their death-marked love / And the continuance of their parents' rage – / Which but their children's end, naught could remove – / Is now the two-hours' traffic of our stage;" (Prologue.9–12).

To modern audiences, used to films whose plots are constructed to keep the audience guessing, with plot twists right up until the end, this is a surprise, and today's reviewers might feel obliged to put in a spoiler alert. Far from spoiling the play for the audience, however, it gives the drive that makes *Romeo and Juliet* a compelling drama. We know exactly what is going to happen to the young lovers as they come together, even though they don't. We know that their love is doomed even as they »

It is perhaps because we must see the pair as innocents that they are so young. Franco Zeffirelli picked up on this in his 1968 film version with Olivia Hussey, just 16 years old, as Juliet.

embark on it with such beguiling charm, innocence, and optimism, and we can hardly turn away as they hurtle blindly towards their fateful end.

Indeed, it is the sense that their love is so powerful and inevitable that it can only end in death that has made their story captivating ever since the play was first performed in the 1590s. For romantics, especially the young, the idea of love flying in the face of a cruel world is intoxicating.

Origins of the story

The basic story in which young lovers choose to die together rather than live apart is an ancient one. The Roman poet Ovid's *Metamorphoses*, for instance, contains the story of the separated lovers Pyramus and Thisbe, which Shakespeare parodied in his next play, *A Midsummer Night's Dream*. In the 3rd century CE, the story of *Ephesiaca*, by the Greek writer Xenophon of Ephesus, sees the 16-year-old Habrocomes and 14-year-old Anthia embark on a suicide pact.

The story of Romeo and Juliet in particular became popular in 16th-century Italy in versions such as Luigi da Porto's 1530 novel *Giulietta e Romeo*. The two feuding families in the story, the Montecchi (Montagues) of Verona and the Capeletti (Capulets) of Cremona, were historical, and the poet Dante writes of them in his *Purgatorio* as being at the centre of civil strife in 13th-century Italy. Shakespeare's immediate source, though, was an English version of the story written as a long poem in 1562 by Arthur Brooke entitled *The Tragical History of Romeus and Juliet*.

Shakespeare's changes

Many of the principal characters in *Romeo and Juliet* are much the same as in Brooke's poem, but Shakespeare's treatment of the story is very different. In *Romeo and Juliet*, the lovers have just one night together after their wedding; in Brooke's poem, Romeo visits Juliet every night for a month or two. Shakespeare's story is faster, and this serves to heighten the tragic brevity of the romance. Shakespeare has a very different attitude towards the lovers. Brooke thoroughly disapproves of them; they are "unfortunate lovers, thrilling themselves to unhonest desire, neglecting the authority and advice of parents and friends." Shakespeare, however, is on their side. In *Romeo and Juliet*, they are innocent victims – Juliet is just 13 – and in the beauty and ardour of their love, they soar far above their parents' bickering and bitterness. It is this large-hearted sympathy that gives Shakespeare such wide appeal, and made his message so subversive at the time.

Elizabethan feuds

Romeo and Juliet was written at a time when England was as divided as it has ever been. King Henry VIII had split from the Roman Catholic church in 1533, and the wounds this had caused were still red raw. The Protestant regime of the reigning Queen Elizabeth I, Henry VIII's daughter, (pictured) was under attack from Catholics both from within the country and from abroad. The regime was fighting back, led by the queen's first minister Robert Cecil. Catholic recusants were hunted down ruthlessly by Cecil's henchmen, while agents of the Catholic Counter Reformation conspired to bring Protestant England back into the fold.

The younger generation, of which Shakespeare was one, were indeed caught between the warring factions – and it may be that *Romeo and Juliet* was intended as a reminder to them of the tragic consequences of their bitter conflict for their offspring. Romeo and Juliet could have found counterparts in England, with Protestants and Catholics replacing the Montagues and Capulets as the feuding neighbours.

The feuding houses of Verona

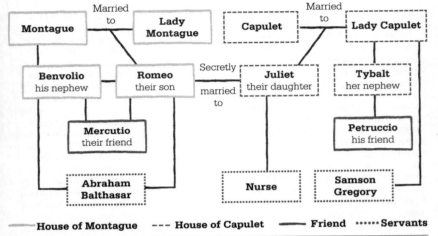

═══ **House of Montague**   --- **House of Capulet**   ━━━ **Friend**   ······ **Servants**

While the characters in Brooke's poem are largely archetypes, in *Romeo and Juliet*, they are much more fleshed out and real. Shakespeare also brings minor characters such as the well-intentioned Friar Laurence and the chatterbox Nurse fully to life. Romeo's quick-witted and earthy friend Mercutio is entirely Shakespeare's creation, one of his most appealing. It is Mercutio's death in a sword-fight at the beginning of Act 3 that wrenches the mood of the play dramatically from comedy to tragedy.

A stage revolution

It is hard to appreciate today just how revolutionary Shakespeare was in bringing this story to the English stage. Italian novels were certainly becoming increasingly popular with the younger generation at the time – Shakespeare was not yet 30 when he wrote *Romeo and Juliet* – but no-one had put this kind of story on stage before. Previously, tragic drama had been mostly about noble lords and mighty warriors in grand settings. Here, the hero and heroine are just two ordinary contemporary teenagers, distinguished only by their love and their way with words, in an ordinary city that happens to be called Verona, but could be

anywhere. The young Shakespeare's play was no slowly unfolding, grand epic as most earlier tragedies had been, but fast-paced, down, and dirty.

In the brief and measured verse with which the Chorus outlines the scenario, Shakespeare seems to be setting us up for the same cautionary tale of misbegotten love as appears in Brooke's version. But as soon as this cautionary rhyme is done, we are plunged into the anarchic reality of the feud, as the formal poetry gives way to a full-scale brawl on the streets of Verona. In the roughest of prose and with rude gestures, two pairs of servants, Samson and Gregory, Abraham and Balthasar, hurl bawdy threats at each other. Samson talks of cutting off the (maiden) heads of the Montague women.

Swords are drawn, fighting begins, and soon the young blades of the families enter the fray, followed quickly by old Capulet, feebly wielding his sword against the equally frail old Montague – as feebly, his much younger wife implies, as he now wields his marital "sword". This is an unruly world of macho posturing in which even the aged who should know better join in, and wisdom and guidance is left in the dubious hands of Friar Laurence and Juliet's nurse.»

What's in a name?

In such a dysfunctional city, "name" is everything, and true substance and feeling is lost. But when Romeo and Juliet later embark on their romance, Juliet realizes a name can be a terrible trap, lamenting famously: "O Romeo, Romeo, wherefore [why] art thou Romeo? / ...That which we call a rose / By any other word would smell as sweet." (2.1.75–86) Juliet yearns for her love to provide a way to transcend the trap of names: "Romeo, doff thy name, / And for thy name – which is no part of thee – / Take all myself." (2.1.89–91) But ultimately even their true love is not enough. "In what vile part of this anatomy /Doth my name lodge?" (3.4.105–106) Romeo asks Friar Laurence after his banishment, likewise realizing the poison in his name and desperate to rid himself of it. That name becomes his death sentence.

Posturing love

In Verona's world of false honour, even love, to begin with, is a posture. When Romeo first appears, wandering distractedly into the aftermath of the brawl, he is in love, not with Juliet – who he has yet to meet, – but with a Capulet girl called Rosaline. She is never fully seen, remaining as insubstantial as Romeo's love for her.

Fittingly, it seems, for a romance set in Italy, Romeo declares his love for Rosaline in a sonnet – a short form of poem in 14 lines, which had been established by the 13th-century Italian poet Guittone of Arezzo and popularized by Petrarch. By the time of Shakespeare, sonnets had become the standard literary form for expressions of love, especially if unrequited – although Shakespeare was soon to invigorate the form with his own verses. Sonnets employed rhetorical devices including oxymoron – the putting together of contradictory words such as "cold fire" and "loving hate". Romeo's sonnet to Rosaline is stuffed with conventional oxymorons: "Why, then, O brawling love, O loving hate, / O anything of nothing first create; / O heavy lightness, serious vanity, / Misshapen chaos of well-seeming forms, / Feather of lead, bright smoke, cold fire, sick health," (1.1.173–177).

Romeo has yet to learn that love, too, must break from these conventions to find something more truthful. Even when he sees Juliet for the first time, he speaks of her in formal couplets: "Did my heart love till now? Forswear it, sight, / For I ne'er saw true beauty till this night." (1.5.51–52).

Breaking convention

When Romeo and Juliet speak to each other for the first time, remarkably, they share the lines of a sonnet with breathless intensity, and the sonnet, conventionally the most personal and unspoken of verses, becomes a tender conversation. The final couplet is shared between the two of them, as if to emphasize their miraculous connection and linked destiny:

"**Juliet:** Saints do not move, though grant for prayers' sake. **Romeo:** Then move not while my prayer's effect I take. [He kisses her.]" (1.5.104–105).

Contemporary audiences will have identified in Mercutio a portrait of the playwright Christopher Marlowe who, like Mercutio, died in a knife fight, in 1593. This illustration dates from 1903.

From this point on, Romeo largely abandons rhyme when speaking to Juliet, and they both now speak mostly in blank verse, finding a new and more truthful way of interacting. It is the young Juliet who matures into this newer expression of love first, and Romeo is drawn in her wake.

The balcony scene
In the balcony scene, a stage metaphor for separated love, Romeo speaks to Juliet from the orchard below her balcony. The device of separating them on stage by the height of the balcony allows them to talk with a passion that would be impossible if they were together, as it could only lead to physicality.

Language of love
Shakespeare finds a new language of love that has a freshness and immediacy that was entirely new in English verse – rich in imagery, yet sincerely personal and new-minted by this earnest young couple, with rich poetic allusions such as Juliet's wish to be a falconer to lure Romeo back like a trained falcon replacing more formal metaphors. In his language, as in his story, Shakespeare moves on from the divisive conventions of the past to a new and more honest and profound mode of expression. Romeo and Juliet's lines resonate with real feeling. Rarely has young love been expressed with such tenderness and such beauty.

Yet that love is doomed from the start. Juliet urgently wishes for time to rush by to bring on the night, "the love-performing night" (3.2.5) that will allow them to be together. But the night is both a time of love and a symbol of death, and the urgent race into the dark is also a headlong charge into the galloping events that bring them to their tragic end.

Romeo and Juliet is full of oppositions – light versus dark, youth versus age, time running fast and time running slow, the moon versus the stars, love versus hate. Juliet describes Romeo to her nurse as "My only love sprung from my only hate" (1.5.137), as if the oxymorons of Romeo's sonnet to Rosaline have taken life.

As we were told it would, it is the darkness that wins out. Romeo and Juliet's love cannot win, for their romantic ideals prove no match for the force of their elders' quarrels. However, in death, they prove the catalyst that brings the quarrels to an abrupt end. Capulet reaches out to Montague "O brother Montague, give me thy hand" (5.3.295), as each praises the other's child. The Prince stands lamenting over their bodies: "A glooming peace this morning with it brings. / The sun for sorrow will not show his head." (5.3.304–305). Those left behind feel a profound shame. ∎

Adaptations

At least 30 operas and ballets have been adapted from Shakespeare's *Romeo and Juliet*, including Prokofiev's 1935 ballet Romeo and Juliet and Gounod's opera *Roméo et Juliette* (1867). Leonard Bernstein and Stephen Sondheim's 1957 stage musical *West Side Story* moves the action to New York's tough Upper West Side, where rival gangs, the Sharks and the Jets, clash. Many other stage shows have been adapted from Shakespeare's play, including French composer Gérard Presgurvic's musical spectacle *Roméo et Juliette: de la Haine à l'Amour* (2001).

More than 60 different film versions have been created, beginning with Clemence Maurice's 1900 production. One of the best known is Franco Zeffirelli's 1968 film, which made an impact with its beautiful teenage leads, including 16-year-old Olivia Hussey as Juliet in a controversial nude scene. Baz Luhrmann's *Romeo + Juliet* (1996, pictured above), starred Leonardo DiCaprio and Claire Danes, and set the action in a modern world of edgy youth on California's "Verona Beach".

THE COURSE OF TRUE LOVE NEVER DID RUN SMOOTH
A MIDSUMMER NIGHT'S DREAM (1595)

In Athens, Theseus is preparing for his wedding to Hippolyta, the vanquished queen of the Amazons, when in bursts Egeus complaining that his daughter Hermia refuses to marry Demetrius. He says that she has been bewitched by Lysander. Theseus commands Hermia to marry Demetrius. Hermia and Lysander decide to elope and agree to meet the next night in the forest. Hermia confides in Helena. Helena is in love with Demetrius. To win Demetrius's love, Helena tells him of the elopement. A band of artisans resolve to meet in the forest to rehearse a play in honour of the wedding.

In the forest, the fairy king and queen, Oberon and Titania, quarrel over a changeling child. Oberon sends mischievous Puck to find the juice of a flower which, when placed in the eyes of a sleeper, makes them fall in love with the first person they see on waking. Oberon drops the juice on Titania's eyes. Demetrius and Helena pursue Hermia and Lysander into the forest. Oberon orders Puck to drop the juice in Demetrius's eyes so that he falls in love Helena – but Puck mistakenly gives the juice to Lysander, who wakes and sees Helena and falls in love with her.

As the artisans rehearse, Puck changes the head of Bottom the weaver for that of a donkey. Bottom's companions flee, but Titania, sleeping nearby, awakes and falls in love with him. As the lovers appear, it is clear something is awry, and Oberon tries to make amends by applying the love juice to Demetrius's eyes. But when Demetrius falls

 O long and tedious night,
Abate thy hours.
Helena
Act 3, Scene 2

in love with Helena, too, she thinks it is all a cruel joke. The boys and girls fight and run through the forest before falling asleep. As they sleep, Puck removes the spell from Lysander's eyes.

Oberon removes the spell from Titania's eyes, and she is appalled when she wakes with Bottom in her arms. Oberon commands Puck to switch Bottom's head back, and Oberon and Titania are reconciled.

Theseus and Hippolyta, out hunting with Egeus, come upon the sleeping lovers. As the lovers awake, Hermia pairs with Lysander and Demetrius pairs with Helena. Theseus ordains that they shall join him and Hippolyta in a three-way wedding. The artisans finish their rehearsal and all return to Athens.

After the wedding, the artisans perform their play *Pyramus and Thisbe*, about two parted lovers. In the play, Thisbe sees a lion and flees, dropping her mantle. Pyramus finds the mantle and stabs himself. Thisbe discovers Pyramus's body, so kills herself, too. The Court can barely contain its laughter, and as the play ends, Theseus calls an end to the revels. Puck leads a fairy procession through the palace. ∎

A *Midsummer Night's Dream* is unique in Shakespeare's varied canon. Full of romance and poetry, humour and beauty, it is a flight of fantasy, a journey into a world of magic that explores love in all its tenderness, excitement, and danger. Its story has resonated across cultures, and the play is widely performed across the world.

The play is set not just on any night, but Midsummer Night. The summer solstice had a mystical significance dating back to ancient times. Shakespeare's England had pagan roots that ran far deeper than its Christian tradition, and this was the night when magic was felt to be in the air, and fairies and sprites were abroad. It is not that everyone believed in fairies, then. Edmund Spenser, who wrote his poem *The Faerie Queene* around this time, declared, "the truth is that there be no such things, nor yet the shadow of the things." Shakespeare simply uses the magic of this night to delve into the interplay between imagination and reality, madness and reason, love and common sense, and tell a story that is both an enchanting delight and a voyage into the dark places of the mind. Spenser's *Faerie Queen*, although set in fairyland, was about the real queen, Elizabeth I, and it is hard not to see Elizabeth, too, in the strong queens of the Dream, Titania and Hippolyta.

Wedding and marriage

It is not known for certain when *A Midsummer Night's Dream* was written, but some suggest that it was a play to celebrate a wedding, possibly the wedding of the young Elizabeth de Vere to the Earl of Derby in 1595. Others dispute this idea, but the play does indeed seem to take the pattern of an elaborate masque. It begins with the announcement of a wedding – so often the endpoint of a drama – and finishes on the night of a triple wedding.

The weddings – in Athens, the world of reality – are brief scenes that frame the wild and spectacular journey into the fairy forest. There is a symmetry and movement between the world of lovers, fairies, and "mechanicals" that is like a marvellous dance, coming together in the magical torch-lit procession that ends the play. The play can be seen both as an exquisite wedding gift and an instruction on the true nature of love that the watching couple must learn before embarking on married life.

City and forest

A Midsummer Night's Dream has a triple structure. It begins in the city, journeys into the forest, and then returns to the city again. The city is the world of order, reason, and discipline, but order in this city has broken down. The characters must voyage into the wild in order to learn lessons for their real work.

In many ways, it is an interior journey – a journey of self-knowledge – but the journey is as much about society rediscovering what matters as it is a personal journey. Clearly, there is much to learn in Athens about marriage. At the opening of the play, Theseus explains how he won Hippolyta, the queen of the Amazons (a tribe of female warriors), by force: "Hippolyta, I have wooed thee with my sword, / And won thy love by doing thee injuries." (1.1.16–17).

Old Egeus calls for the death penalty if his daughter Hermia refuses to marry Demetrius. Even Theseus's "reprieve" only offers Hermia the choice of life in a nunnery instead. It is clear that Theseus and Egeus may have the law on their side, but their world of "reason" and "sense" has little understanding of human love and feelings. Indeed, Theseus's vision is entirely out of sympathy with imagination and poetry, as well as love, which he equates with a kind of madness: "The lunatic, the lover, and the poet / Are of imagination all compact" »

An English idyll

The forest in *A Midsummer Night's Dream* is said to be outside Athens, but it is really an English wood, like the forest of Arden Shakespeare knew so well. The play can be seen to be a hymn to England, full of magic, yet down-to-earth and real – a reminder, perhaps, to distant rulers of what really matters.

The wild flowers Oberon, the king of the fairies, tells of are those of an English wood, brought to life with a tenderness and knowledge of a writer who had walked those woods since childhood. Shakespeare gives Oberon these words: "I know a bank where the wild thyme blows, Where oxlips and the nodding violet grows, Quite over-canopied with luscious woodbine, With sweet musk-roses, and with eglantine" (2.1.250–253).

The fogs and sodden fields and the tired ploughman that the queen of the fairies, Titania, describe are scenes from England, not from Athens, and the artisans who put on the play are as solidly English as one can imagine.

(5.1.7–8). Love, for Theseus, is a frantic delusion. Poetry is a frenzied rolling of the eye.

Parallels with Verona

In some ways, the Athens of Theseus is as unhealthy as the feuding Verona that brings such tragedy to *Romeo and Juliet* (which was written at much the same time). Like Romeo and Juliet, Hermia and Lysander are star-crossed lovers, doomed to separation by foolish and tyrannical parents. When Lysander laments that "The course of true love never did run smooth" (1.1.134), it is almost as if he is talking of Romeo and Juliet. The journey into the forest in *A Midsummer Night's Dream* is the journey the Montagues and Capulets needed to embark upon if Romeo and Juliet were to have a happy outcome.

A forest of the mind

The forest that the four lovers enter, along with the artisans, is a place of the imagination, a place of fantasy and dreams, where the normal order of things is turned upside down. Nowadays, psychologists might talk of the realm of the unconscious, and critics explore the psychological symbolism of the play and its expression of sexual desires and gender issues. In Shakespeare's time it is simply the world of dreams and faeries. Indeed, the whole play is presented as a dream that we have strayed into. As Puck says at the end: "If we shadows have offended, / Think but this, and all is mended: / That you have but slumbered here, / While these visions did appear; / And this weak and idle theme, / No more yielding but a dream" (Epilogue.1–6).

The forest of dreams is a place where normality is subverted. But it is more of a nightmare than a dream. Characters play parts, wear masks and costumes, change roles, behave out of character, suffer delusions, swap status or lovers – and even, as in the case of Bottom the weaver, acquire the head of an ass. Here the world of reason and "common sense" – what is normally sensed – vanishes and nothing is certain. Identities continually shift and transform.

Troubled identity

The loss of identity is disturbing, often terrifying. What is love, when it can shift so easily? Isn't love attached to a person's identity? Hermia, the most constant of the lovers, begins to question who she really is, as Lysander, who once professed to love her, suddenly seems to hate her – "Am I not Hermia? Are you not Lysander?" (3.2.274). Yet Helena lamented at the beginning of the play that she would have been happy if she could only be Hermia and so be loved by

Adaptations

The play's unusual structure means it has not always been treated gently by adaptors. In the 17th century in particular, many productions took liberties, for example by staging the comic elements alone. The pageant-like nature of the play has inspired many to add music. One of the best was the *Fairy Queen* by English composer Henry Purcell (1692), which inserted exquisite musical masques between each scene. In 1842, Felix Mendelssohn wrote beautiful incidental music to a production that includes the famous Wedding March.

In the 20th century, adaptors have been more interested in the psychological and sexual symbolism. Peter Brook's 1970 version was performed in a plain white box, and focussed on the adult themes over spectacle. Benjamin Britten's 1960 opera had a fairy chorus of boy trebles as a chaste counterpoint to the libidinous adults. Film versions have included Max Reinhardt's epic and visually sumptuous rendering of 1935 and, more recently, Michael Hoffman's 1999 soap opera-like version set in Tuscany.

Demetrius – that she would give the world to be Hermia "translated".

In the forest, they are all "translated" under the influence of mischievous, shape-shifting Puck, and the effect is decidedly nightmarish. The magic love juices turn them this way and that, love to hate, hate to love, in an extreme fashion. Bottom is the most dramatically translated of all, yet he is the one who stays most constant. He may gain the head of an ass, but he is unfailingly courteous to Titania and to all the fairies who tend on him, and the relationship between him and Titania, though in some ways an illusion, is the gentlest and most tender in the play. Indeed, it is Bottom who has the sanest insight into love, telling Titania: "Methinks, mistress, you should have little reason / for that [loving me]. And yet, to say the truth, reason and love / keep little company together nowadays." (3.1.135–137).

Happy resolution

The artisans show the truest understanding of love, and pass through the madness of the forest with their identities intact. Even when they are playing characters in their play, they stay steadfastly themselves. Snout doesn't become the Wall, he simply, as Snout, "presents" it.

It is only fitting that these simple men bring the drama down to earth and good humour again at the end, leaving the realm of dreams to the fairies, with proper separation restored. At the end, everyone retires to bed, thankful to put this wild night behind them. The fairies reinhabit the house as protective dreams: "But all the story of the night told over, / And all their minds transfigured so together, / More witnesseth than fancy's images, / And grows to something of great constancy; / But, howsoever, strange and admirable." (5.1.23–27). ∎

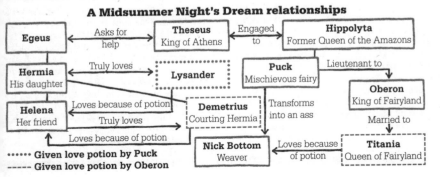

A Midsummer Night's Dream relationships

THERE IS NO SURE FOUNDATION SET ON BLOOD

THE LIFE AND DEATH OF KING JOHN (1596)

> 66 Mad world, mad kings, mad composition!
> **Philip the Bastard**
> Act 2, Scene 1 99

England and France prepare for war. Robert Falconbridge quarrels with his brother, Philip. They both claim to be the heir to their father's estate. Robert insists that his brother is the illegitimate son of Richard I, "the Lionheart". Queen Eleanor recognizes her son's features in Philip and renames him Sir Richard Plantagenet, although he continues to be known as the Bastard.

Outside the city of Angers (in France, but owned by the English), the French and English kings demand that the gates be opened to them. A battle is waged, with both sides claiming victory. Peace is made by the marriage of the dauphin to John's niece, Blanche, with all of England's French territories, except Angers, as her dowry. The arrival of Cardinal Pandolf, the Pope's legate, causes renewed conflict. When King John defies the Pope's authority, Pandolf excommunicates him. King Philip breaks his allegiance with England.

The Bastard decapitates the Duke of Austria (who had killed his father, Richard I), and rescues Queen Eleanor. Arthur is taken prisoner by King John and placed in the custody of Hubert, who is ordered to murder him. The Cardinal is cheered by the fact that King John will have to kill Arthur, which will turn the English against him. He recruits Louis the Dauphin to march on England.

Hubert cannot bring himself to kill Arthur and instead promises to tell King John that he is dead. John has had himself crowned for a second time. When the king announces that Arthur is dead of a sudden sickness, the nobles angrily renounce him. A messenger tells the king that French troops are about to land on English soil. The Bastard brings in Peter of Pomfret who prophesies that John will give up the crown by noon on Ascension Day. John throws him in prison. John is relieved when Hubert confesses that the prince is still alive. But Arthur falls to his death. His body is found by Pembroke, Salisbury, and Bigot, who don't believe the death was accidental.

John submits to the authority of the Pope on condition that Cardinal Pandolf disarm the French. It is Ascension Day when John resigns his crown into Pandolf's hands only to have it returned. The Bastard condemns this and insists that the king should continue to defy the dauphin. The latter is eager to fight, and refuses to be deflected by the Cardinal. The French are weakened by a loss of supplies and the defection of English nobles. As fortune turns in the favour of the English, King John is ill. He dies in the presence of his son, now King Henry III. English nobles offer their allegiance to the new king, and the Cardinal negotiates a truce. ■

IN CONTEXT

THEMES
Inheritance, identity, kingship, loyalty

SETTING
The English court, Angers in France

SOURCES
1587 Holinshed's *Chronicles of England, Scotland, and Ireland*.

c.1589 Anonymously authored play *The Troublesome Reign of King John* may have been an influence on Shakespeare.

 I am amazed, methinks, and lose my way Among the thorns and dangers of this world.
Philip the Bastard
Act 4, Scene 3

When King John asserts that there is "No certain life achieved by others' death" (4.2.105), he alludes to his decision to kill Arthur – the young rival to his throne. Rather than confirming John's authority, the murder has undermined it, for England's nobles will no longer follow "the foot / That leaves the print of blood where'er it walks" (4.3.25–26).

Blood follows blood

The doctrine that blood follows blood, and that murdering other royal claimants does not secure one's grip upon the throne, resonates throughout Shakespeare's English history plays. For example, in *Richard II*, the murder

of King Richard continues to generate new enemies for the usurper Henry IV. What is unusual about *King John* is the joke that is being played against the king when he makes this assertion, for, as the audience already knows, Arthur isn't really dead. The audience is allowed to think that John has won a lucky reprieve. But at the very moment when Hubert is hurrying after the earls to tell them that Arthur is not dead, they discover his body at the foot of the prison walls. This episode illustrates one of the distinct features of *King John*; why it appears to stand alone tonally as well as structurally.

The play undermines the ambitions and actions of the great, wrong-footing them at every turn. For example, the motives of the King of France may be morally suspect when he makes peace with England, »

The play includes John's disputes with his nobles, but omits the resolution – forcing him to sign the Magna Carta in 1215. John died a year later at Newark Castle, Nottinghamshire, shown here.

Philip The Bastard

Philip Falconbridge has more lines than any other character in *King John*, and is often described as the play's hero. Bastards in Shakespeare are usually villains (Don John, Iago, Edmund). The status of "bastard" was equated with a moral deficit, his inability to inherit wealth leaving him with a ruthless streak. However, the Bastard of *King John* is a comic figure: "Why, what a madcap hath heaven lent us here!" (1.1.84). He acts as both a satirical chorus, exposing the protagonists' true motives, and a heroic figure. In Maria Aberg's 2012 production for the RSC, Philip's gender was changed, and he was played with a mixture of tenderness and scorn by Pippa Nixon (above, left).

Philip is aware of the irony of a bastard defending the moral order, and at the end of the play Salisbury advises the new King Henry that it is his duty "to set a form upon that indigest" (5.7.26). That Philip speaks the play's final lines may testify to his charisma and rapport with the audience, or to the difficulty that subsequent kings will find in imposing this ideal "form".

as the Bastard points out, but an Anglo-French marriage at least prevents further bloodshed. However, Philip's vows of allegiance have barely been made before he is forced by Cardinal Pandolf to declare war once again. It seems impossible for the major characters to maintain a consistent policy on anything, and, as a result, the play struggles to achieve any kind of tragic effect (it may be worth noting that the term "Tragedy" is absent from the title). Tragedy depends on a kind of heroic consistency and self-assertion in the face of cosmic opposition or unlucky chance – and this is not the story of King John.

Disputed succession

John's assertion that "There is no sure foundation set on blood" (4.2.104) also relates to ideas of identity and inheritance. The play's opening dispute is about who stands next in line to the throne after the deaths of Richard and Geoffrey, Queen Eleanor's elder sons. There is disagreement about whether a son (Arthur) or a brother (John) should inherit, with even Eleanor implying that Arthur might have the superior claim.

The situation is made more complicated by the larger difficulty of determining paternity. This anxiety is focused on Philip the Bastard, who is proven to be the illegitimate son of Richard the Lionheart by physical resemblance. Philip is left in the position of choosing his identity – whether to inherit Sir Robert's estate, or suffer the stigma of illegitimacy in order to be recognized as Richard's son. He chooses the latter, but the arbitrariness of his choice reinforces the point that "all men's children" (1.1.63) must doubt their paternity. In the verbal battle between Eleanor and Constance (2.1), both Arthur and Richard the Lionheart stand accused of being bastards.

It seems then that neither ruthless political action nor an unquestioned blood right to the throne are enough to render kingship secure. The play advises the necessity of maintaining loyalty, particularly among one's nobles. The new King Henry III is brought to tears by the sight of Salisbury, Pembroke, and Bigot kneeling before him. A cynical response to this display – given their betrayal of King John and then the dauphin – seems to be deliberately averted by the Bastard's final words, which emphasize the need for unity: "Naught shall make us rue / If England to itself do rest but true" (5.7.117–118). It is one of the play's deepest ironies that the man who carries the blood of Richard the Lionheart in his veins is denied the chance to rule the nation he loves more than its legitimate kings do. ∎

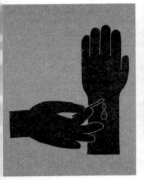

IF YOU PRICK US DO WE NOT BLEED?
THE MERCHANT OF VENICE (1596)

In Venice, the merchant Antonio is sad, but agrees to help his friend Bassanio raise the money he needs to woo the beautiful heiress Portia. In Belmont, meanwhile, Portia is sad too. By her father's will, she must marry the man who chooses the correct one of three caskets – gold, silver, and lead. When Shylock hesitates to lend Bassanio money, Bassanio promises Antonio as guarantor. Shylock sees a chance of revenge on Antonio, who has previously mocked him. He stipulates that the bond be a pound of Antonio's flesh.

In Belmont, the Prince of Morocco arrives to try his luck with Portia. In Venice, Shylock's servant Lancelot decides to leave his master and serve Bassanio. Shylock's daughter Jessica is sad that Lancelot is leaving and decides to run away. She gives Lancelot a message for Lorenzo, who is staying with Bassanio. Shylock is invited to dinner with Bassanio, and while he's out, Jessica steals his money and escapes to Belmont disguised as a boy. In Belmont, the Princes of Morocco and Aragon fail the casket test, choosing gold and silver.

In Belmont, Portia asks Bassanio to delay choosing caskets to prolong their time together. But to his and Portia's joy, he chooses the lead casket containing a portrait of Portia. Bassanio's friend Graziano and Portia's maid Nerissa decide to marry. This happiness is marred by news that Shylock is claiming his flesh from Antonio. Portia offers to repay the debt "twenty times over", and Bassanio sets off for Venice. Portia follows Bassanio disguised as a male lawyer, accompanied by Nerissa disguised as "his" clerk.

In a Venice courtroom, Shylock demands his pound of flesh. Balthasar (Portia in disguise) arrives to adjudicate. Balthasar says Shylock should be merciful, but the law is in his favour. Shylock delightedly prepares to take his pound of flesh. Then Balthasar informs him that in doing so he may not spill Antonio's blood. Stunned, Shylock accepts Bassanio's money. But Balthasar is relentless. As an alien threatening a Venetian, she tells Shylock, he faces the death penalty, which can only be averted by giving up all his wealth. The Duke pardons him, providing he pay half his wealth to Antonio. Antonio simply asks that Shylock give the money to Jessica and Lorenzo on his death. Balthasar asks in payment from Bassanio only the ring Portia gave him.

Lorenzo and Jessica bask in their love as Portia and Nerissa return. The girls berate Bassanio and Graziano for giving their rings to other women. Antonio defends them, and Portia and Nerissa admit the truth. Portia tells Antonio his boats are safe, and Nerissa gives Lorenzo and Jessica Shylock's new will. ∎

IN CONTEXT

THEMES
Prejudice, revenge, justice, money, love

SETTING
Venice and the fictional town of Belmont, in Italy

SOURCES
The main elements of the plot, the flesh-bond and the story of the caskets, are taken from folk tales. The character Shylock is inspired by the following:

14th century Italian Giovanni Fiorentino's collection of tales *Il Pecorone* ("The Dunce").

1589 Christopher Marlowe's *The Jew of Malta*.

F ew of Shakespeare's plays have caused quite as much disquiet as *The Merchant of Venice*. The story is a blend of two old folk tales – that of the mean moneylender who demands an extreme payment, a pound of flesh, from his creditor, and that of the young princess who finds her true love through the test of three caskets. *The Merchant of Venice* has a happy ending for most, with the young lovers united, and in Portia, Shakespeare creates an appealing heroine, humble and loving yet brilliant and incisive in the court scene. But the moneylender Shylock, whose Jewishness is so crucial to his portrayal, and for whom the play does not end well, continues to arouse deep anxiety among audiences and performers.

The stereotypical Jew
The anxiety hinges on whether the play is anti-Semitic. A rapacious, skinflint moneylender, Shylock certainly conforms to a negative stereotype of a Jewish character that was already well used by the time Shakespeare wrote his play around 1597. Indeed, Christopher Marlowe had a huge hit with such negative stereotypes around 1590 with *The Jew of Malta*. There are clear parallels between Shylock and

Marlowe's Jew, Barabas, who, like Shylock, is a widowed father with a single beautiful daughter who rejects her father's "misplaced" Judaism and converts to Christianity. It is likely that neither playwright was writing from direct experience, however, since Jews had been banned from England long before. As a result, both Barabas and Shylock are perhaps best seen as stock villains.

There is no doubt that *The Merchant of Venice* has done a great deal to reinforce negative stereotypes of Jews over the centuries. Originally, perhaps, this was in a mostly comic vein, with Shylock played as a pantomime baddy. But more disturbingly, *The Merchant of Venice* was staged deliberately in Nazi Germany in the late 1930s to help justify the attacks on Jews. Critics, however, have been divided over whether this can be blamed on Shakespeare, or those who misuse the play. Many critics defend Shakespeare against the charge of anti-Semitism by underlining the play's nuances. Others have suggested that we should bear in mind the context of Shakespeare's age, when few people had the political and racial awareness

In the 16th-century, Venetian Jews were confined to a ghetto, and Shylock would have been forced to live here. In this early 17th-century map of Venice, the ghetto is marked with a star.

> In sooth, I know not why
> I am so sad.
> It wearies me, you
> say it wearies you
> **Antonio**
> Act 1, Scene 1

we do now. Shakespeare was writing, as when he wrote of Othello, about storybook figures in tales from abroad. The problem, perhaps, is more for us today – how do we deal with characters such as Shylock with our awareness of the dangers such stereotypes pose?

The victim of prejudice

Since the Holocaust, most stagings of the play have been acutely aware of the dangers of portraying Shylock simply as a villain and have instead looked at the character more as a tragic victim of racial and religious prejudice. Shylock is seen as an outsider who is abused by the Christians of Venice, robbed and abandoned by his daughter, and finally humiliated by the loss of his fortune and good name and forced to convert to Christianity. Such is Shakespeare's skill as a playwright that his tragedy can be found in the play. In a famously telling speech, Shylock rails against the abuse he has suffered: "I am a Jew. Hath not a Jew eyes? Hath not a Jew hands, organs, dimensions, senses, affections, passions; fed with the same food, hurt with the same weapons, subject to the same diseases, healed by the same means, warmed and cooled by the same winter and summer as a Christian is? If you prick us, do we not bleed?" (3.1.54–59).

This speech is often quoted out of context as a heartfelt cry against racial prejudice – or the bitter cry of anger of the whole Hebrew race. But perhaps it is not quite so simple as that. When Shylock says, If you prick us, do we not bleed?" he is not just saying that Jews have the same blood, but also referring to the common test for a witch, which was to prick the thumbs to see if they bleed. Is this speech a plea for human rights or a justification for revenge –

Dustin Hoffman took on the role of Shylock in a 1989 production directed by Peter Hall. Hoffman portrayed the moneylender as a good man driven beyond endurance by mistreatment.

another stereotype of Jewish villainy? Either way, Shakespeare's audiences may have been surprised by how much they were moved by the words he placed in the mouth of the play's stock villain.

The melancholic merchant

Shylock often draws so much attention from critics that he is sometimes assumed to be the merchant in the play's title. But of course Shylock is a moneylender, not a merchant. The merchant of the title is Antonio. He plays a comparatively peripheral role in a play that is, in the main, a comedy about the nature of love.

In the very first line of the play, Antonio laments: "In sooth, I know not why I am so sad." His friends try to find an explanation for his sadness, but there is none. In a telling parallel, Portia opens the very next scene »

> Tell me where is fancy bred,
> Or in the heart, or in the head?
> **Singer**
> Act 3, Scene 2

> 66 This night, methinks
> is but the daylight sick.
> **Portia**
> Act 5, Scene 1 99

saying: "By my troth, Nerissa, my little body is aweary of this great world."

There is something that has cast a gloom over the world, and the comic journey of the play is to lift this gloom through the redeeming power of love, just as it is in *Twelfth Night*, in which it is Viola's task to lift the gloom into which Orsino and Olivia have sunk. In both plays, the heroines, Portia and Viola, must dress as men to win through, released by their disguise to reveal their true brilliance. In both plays, too, a misanthrope – Malvolio in *Twelfth Night* and Shylock in *The Merchant of Venice* – is left out of the general happiness at the play's end.

So what is the reason for this gloom? It may be no accident that Shakespeare's play is set in Venice, the commercial capital of Europe at the time, and the play focuses on a merchant. It is perhaps the restless quest for money and the commodification of relationships that

has robbed the world of joy. When his daughter Jessica leaves, what is uppermost in Shylock's mind is the financial cost, and the plot of the play hinges on Bassanio's need to borrow money to even woo Portia.

The value of life

In the test of the three caskets, Portia will not find true love in the precious gold or silver caskets, but only the poor lead casket. When Bassanio makes the right choice of the lead casket, Portia explains that she has herself has little monetary value: "the full sum of me / Is sum of something which, to term in gross, / Is an unlessoned girl, unschooled, unpractiséd, / Happy in this, she is not yet so old" (3.2.157–160).

For Shylock, this would make her utterly worthless. For him, without money, there is no life. "Nay, take my life and all," he wails when the Duke threatens to take all his wealth in punishment for his crime, "you take my life / When you do take the means whereby I live." (4.1.373–374).

But the Christians in Venice are perhaps only slightly less obsessed with the making and spending of money. To achieve a happy ending, all the couples must leave the commercial world of Venice behind entirely and escape to the paradise of Portia's home in Belmont. Only there can Lorenzo and Jessica see that the real riches are in the beauties of the night and music: "the floor of heaven / Is thick inlaid with patens of bright gold." (5.1.58–59). It is also in Belmont that Antonio receives the happy news that his

Darko Tresnjak's 2007 production had a futuristic setting. At the end, it hints that the marriages will not turn out well, so it is not only Shylock (F Murray Abraham) who will suffer.

THE LORD CHAMBERLAIN'S MAN 79

The friends in Venice

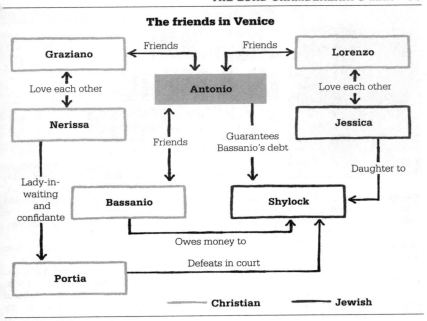

Christian ——— Jewish

ships are safe, after Portia assures him with a letter that she has mysteriously acquired. But this happiness has come at a cost.

Back in Venice, Shylock is a lonely and broken man, humiliated and vilified, with most of his money gone, his renegade daughter absent and waiting upon his death, when she will inherit what wealth of his remains. Elizabethan audiences may have seen this outcome as just deserts for the Jew. But Shakespeare manages to portray Shylock's fall as an all too human event. ■

Demonized Jewry

Jews had been banished from England since 1290, and they remained banished until 1655, when the Jewish scholar Manasseh ben Israel gained Oliver Cromwell's assent for Jews to return. There were a handful of Jews in London in Elizabethan times, but none would have been able to profess their religion openly, on pain of death. London Jews in the 1590s were mostly Marranos – descendants of forced Jewish converts from Portugal and Spain – including the queen's doctor Rodrigo Lopez, who was hung, drawn, and quartered in 1594, accused of conspiring to poison the Queen. Some scholars believe Lopez was the inspiration for Shylock, but there was no shortage of negative role models for Shakespeare to draw on, not least Marlowe's Barabas. With the Christian ban on usury, Jews had long been forced into the role of moneylenders. Prejudice was rife, partly because Jews were blamed by Christians for the betrayal of Christ. Jews were demonized in many ways – blamed for spreading the plague and associated with witches.

HONOUR IS A MERE SCUTCHEON

HENRY IV PART 1 (1596–1597)

The troubles that plague Henry IV's reign begin with his overthrow and murder of Richard II in the earlier play of that name. Plagued by guilt, which he longs to expiate with a crusade to the Holy Land, Henry is kept frustratingly at home by the threat of rebellion in Wales and in the north.

In Wales, the warlord Owain Glyndw^r has thrown his forces behind the claim of Glyndw^r's son-in-law, Edmund Mortimer, to be Richard's rightful heir. In the north, those barons who helped Henry to the throne, led by the Earl of Northumberland, fear his appropriation of their feudal rights. Henry has already demanded the Scottish prisoners captured for ransom by Hotspur. Faced with Henry's ultimatum, the fiery Hotspur vents his fury. The barons harness the young man's anger by recruiting him to their cause. Stung by Henry's ingratitude, they plan to join with Mortimer and the Scots against him.

Henry's son, Prince Hal, adds to his father's woes. He sidesteps all responsibility as Prince of Wales and wastes his time in the seamy underworld of Eastcheap. There his surrogate father, Sir John Falstaff, holds sway over a tavern-court of drunkards, thieves, and prostitutes. Hal joins in the revelry, but only, he tells us, to shine the brighter when, like the prodigal son, he turns away from fleshly pursuits to take up his royal role.

Hal's eventual return to face his father is rehearsed in the tavern where, speaking as Hal, Falstaff defends his own licentiousness as a celebration of life. But Hal, speaking as his father, calls such vice life-threatening, and admits he'll banish Falstaff one fine day. He seems to speak both as the king and as himself in this.

With the rebellion gathering pace, Hal returns to court and plays the tavern scene for real. When he promises to defeat Hotspur and appropriate his honours, Henry is reassured, finally seeing something of his own ambition in his son. Together they meet the rebels in a parley. Hal offers to fight Hotspur in single combat but the unbending Henry refuses, dismissing the rebels' claim of broken promises and repeating his demands.

The two sides fight at the Battle of Shrewsbury, where Hal fights Hotspur one-to-one. After killing his rival, the prince praises his nobility. Then, seeing the body of Falstaff, he grieves the loss of his less noble friend. True to form however, Falstaff is feigning. Once Hal has left, the wily knight sees the chance for profit and takes the body of Hotspur off as his own kill. Meeting Hal as he goes, Falstaff persuades the Prince to condone the lie. Meanwhile, news of further rebellion leaves the resolution of Henry IV's political difficulties to Part 2. ∎

There is little honour in the deposition of a king. The crown that Henry IV wears is one he took from the weak King Richard II, with the help of a group of independent warlords led by the Earl of Northumberland. Now he wants to unite England as a nation marching "all one way" (1.1.15). Unfortunately, this means replacing those same warlords' feudal powers with a centralized form of rule, and they are not pleased. Their threatened rebellion challenges Henry in the north and the west.

Henry doubly needs the support of these barons – not only to defend the borders but, importantly, to maintain his right to rule. He cannot claim to have inherited the throne. His right depends on might, and therefore on their support. Henry's dilemma as king is how legitimately he can quell their rebellion when his legitimacy is derived from rebellion itself.

Politics and chivalry

Shakespeare reinvents Henry here as a Renaissance prince rather than the medieval monarch that he was. His attempt to forge a nation-state under the crown, which was in fact a later Tudor project, is the strategy of a politician. Such shrewd tactics cut clean across the chivalric code of honour with its escutcheons (shields bearing coats of arms) and heraldic etiquette on which the court of his predecessor, Richard II, was built.

Among the rebels, Richard is remembered as the perfect king. They conveniently forget his self-interested neglect of England, and now heap blame on his usurper for destroying the ideal. This illusion of chivalry fires the imagination of young Hotspur to pursue honour wherever it lies: "To pluck bright honour from the pale-faced moon…And pluck up drownèd honour by the locks." (1.3.200, 203). But the fact that it is unreachable shows how vulnerable it is.

Old men and the young

The play presents the conflict between this imagined past and Henry's coldly realistic present through a series of real and surrogate father-son relationships. Northumberland and Worcester, those powerful warlords who want to reinstate the past, are happy to recruit their valiant young kinsman Hotspur to the cause. They see a political naivety in his idealism that they can use. But they keep him well away from policy decisions and, doubting the king's word, deny him the details of Henry's terms for peace. In the end, though, it is Northumberland who can't be trusted. He and Glyndwˆr fail to send Hotspur essential reinforcements before the battle at Shrewsbury. Typically, Hotspur puts a brave face on this, arguing that it adds a "larger dare to our great enterprise" (4.1.78). But single-minded valour is no substitute for political strategy. And the consequence is fatal.

Henry sees in Hotspur the man he'll never be. He represents the knightly virtue that Henry stepped away from when he seized the crown. In this respect he is Henry's lost ideal, and the son that he would wish for: "A son who is the theme of honour's tongue" (1.1.80). His own son, Prince Hal, is a rebellious youth whom Henry needs to conform, for a noble heir would let him reinstate the line of legitimate inheritance that he himself usurped, and restore England's true order.

For the present, Hal chooses disorder. He spends his days far from the uneasy court, in the stews of the Eastcheap » taverns, where excess, licentiousness, and dissipation are the norm. The whole is epitomized in the expansive and unconstrained fleshiness of Falstaff, the emblem of physical, moral, and spiritual disorder and of occasionally letting go. If Hotspur is true honour then Falstaff, as his name suggests, is its opposite. He sees honour as an empty word, a symbol that serves no material good. In this respect, Falstaff is a parody of Henry. Wit and low cunning are his tools, as political craft is the king's. And both of them are thieves.

Three worlds

Shakespeare constructed his own narrative using details from Holinshed's account of Henry's "unquiet reign" but much of the plot is his own invention. The result is a tightly structured, three-part story focusing on the relationships between a troubled monarch, his ambitious warlords, and his wayward heir. This gives us three clearly defined worlds in the court, the rebel camp, and the Boar's Head Tavern. The first two present events in historical time while the third, a wholly invented comic alternative to recorded history, acts as a foil. It's both a rebel space, and a topsy-turvy court, and offers a subversive commentary on the two. Falstaff's principles are the same as Henry's but applied to the realm of private life, as we see in the second scene (1.2). Some directors have made this clear in the scene transition, as the court figures leave by passing through the entering tavern folk, and Falstaff sits on what was Henry's throne. Where the court is factional and serious, in the tavern laws are joyously broken and honour mocked. And while the infestations of Eastcheap parody the dis-ease of Henry's court, in Falstaff they indicate a greed for pleasure more than power.

Hal's destiny

Hal may prefer to spend his time in Eastcheap, but he's not entirely unlike his royal father. His appearance as the wayward prince is part of a long-term plan, as he tells us privately at the scene's close. He's wasting time with the common people in order to reform himself when the

moment's right. He'll shine the brighter because of what he seemed to be. Critics are divided as to how we might respond to this, and much depends on individual performance. Should princes know their subjects' lives in order to govern better? If so, then Hal's calculation is wise. It shows him following a path between Hotspur's unquestioning pursuit of honour and Falstaff's selfish dismissal of it. The opposite view is that Hal is as crafty as his father and knows precisely how to make a show. In a world where chivalry is dying and honour a "mere scutcheon" (5.1.140), Hal deploys the tactics of a politician.

The Eastcheap world extends Hal's range of roles. Mimicking the tavern drawer (barman), he shows that he can "drink with any tinker in his own language" (2.5.18–19). The multi-layered tavern scene (2.5) draws the clearest parallels between kingship and acting when he and Falstaff rehearse Hal's interview with his father. Playing the king with a cushion for a crown, Hal responds to Falstaff's appeal against banishment with simple honesty: "I do; I will" (2.5.486). The moment is rich with possibilities, not least that Hal speaks for himself here and the threat of banishment is real. The knocking at the door that follows underlines the cold reality of Hal's words: that time will intrude upon this comic world and judgment will catch up with them all.

This parallel between politics and performance is acknowledged by the king himself when he and his son meet for real. He tells Hal that, as Bolingbroke, he rationed his appearances, and was so courteous in public that he soon had Richard's audience in his hands. He fears that the Prince is too familiar with his people and will be as vulnerable as Richard was. But Hal already has his plan. He assures his father that, as Henry used Richard, so he will use Hotspur and appropriate his reputation for himself: "Percy is but my factor, good my lord, / To engross up glorious deeds on my behalf" (3.2.147–148). Hal's language of commodity sounds more like a Renaissance merchant than a medieval knight. The politician prince will fashion his heroic image out of Hotspur's coat of arms.

The two meet at Shrewsbury in battle. On stage, it's a chance to thrill the audience with swordplay. The opponents are equally matched and by the end almost admire each other's fighting skills; this makes Hotspur's death all the more poignant, as Hal admits: "Fare thee well, great heart…When that this body did contain a spirit, / A kingdom for it was too small a bound" (5.4.86, 88–89).

Ambiguous ending

As Hal turns to leave, he sees Falstaff's body nearby and bids a brief farewell to his surrogate father. But once he's gone, the fat knight rises from the ground in high indignation at Hal's farewell. This comic coda alters the tone of the ending. We laugh, happy that Falstaff only pretends death. But we are also invited to consider Falstaff's feigning as a comment on Henry's tactical success. For the king used decoys in the battle, men dressed as him and carrying his escutcheon. It's a ploy that only confirms the rebels' view of him as a counterfeit king.

When Falstaff then heaves Hotspur's body on his back and goes off to spin tales of how he killed the hero, we watch story-telling take up what's left of chivalry. And as Hal meets Falstaff taking off the body, he agrees to "gild" (5.4.155), the old man's lie, which makes for an ambiguous, downbeat ending. It's a sign that Hal has yet to separate himself from his former life, and both his less-than-honourable father figures. ∎

Prince Hal is caught between, and is under pressure from, the "three worlds" of the play – the tavern and his surrogate family, the royal court and duty to his father, and the rebel camp, where Hotspur represents an ideal of knightly honour Hal knows he cannot attain.

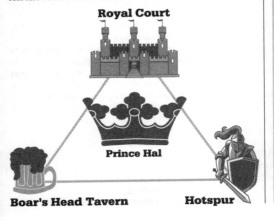

Royal Court

Prince Hal

Boar's Head Tavern   **Hotspur**

Censorship

Sir John Falstaff (above right, played by Antony Sher in a 2014 RSC production) is one of Shakespeare's bawdiest dramatic creations. His comic profanities were part of a long tradition of stage swearing. However, by the late 16th century, this was increasingly offending Puritan sensibilities. Shakespeare had already got into trouble by originally naming the character Sir John Oldcastle, which was also the name of a Protestant martyr. The outraged lord chamberlain (a descendant of Oldcastle's) forced Shakespeare to change the name and apologize.

Players came under pressure to clean up their language, then the 1606 "Act to Restrain the Abuses of Players" formally banned all onstage ribaldry and cursing. From then on, the plays were purged of any off-colour or irreligious language, a legacy that continued into the 20th century. The most drastic clean-up was, perhaps, the 1818 *Family Shakespeare* edited by the Reverend Thomas Bowdler, whose cuts were so severe that some plays, in particular *Othello*, were rendered nonsensical.

WIVES MAY BE MERRY AND YET HONEST TOO

THE MERRY WIVES OF WINDSOR (1597–1598)

In Windsor, Justice Shallow threatens Falstaff for poaching deer. Falstaff cheerily admits his misdemeanours and trouble is averted. Shallow's nephew Slender is advised to marry young Anne Page for her money. At the Garter Inn, Falstaff laments his lack of funds, and plans to send letters to mistresses Page and Ford in a bid to get at their husbands' money.

Dr Caius is enraged when he sees a letter from parson Evans backing Slender's hopes to marry Anne Page. Caius is hoping to marry Anne himself.

Young Fenton then arrives, also hoping to marry Anne. Mistresses Page and Ford receive identical love letters from Falstaff and decide to teach the fat knight a lesson. Pistol, annoyed by being sacked by Falstaff, tells Ford about Falstaff's letter to his wife, while Nim tells Page. Page is not bothered, but the enraged Ford disguises himself as "Brooke" to meet Falstaff at the Garter Inn.

Mistress Ford invites Falstaff to her house when her husband is out. Brooke pretends to be a suitor of Mistress Ford himself and offers to pay Falstaff to seduce his wife on his behalf. Unaware of the plans the mistresses Ford and Page have for Falstaff, Ford angrily follows him on his assignation with Mistress Ford. As Ford comes home, Mistress Ford (as planned) tells Falstaff to hide in a basket of filthy linen, which is then dumped in the river. Recovering later at the Garter, Falstaff is told by Mistress Quickly that it was all a big mistake and Mistress Ford wants to meet again. Ford (as Brooke) finds out. At Mistress Ford's house, Falstaff is persuaded to dress as an old woman in order to escape Ford, but Ford thinks it's his hated aunt and beats him black and blue.

Mistresses Ford and Page tell their husbands what has been going on, and together they plot Falstaff's final humiliation. They invite him to dress as the mythical stag spirit Herne the Hunter, and to meet them at night in the forest. Page arranges for Slender to elope with Anne, while Mistress Page, unaware, arranges for Caius to elope with Anne. Meanwhile, Anne elopes with Fenton. Page tells Slender that Anne will be in the forest dressed in white. Mistress Page tells Caius that Anne will be in the forest dressed in green.

In the forest, Falstaff is terrified by "fairies" (really children trained by Evans), who pinch him while Pistol and Nim tease him with burning tapers. Caius runs off with a boy dressed in green and Slender with a boy dressed in white. The wives reveal their pranks to Falstaff who admits he has been made a complete ass – as Caius and Slender return to acknowledge that they too have been made fools of. Fenton arrives, married to Anne. ∎

IN CONTEXT

THEMES
Love, fidelity, forgiveness

SETTING
Windsor, a town on the River Thames near London

SOURCES
There are no direct sources for the play, which was largely a spin-off from the *Henry IV* plays. It is one of the very few of Shakespeare's plays to be set wholly in England, and much of the comedy draws from English in-jokes of the period.

The *Merry Wives Of Windsor* is one of the most enjoyed but least celebrated of Shakespeare's plays. Its tale of a lovable rogue getting his comeuppance at the hands of the women he hopes to take advantage of is a comic formula that has been recycled again and again, in everything from Restoration comedies to stage farces and TV sitcoms. The rogue is, of course, Shakespeare's unique creation, the "fat knight" Sir John Falstaff.

Suburban comedy

The remarkable thing, however, is that Shakespeare's play was one of the originals, the blueprint for all these later comedies. At the time Shakespeare wrote *The Merry Wives*, plays were mostly about aristocratic, mythical, or heroic figures. The idea of a comedy about the foibles of a "suburban" middle class was unheard of. Although younger English playwrights such as John Fletcher and Ben Jonson quickly followed with sharp "city" satires, the suburban comedy was Shakespeare's idea.

A story goes that Elizabeth I so liked the character of Sir John Falstaff in *Henry IV Part 2* that she wanted to see "Falstaff in love", and *The Merry Wives* was Shakespeare's rather off-beat response. There is no reliable source for this story, however. Another speculative theory is that the play was performed in front of the queen in April 1597 in Windsor, prior to the annual feast for the knights of the Garter at Windsor Castle, or that *The Merry Wives* makes good the promise in the epilogue for *Henry IV Part 2* to "continue the story, with Sir John in it".

The fat knight's frolics

Scholars have debated the question of when in Falstaff's life the story is set. It's clearly before his reported death in *Henry V*, but is it before his drinking days in Eastcheap with Prince Hal in *Henry IV*, or after? It probably doesn't matter, because Shakespeare omits any reference to 15th-century historical events in *The Merry Wives* – it really feels as if Falstaff has been plucked from his own century and dropped amid the citizens of Shakespeare's time.

Falstaff is definitely the star of the play, and the comedy comes from this rambunctious character, who drops into the dull world of Windsor life and causes chaos. He imagines he is going to lord it over this provincial backwater with his knighthood and his eloquence but he's in for a surprise. The very biddable housewives who he thinks will make easy pickings, mistresses Page and Ford, quickly turn the tables on him and he is humiliated again and again.

What makes Falstaff so appealing is the manner in which he bounces back from each setback with irrepressible optimism. Even at the end, when made a complete fool in the forest, he has a comeback – "Have I lived to stand at the taunt of one that makes fritters of English?" (5.5.141–142). Throughout the play, his wit shines while all the other men mangle language so badly that it is often impossible for modern audiences to follow. »

> ❝ Why then, the world's mine oyster,
> Which I with sword will open.
> **Pistol**
> Act 2, Scene 2 ❞

Mangled words

There are malapropisms and mispronunciations galore – and they are frequently bawdy. Mistress Quickly laments, "she does so take on with her men; they mistook their erection" (presumably meaning "direction"), to which Falstaff ruefully responds, "So did I mine, to build upon a foolish woman's promise" (3.5.39–40). While when Hugh Evans is teaching the boy William his Latin, he talks of the "focative" case, not the vocative, saying, "Remember, William, focative is caret" – to which Mistress Quickly knowingly replies, "And that's a good root." (4.1.48–49).

Most of the play is about the wives asserting their control over the town. They are not easily fooled, and they are worthy of more respect than their husbands give

In this 2008 production at the Globe Theatre, London, Christopher Benjamin's self-deluding Falstaff fancies he sees the "leer of invitation".

them. They show, too, that they have a great sense of fun. But having fun does not make them disreputable; they do not have to be melancholy nuns or unattractive prudes to be good wives. As Mistress Page says, "Wives may be merry, and yet honest, too." (4.2.95).

A triumph for love

Yet even as the wives come out on top with their husband's apologies and Falstaff's humiliation, they are caught by surprise, as Fenton and Anne show the real victor to be love. While the wives have been off teaching the men a lesson and the Pages have been trying to set up their daughter Anne in marriages she doesn't want, Anne has eloped with Fenton. "You would have married [Anne], most shamefully, / Where there was no proportion held in love" (5.5.213–214), Fenton tells them, and stresses how their love match will save Anne from "A thousand irreligious cursèd hours / Which forcèd marriage would have brought upon her." (5.5.221–222). The message still resonates today. ∎

> 66 ...here will be an old abusing of God's patience and the King's English!
> **Mistress Quickly**
> Act 1, Scene 4 99

WE HAVE HEARD THE CHIMES AT MIDNIGHT

HENRY IV PART 2 (1597–1598)

The presenter Rumour begins the play by revealing the lie that's on its way to old Northumberland: that Hotspur has defeated King Henry's forces at the Battle of Shrewsbury. This happy news reaches him moments before it is contradicted by the truth: that Hotspur was killed, the rebels routed, and the king's men are marching north towards him. Despite his grief, Northumberland agrees to join the Archbishop of York's forces in a renewed fight. By the time the forces gather, however,Northumberland has fled to Scotland and left his fellow rebels vulnerable. They agree to a parley, and present their grievances to Prince John who promises redress on behalf of his father. Although Mowbray remains unsure, the other lords dismiss their troops and prepare for peace. No sooner have their men dispersed than John arrests the rebels for high treason and condemns them all to death.

Deception also flourishes elsewhere. Falstaff should be with Prince John in the north but consumption, physical and financial, keeps him in London. There the Lord Chief Justice rebukes him for dishonourably misleading Prince Hal, and Mistress Quickly has him arrested for debt. He mollifies her with further empty promises and borrows more; and then maligns Prince Hal, who overhears these potential words of treason. Amid the rising noise and chaos of the Eastcheap underworld, a sudden call to his father's sickbed delivers a timely rebuke to the wayward Prince for this irresponsible waste of time.

Sensing his own mortality, Falstaff seeks comfort from Doll Tearsheet before departing for duty. He is tasked with a recruiting drive in Gloucestershire. But since Falstaff takes bribes to exempt certain conscripts, his fighting force retains the poorest men in every sense.

At court, the wakeful king is troubled by his betrayal of those same warlords who helped him to the crown, and by fears for the future once the unpredictable Hal is king. He asks that the crown lie on his pillow as he sleeps. When Hal arrives and takes the crown believing the king has died, the king is all the more convinced his son desires his death. Hal assures his father that he dreads that event, and promises that, when it comes, it will herald a just reign.

Henry dies, and Falstaff hopes for influence at court. But Hal keeps his word. Promising the Lord Chief Justice to defend the law, he dismisses Falstaff when his old friend hails him at the coronation. As Falstaff is arrested for debt, Prince John mentions a rumoured war with France and we know that Agincourt beckons. ∎

Falstaff remembers hearing London's church clocks chiming midnight when, as a student at the Inns of Court, he burned the candle at both ends. In those days, the lateness of the hour signalled a young man's liberty. Now, remembered in old age, it marks the end of things. With their blend of warmth and wistfulness Falstaff's words capture perfectly the bitter-sweet quality of this play, in which for king, rebels, and common folk alike, midnight chimes finality and judgment.

The title *Henry IV Part 2* leads us to expect a sequel to Part 1, and to a degree it is. As the title page to the 1600 quarto promises, we are to see again the comic knight John Falstaff, meet his new companion, Pistol, and follow the history to Henry's death and the coronation of the hero-king Henry V. It was a winning combination for the Elizabethan audience who had delighted in Part 1. But while there is comedy in Part 2, the mood is darker, and the historical events are less valiant, tainted as they are with political trickery.

The play appears to have been written for an audience that has seen Part 1, and it therefore uses similarities between the two in narrative and structure to make the differences stand out. While this play looks forwards to the coronation of Henry V, its main focus is retrospective. It revisits issues and relationships from Part 1 and reflects on them at a slower pace and in a more nuanced way.

Subjects to time

The three worlds of Part 1 – the court, the tavern, and the rebels – now feel the debilitating effects of time and mortality. Plump Jack Falstaff, Hal's father-substitute and tavern-king, is in physical decline: his first words in Part 2 are to enquire about the health of his urine. The king himself swaps the robe of majesty for a nightgown as sleepless anxiety about rebellion and his inheritance contributes to his deteriorating health. And the rebels, too, admit that their long dispute with the king has made them ill: "we are all diseased, / And with our surfeiting and wanton hours / Have brought ourselves into a burning fever, / And we must bleed for it" (4.1.54–57). Even when the central scenes take us to Gloucestershire, where pippin apples land appears as a society in its twilight years where elderly men ponder sheep prices and tally the deaths of old friends.

Not even Hal is untouched by this pervasive malaise. He admits when he first appears that he is "exceeding weary" (2.2.1) and seems bored with his wastrel life. Keeping up the image of the wayward scapegrace has become harder since his father's illness, and the prince confides to Poins that his heart "bleeds inwardly"

In an intriguing theatrical dynamic, a dotard Falstaff was played by British actor Timothy West alongside a cynical Prince Hal, played by West's son Samuel, at the Old Vic, London, in 1997.

From the medieval kings to Elizabeth I

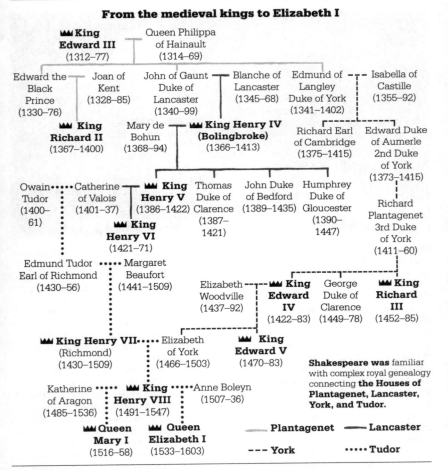

Shakespeare was familiar with complex royal genealogy connecting **the Houses of Plantagenet, Lancaster, York, and Tudor.**

——— Plantagenet ——— Lancaster

--- York ••••• Tudor

(2.2.41) for the king. He is concerned, too, about how his friends perceive him. He knows that Falstaff hopes for future influence at court, but now he learns that Poins, his close companion, might have misused their friendship by claiming that his sister Nell and Hal will marry. Though Poins dismisses this as Falstaff's lie, there is a new unease in Eastcheap.

Time is running out, flesh is weak, and dreams decay. This vulnerability to time and its deceptions is described in the Induction to the play, which is spoken by the figure of Rumour, possibly wearing a robe decorated

with tongues. He not only reveals the lie about Hotspur's death, but says that the greater danger comes from the lies we tell ourselves: "smooth comforts false, worse than true wrongs" (Induction.40–41).

Looking back

Characters spend much time revisiting and revising the past in this play, and almost unthinkingly rework history to suit the present. For example, the barons justify their continued rebellion with reference to the death of Richard II, and promises made but not fulfilled by Henry since »

Thinking his sleeping father (David Yelland) dead, Hal (Tom Mison) tries on the crown for size in this 2011 production directed by Sir Peter Hall.

becoming king. They overlook their own complicity in Henry's rise to power and dangerously underestimate how far the king will go to "wipe his tables clean" (4.1.199). Fearful and unable to sleep, Henry also looks back at that time and marvels at how easily the barons seem to switch allegiance. In doing so, he forgets how he, too, betrayed a king.

Meanwhile, profiting from the lie that he killed Hotspur, Falstaff has recast himself as a gentleman and adopted airs and graces he can ill afford. He is confronted in the street by the Lord Chief Justice who is unamused by the wit with which the fat knight usually extricates himself from trouble. Now Justice itself warns Falstaff

> 66 Sir John, Sir John, I am well acquainted with your manner of wrenching the true cause the false way.
> **Lord Chief Justice**
> Act 2, Scene 1 99

that time is short and judgment inevitable. At the play's end this same Justice will imprison Falstaff for debt.

The rebels also find that time is not on their side. Northumberland hears the falsehood of his son's victory before learning of his death, and news of his own departure for Scotland reaches his fellow barons too late for remedy. Prince John takes advantage of this weakened position to spring his trap. Although Mowbray is uneasy, the other rebel leaders trust the Prince's word and rashly dismiss their forces before establishing the details of his promised redress. Once the lords are powerless, John condemns them all to death. Timing is everything. As Lord Hastings puts it, "We are time's subjects, and time bids be gone" (1.3.110). Thanks to Prince John's tactics, by the middle of the play, all of Henry's enemies are gone.

Inheritance

Shakespeare alters history to implicate the king in this deception by tasking his son with the trick. The chronicles ascribe it to one of his nobles. In political terms, John has acted wisely in avoiding bloodshed. Yet, as the scene closes, his insistence that "God, and not we, hath safely fought today" (4.1.347) recasts his political stratagem as a battlefield victory by infusing it with honour that it hardly deserves. John has evidently

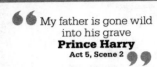

> ❝ My father is gone wild into his grave
> **Prince Harry**
> Act 5, Scene 2 ❞

inherited his father's calculation. He is, in Falstaff's words, a "sober-blooded boy" (4.2.84–85), lacking a sense of humour or taste for drink. In his lengthy praise of sack, or sherry, the fat knight says that Hal, who also shares his father's cold-bloodedness, has warmed it with the wine of tavern life.

Hal shows his ability to sidestep the kind of confrontation that his brother seems to relish when he eventually meets the king. Henry has placed the crown beside him on his pillow and, mistaking sleep for death, Hal has briefly tried it on. Now it sits between them as they talk. The prince tells Henry what he wants to hear, but he does so by reworking slightly what happened when he briefly took the crown away. In his earlier words, he described his father as using the crown like armour, to serve himself. Now he says to the king that it is he, the king, who has protected the crown and suffered in its service. Henry takes up this flattering falsehood when he

describes himself as meeting rather than seizing the crown, as if he took no active part in usurping Richard II. And Hal confirms the fiction that the crown has rightfully passed to Henry when he casts himself as its true inheritor: "You won it, wore it, kept it, gave it me; / Then plain and right must my possession be" (4.3.350–351). This revision by father and son of the central problem of Henry's reign exemplifies Shakespeare's major theme in the play – that of re-reading the past.

Having placated his father with this promise of loyalty, the prince receives his advice. Once king, says Henry, Hal should bring the people together in a foreign war.

Sombre finale

Shakespeare closes the play in the minor key. Falstaff is finally dismissed when Hal establishes his power in the rule of law. His rejection of his old friend is the final playing out of that promised moment from the comic tavern play in Part 1. Hal's new regal style now silences Falstaff's familiar greeting: "I know thee not, old man" (5.5.47). And when John mentions rumours of war, we remember Henry's deathbed advice to his son. We know this war will end with victory at Agincourt and see Hal fulfil his father's project of uniting the nation under the crown, however briefly. ■

Language and place

The Eastcheap tavern is a place of transit through which pass characters whom Shakespeare identifies by their idiosyncrasies

of speech: Ensign Pistol's empty bombast; Mistress Quickly's sentimental picturing of the past; Bardolph's monosyllabic utterances, and Doll's abuse.

In contrast, Gloucestershire folk are rooted to and identified by place: John Doit of Staffordshire; Will Squeal, a Cotswold man; Clement Perkes o'th'Hill. Unlike Eastcheap, there is a deep sense of continuity in the country, and of events driven more by the seasons than by man. Falstaff contaminates this

English idyll. In a telling moment, Feeble, a woman's tailor, speaks out against Falstaff's corrupt recruiting practices and declares that he is proud to die for King and country: "No man's too good to serve's prince... Faith, I'll bear no base mind." (3.2.234–235,238). Feeble's simple integrity puts Falstaff's enterprise to shame. It also rejects the calculating baseness of mind that ultimately derives from the very king whom Feeble would give his life for.

OUT ON THEE SEEMING I WILL WRITE AGAINST IT
MUCH ADO ABOUT NOTHING (1598-1599)

News comes to Leonato, Governor of Messina, that the victorious Don Pedro of Aragon will shortly return from war and that Claudio, a young member of his company, has distinguished himself in battle. Beatrice's playful enquiry after another officer, Benedick, sets the theme of their love-hate relationship. The couple's witty banter cuts through the welcoming formalities and sharply contrasts with Claudio's nascent adoration of Hero, Leonato's only heir. Claudio confesses this infatuation to Don Pedro and Benedick, as if seeking reassurance. But while Benedick, the avowed bachelor, ridicules idealized love, Don Pedro offers to win Hero's hand for Claudio at that evening's masked ball. With their identities disguised, the maskers indulge in innuendo, sexual banter, retribution, and deceit. And Don John, seizing the chance to play mischievously on Claudio's insecurities, insinuates that Don Pedro is wooing Hero for himself.

The lie is exposed, the match is made and, delighted, Leonato gives his blessing. All that remains is for Claudio and Hero to speak to one another for the first time. While they whisper together, Beatrice fends off a throwaway marriage proposal from Don Pedro.

Until the wedding, Don Pedro takes up matchmaking. Detecting compatibility in opposites, he decides to trick Beatrice and Benedick into admitting they love each other. Two scenes are set: Benedick eavesdrops as Don Pedro, Claudio, and Leonato discuss Beatrice's feelings. Meanwhile, she overhears Hero and Ursula revealing Benedick's love.

Borachio feeds Don John's malevolence with a plot to thwart the marriage. He'll speak to Margaret, dressed as Hero, at her window the night before the wedding, while Don John ensures that Claudio and Don Pedro witness the encounter. At the altar, Claudio cruelly rejects Hero, claiming that she's no longer pure. Hero faints. Claudio and Don Pedro leave. Unlike Leonato, the Priest believes in Hero's innocence and proposes a rescue plan. Benedick stays behind, concerned for Hero and Beatrice. Overwhelmed by emotion, he and Beatrice confess their love. She then asks him to kill Claudio.

The duel does not take place because by chance the bumbling watchmen have overheard Borachio bragging about the plot. They bring the truth to light and clear Hero's name. Believing her to be dead as the Priest suggests, Claudio agrees to mourn at her "tomb" and to marry her "cousin", sight unseen. When this lady unveils, she is, in fact, Hero. The play ends with news of Don John's arrest, and a dance before the double wedding. ■

IN CONTEXT

THEMES
Social codes and status, love, marriage, deception

SETTING
Messina, a port city in Sicily under Spanish rule

SOURCES
There are no direct sources. The Hero plot, based on an old tale, is indirectly indebted to:

1516 Ludovico Ariosto's *Orlando Furioso* (Italian verse translated into English, 1591).

1554 Matteo Bandello's *Novelle* (Italian prose adapted into French, 1569).

Much *Ado About Nothing* presents "seeming" in several guises. The wordplay on nothing/noting in the title would have alerted the play's first audience to the theme of observation. And the messenger's reports in the first scene make it clear that Messina is a society where appearances matter. But what's built on appearance, report, and hearsay is fragile, open to conflicting interpretations, and easily destroyed.

Appearing and observing

Both love stories in the play hinge on appearance and observation. Claudio has fallen in love with Hero because she seems to him a sweet, modest young woman. But he's unsure of his own judgment and seeks confirmation from the older Benedick and

For his 1993 film, Kenneth Branagh cut the text to keep the action moving. A star-studded cast included Kate Beckinsale, Denzel Washington, Keanu Reeves, and Branagh himself.

Don Pedro. Benedick differentiates between noting Hero and looking at her. His replies draw attention to the subjectivity of perception, as simply looking at her does not reveal any extraordinary traits in the young woman; Claudio's noting, however, marks her as priceless: "Can the world buy such a jewel?" (1.1.171). With no assurance for his budding love from Benedick, Claudio is reluctant to reveal his admiration for Hero to Don Pedro. Only when the Prince insists that he's serious in thinking "the lady is very well worthy" (1.1.207–208) does Claudio admit his love.

The courtship of Claudio and Hero follows a very formal pattern. First the lovers admire each other from a distance. Claudio does not even woo Hero himself, but leaves this to the Prince. The lovers do not speak to each other until their elders have agreed on the marriage and Leonato has given his blessing. Even at this point, Hero doesn't have any lines, although the text suggests that she takes the liberty of kissing Claudio in public.

Constrained by the formality of their courtship, Claudio and Hero hardly know each other. It's not surprising, therefore, that Claudio's faith in Hero is easily shaken when Don John tells him that his brother has wooed her for himself. Claudio does not doubt for a minute that Hero has accepted Don Pedro. The report is quickly revealed as false and laughingly dismissed by the Prince and Leonato. But Don John is still determined to prevent the marriage and, thanks to Borachio's plot, he makes it appear to Claudio and Don Pedro that Hero entertained a man on the night before the wedding. Mistaking Margaret for Hero, Claudio is instantly convinced that she is unfaithful and his idolising adoration quickly turns into hatred and disgust.

The formal, stylized nature of the courtship finds its counterpart in Claudio's public rejection of Hero in the disrupted wedding ceremony. As in the scene at Hero's window, Claudio misinterprets what he observes. Having rejected Hero as a "rotten orange" (4.1.32), he's convinced that "Her blush is guiltiness, not modesty" (4.1.42). Incapable of seeing her as the » person she really is, Claudio falls from one extreme: Hero as chaste, pure, and innocent, to another: Hero as loose and wanton. The way she appears to him is determined by what others want him to believe. So it's no surprise that when, eventually, Borachio confesses the plot, Claudio instantly reverts to the first image he had of her.

Tricks and truths

While appearances give the love story of Claudio and Hero an almost tragic turn, they are put to comic use in the love story of Beatrice and Benedick. Here are two people who seem to detest nothing so much as each other. Yet we cannot help feeling that behind their battle of words they are hiding wounds caused by rejected love, hints of which can be heard in their banter: "You always end with a jade's trick. / I know you of old" (1.1.138–139).

Their friends are convinced that they will make a perfect couple and, in the two eavesdropping scenes, use report and hearsay to trick them into admitting their love. Claudio, Don Pedro, and Leonato paint the picture of a Beatrice desperately in love. But they think it best for her not to admit it for fear of being mocked by an unfeeling Benedick. Convinced that the three men tell the truth, because "The conference was sadly borne" (2.3.210),

Benedick is determined that Beatrice's love will be requited. Even the prospect of being mocked by his friends for changing his mind about marriage does not deter him.

Hero and Ursula, in turn, praise Benedick as "the only man of Italy" (3.1.92). They reproach Beatrice for being proud and disdainful since, as a confirmed bachelor, she always finds things to criticize in even the most perfect of men. If she learned of Benedick's love, then she would "make sport at it" (3.1.59). Sobered by this criticism, Beatrice is prepared for "taming my wild heart to thy [Benedick's] loving hand" (3.1.112). Benedick can confirm that Beatrice is fair, virtuous, and wise, and Beatrice does not need reports of Benedick's merits to know that he is deserving. It is clear to us that, unlike Hero and Claudio, Beatrice and Benedick know each other well.

Language and reality

The play's language is characterized by wordplay, banter, and repartee. Beatrice and Benedick are involved in linguistic fencing matches from the moment they meet in the play: "**Benedick:** What, my dear Lady Disdain! Are you yet living? **Beatrice:** Is it possible disdain should die while she hath such meet food to feed it as Signor Benedick?" (1.1.112–115). Conversation between Don Pedro and his

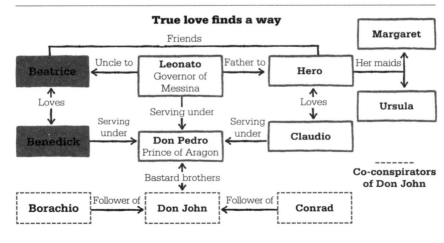

True love finds a way

Friends

Beatrice ←Uncle to— **Leonato** Governor of Messina —Father to→ **Hero** —Her maids→ **Margaret**

Beatrice ↕ Loves

Hero ↕ Loves

Hero ↔ **Ursula**

Benedick —Serving under→ **Don Pedro** Prince of Aragon ←Serving under— **Claudio**

Benedick Loves Beatrice

Don Pedro ↑ Bastard brothers

- - - - - - -
Co-conspirators of Don John

Borachio —Follower of→ **Don John** ←Follower of— **Conrad**

men is predominantly light-hearted, blokeish joking, especially about Benedick's mistrust of women and rejection of marriage:
"Don Pedro: 'In time the savage bull doth bear the yoke.'
Benedick: The savage bull may, but if ever the sensible Benedick bear it, pluck off the bull's horns and set them in my forehead, and let me be vilely painted…'Here you may see Benedick, the married man'." (1.1.243–250). This expresses the deeply rooted fear in Messina society of being cuckolded. Even Leonato jokes about the legitimacy of his daughter. Where marriage brings fears of cuckoldry, Don John's accusation against Hero is readily believed. In the wedding scene, the language switches from jests to calculated insults as Claudio uses the very form of the marriage service to reject and humiliate Hero. The studied nature of his rejection is matched in the formal mourning ceremony at Hero's tomb. The readiness with which Don Pedro and Claudio dismiss the musicians and leave for a second wedding can make us wonder how much of Claudio's grief is merely "seeming".

Language is also used as a means of establishing social equality. In her conversations with men, Beatrice uses witty repartee to meet them on an equal footing. Both Margaret and Dogberry see language as having the potential to bring them level with their masters. Margaret's brief conversation with Benedick (5.2), a dialogue that condenses many of the play's concerns about class and gender conflict, reveals her desire to move up socially. In the RSC production in 1996, she was caught at this point by Benedick with one of Hero's dresses. Access to these outward signs of social status makes her a threat in a society that depends so much on signs. However, Constable Dogberry's efforts to sound like his betters fail miserably. He epitomises a society distracted by surfaces, where words are easily divorced from their meaning.

Pairs and frames

The play is structured around pairs: Leonato and his brother Antonio; Claudio and Don Pedro; Borachio and Conrad; Dogberry and Verges. And Messina is a society where marriage is the rule.

The banter between Benedick and Beatrice is central to the play's charm. In the 2007 production at London's National Theatre, Simon Russell Beale and Zoe Wanamaker played the pair.

Don Pedro's scheme to make Beatrice and Benedick pair up, therefore, is not purely comic. It brings firmly into line two individuals who otherwise stand out uncomfortably against Messina's values in their preference for the bachelor life. Claudio and Hero are easily reconciled once her innocence is proven. But Beatrice and Benedick seem determined not to admit their love. In her final lines, Beatrice hints that she might yet refuse to be neatly paired off. Most productions follow the editorial tradition and attribute the reply, "Peace! I will stop your mouth" (5.4.97) to Benedick, as he kisses Beatrice. But the Quarto and Folio texts give this line to Leonato, who may be using his patriarchal authority to bring Beatrice to heel. Like *The Taming of the Shrew*, there is ambiguity in the ending.

By the end of the play, Don Pedro is the only single man left. Without an heir, he leaves his estate vulnerable to the plotting of others such as his bastard brother Don John. A born outsider, John refuses all efforts to be framed in Messina's codes. In a world of wordplay he guards his silence: "I am not of many words" (1.1.150). Refusing to perform, he is what he seems. News of his recapture darkens the festive mood. In the 1990 RSC production, he stood at the edge of the stage, and stared at Don Pedro as if reigniting the conflict suggested at the beginning of the play. ∎

ONCE MORE UNTO THE BREACH DEAR FRIENDS, ONCE MORE
HENRY V (1599)

The Chorus pleads with the audience to overlook the theatre's limitations and to picture the epic events to come. King Henry V, reformed from his wild youth, is assured by the Archbishop of Canterbury that his claim to the French throne is just. When the French ambassador brings him a mocking gift of tennis balls, Henry's riposte is that he will strike the French crown out of play.

In Southampton, the Chorus describes how the youth of England are eager to fight, but warns that there are three traitors. Henry's old drinking pals meet in a tavern. Bardolph stirs up trouble between Nim and Pistol, now married to Nim's former betrothed, hostess Nell Quickly. Henry unmasks the traitors and sends them for execution. Nell describes the death of old Falstaff, broken by Henry's rejection of him, and the three pals embark for France with Henry.

In France, the French king, Charles VI, and his son, the Dauphin, prepare for battle, mocking the wild youth of Henry. Henry's ambassador Exeter warns the French against resistance.

In France, Henry launches an attack on Harfleur and threatens dire repercussions if the townspeople do not yield. Meanwhile, Bardolph and his associates argue about joining the fight. In the French palace, the French king's daughter Catherine tries to learn English. The king rails against Henry while the Dauphin condemns French women for fraternizing with the English.

In the English camp, Bardolph is caught looting and executed on Henry's orders. Henry refuses an embassy from the French to persuade him to withdraw. Henry, disguised as Henry Le Roy, argues the rights and wrongs of the battle with the soldier Williams. The next morning, Henry, his army outnumbered 5 to 1, gives a speech pledging that those who fight with him will be forever remembered on this, St Crispin's Day.

As the French attack again, Henry orders the slaughter of French prisoners to free up the men guarding them. Gower reports that the French have slain English boys, and Henry swears the French no mercy. Henry wins the day, with 10,000 French slain and only three English lords. Henry prepares to return to England victorious.

In the French palace, Charles receives Henry. Henry agrees to peace only if his demands are met – including the hand of Princess Catherine. Henry starts to woo the French princess in a conversation made difficult by his poor French and her poor English. It ends with Henry kissing her. The Chorus recounts how destiny unfolds as Henry and Catherine's son becomes Henry VI and how his courtiers lost France again. ■

THE LORD CHAMBERLAIN'S MAN 97

IN CONTEXT

THEMES
War, patriotism, kingship

SETTING
London and Southampton in England; the palace of the French king; Harfleur and Agincourt in France

SOURCES
1577 Edward Halle's *Union of the Two Noble and Illustrious Families of Lancaster and York*.

1587 The key source is the *Chronicles of England, Scotland, and Ireland* edited by Ralph Holinshed.

Henry V is often described as Shakespeare's war play. Unlike most of his plays, there is no unfolding of complex personal journeys or relationships. It appears to be a simple, thrilling story of how the heroic young soldier-king Henry V triumphs at Agincourt against all the odds, packed with stirring war poetry.

In the past, many regarded it as Shakespeare's most patriotic play – a glorification of a high point in England's history, when a small "band" of Englishmen defeated a large army of the cream of French knighthood. At the centre of it all is an uplifting portrait of a matchless hero, leading his men to an unlikely victory. Speeches have often been culled from the play to inspire troops at moments of crisis. Most famously, British Prime Minister Winston Churchill echoed Henry's speech "We few, we happy few..." (4.3.60) in his broadcast telling the public of the debt owed to the "few" fighter pilots who saved the country in the Battle of Britain of 1940.

Changing perspectives

Attitudes towards the play have changed considerably through time, along with attitudes to war and nationalist fervour. Critics and theatre directors now treat the play much more warily than in the past. They often look for a subversive political

message that parodies militarism – staging the play not in historical England, for instance, but in charged contemporary situations, such as the war in Iraq. Or they look to focus on the human cost of war implicit in the play. Many critics have gone further, and suggested that *Henry V* has been misread. Far from glorifying war, they say, the play is a complex exploration of the miseries of war and the power of propaganda.

What is clear is that the play is by no means a simple narrative of Henry's big moment. It tells the story from at least four different perspectives. Not only is there the straight sequence of scenes that places Henry at the thick of things; there is also the Chorus, which prepares us for each act; there are the trials and tribulations of the Eastcheapers; and there are the tough experiences of the ordinary soldiers. There is even a French perspective. These multiple viewpoints suggest there is much more going on than merely Henry's heroism, as each interweaves with the central Henry narrative.

Proclaiming Henry

The Chorus that opens the play puts the illusory theatre experience at the forefront, with its evocative mentions of "this wooden O" – the term often used for the round, timber-framed playhouses of Shakespeare's time, one of which has been accurately reconstructed today in the form of the Globe Theatre. The Chorus apologizes for the theatre's limitations in staging such an epic story, but the apology is uplifting: "O for a muse of fire that would ascend / The »

Laurence Olivier's morale-boosting film, made during World War II, left out some of Henry's more vicious acts, such as the hanging of Bardolph, to portray Henry as a heroic figure.

brightest heaven of invention: / A kingdom for a stage, princes to act, / And monarchs to behold the swelling scene." (Prologue-1–4).

The Chorus may be saying sorry, but at the same time, he is whipping up the crowd for the coming event with no less fervour than Henry will do when he later rouses his troops with his famous Crispin's Day speech. "Can this cock-pit hold / The vasty fields of France?" the Chorus asks (Prologue.11–12). The words conjure the same illusion as Henry will when he, beginning with the same false modesty, rouses his men with the promise of great memories for the future.

Beyond the banner

What follows the Chorus's prologue is not scenes of heroism but a shady debate between England's two church leaders. These men of the cloth do not discuss high moral matters, but a backstairs collusion to escape taxes by supporting Henry's claim to the French throne. If the church leaders' motives are so venal, maybe one should question their assessment that the erstwhile tearaway Prince Hal has had an almost religious conversion to the straight and narrow on becoming king: "Consideration like an angel came / And whipped th'offending Adam out of him." (1.1.29–30). Throughout the narrative, Henry presents himself as a Christian king, armed by God. After the seemingly miraculous triumph on the battlefield at Agincourt, he declines to take credit, offering the victory to God – "Take it God, / For it is none but thine." (4.8.111–112). But is this all image-building, part of a necessary display of kingship? We never actually see Henry on the battlefield, nor do we ever hear of any strategic skill. Instead, Henry dazzles with rhetoric.

Henry the orator

Two speeches in particular show Shakespeare's language at its most muscular. The first is when Henry urges his men on outside the walls of Harfleur: "Once more unto the breach, dear friends, once more, / Or close the wall up with our English dead." (3.1.1–2). The second is his address before the battle, when he promises: "And Crispin Crispian shall ne'er go by / From this day to the ending of the world / But we in it shall be rememberèd, / We few, we happy few, we band of brothers" (4.3.57–60).

Ruthless leader

The picture presented of Henry is far from simply heroic. Shakespeare shows him to be not just an inspiring leader, but a tough, even brutal, one too. His way with justice is ruthless. The traitors are tricked into urging their own death sentence, while

Historical Agincourt

The focus of *Henry V* is the Battle of Agincourt, a landmark English victory in a series of conflicts known as the Hundred Years War, which lasted from 1337 until 1453. It was fought between the English and French ruling families, the Plantagenets and the Valois, for control of the French throne.

The battle took place on 25 October 1415 near present-day Azincourt in northern France. Henry V did indeed fight in the battle. The outnumbered English forces possessed both technology and luck. Henry's archers could shoot up to six arrows a minute using the longbow, whereas the French possessed the slower, heavier crossbow, and, weighed down with armour, had chosen a muddy field for their attack.

The battle was not as one-sided as Shakespeare makes out, although the killing of the prisoners did take place. Neither was the impact of the battle as decisive as the play suggests. It took five more years of war before Henry reached a settlement with the French. He died at the age of 35 before ever becoming king of France.

Henry brusquely confirms the death sentence on his drinking friend Bardolph for stealing from a church, despite pleas for clemency. Indeed, Henry's old Eastcheap pals – Bardolph, Nim, and Pistol – are as unheroic an image of soldiering as can be.Disreputable, lazy, cowardly, and argumentative, very often they seem to parody Henry's rhetoric, with Bardolph proclaiming, "On, on, on, on, on! To the breach! To the breach!" (3.2.1–2). In the prequel, *Henry IV*, these were entertaining characters, a comic counterpoint to the main action led by the irrepressible Sir John Falstaff. But in *Henry V*, much of the humour has drained away and the lovable rogues of the earlier play become victims, bearing the cost of war more than the other characters.

Falstaff dies without ever even appearing – a victim, so Mistress Quickly insists, of Henry's neglect: "The King has killed his heart" (2.1.84). Bardolph and Nim are hanged offstage for the same roguery that made them endearing in the earlier play. Finally, Mistress Quickly dies of the French malady (venereal disease), again offstage. Only Pistol survives, and even he is humiliated by being forced to eat leek by Fluellen. The juggernaut of Henry's heroic new age has rolled on and left these characters of an earlier time in its wake.

Henry the king
The portrait of a king in *Henry V*, then, is an ambiguous one, more so than the stirring speeches would suggest. What is certain is that Henry is no unthinking military leader. He has a keen insight into his role as king. As he explains to Bates and Williams when in disguise, "All his senses have but human conditions. His ceremonies laid by, in his nakedness he appears but a man" (4.1.103–105).

Henry knows that he is, underneath the crown, just a man. But he is keenly aware that, as king, he cannot behave as other men do. "We are no tyrant," he insists, "but a Christian king, / Unto whose grace our passion is as subject / As our wretches fettered in our prisons" (1.2.241–243). The image of his human emotions as a wretched prisoner in chains is disturbing, but his view of the need for self-control and

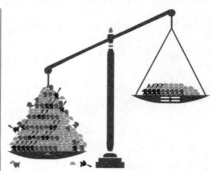

The Battle dead: 10,000 French, including 126 nobles, 8,400 knights, 1,600 common soldiers; 29 English, including 4 nobles and 25 knights/common soldiers.

KEY

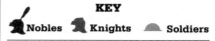

Nobles   Knights   Soldiers

self-sacrifice is clear. The result is that Henry's personality remains largely hidden. He has just one moment of personal revelation – a long soliloquy at the end of his nightwalk about the camp – and even here his argument about the burdens of kingship seem more theoretical than emotional. Henry is a consummate actor, able to be whoever his people need him to be – from theologian with the bishops to common man with the soldiery, to charming, unschooled lover with the princess Catherine.

The Henriad
Henry V was the fourth play of the Henriad, a quartet of history plays, following *Richard II* and *Henry IV* Parts 1 and 2. Together with the first quartet (comprising *Henry VI* Parts 1, 2, and 3, and *Richard III*), it forms a complete chronology of English history from the time of Richard II (1377–99) to the time of Richard III (1483–85). Henry V provides a contrasting figure to the quartet's first king, Richard II, whose weaknesses are transformed into Henry's strengths. Richard smashes a mirror when he loses his throne. But as the English prepare for battle, the Chorus holds Henry up as "the mirror of all Christian kings" (2.0.6). Henry is our own reflection, the king we want him to be, which may explain why our view of this hero is so hard to pin down. ∎

THERE IS A TIDE IN THE AFFAIRS OF MEN WHICH, TAKEN AT THE FLOOD, LEADS ON TO FORTUNE

JULIUS CAESAR (1599)

In Rome, the people celebrate a holiday, the Lupercal, and also rejoice in the triumph of Julius Caesar over the former leader, Pompey.

While greeting his followers, Caesar is warned by a soothsayer to beware the ides (15th) of March. Caesar ignores this warning and dismisses the soothsayer as a dreamer. As he leaves, Cassius draws Brutus aside to convince him that Caesar has become too self-important and that Brutus himself would be a better leader, being of equal standing and as respected by the public. After this, Cassius and Brutus learn from Casca that Caesar has been offered a crown three times, but refused it, albeit unconvincingly, each time. He finally accepts the offer, agreeing to become king and sole leader of Rome. Cassius, left alone, admits that he will use whatever deception necessary to convince Brutus to overthrow Caesar.

During a thunderstorm the night before Caesar is to be crowned Casca notes that many ill omens have appeared. The conspirators meet at Brutus's home and agree to murder Caesar in order to liberate the country from his dictatorship. Brutus has reservations, but he agrees that it must be done to put a stop to Caesar's ambition.

The next day, on the fateful ides of March, Caesar is convinced by Decius that he should go into the city, where he is stabbed by each of the conspirators. When the great soldier Mark Antony hears of this, he laments the death of Caesar, but he shows respect for the people who murdered him, asking them if he can give a speech to the people before Caesar's funeral. Brutus agrees to let Antony do this, in spite of Cassius's warning that it would be dangerous to let him rally the public in Caesar's name.

After Brutus gives a speech to the people, Antony convinces them that Caesar was unjustly murdered by the conspirators, and that this injustice must be avenged. The people then take Caesar's body to be buried, and start a public mutiny. When Caesar's son Octavius returns to Rome, he and Antony start a war against Brutus and the conspirators.

Brutus sees the ghost of Caesar, and acknowledges that he will lose the battle. After he finds Cassius dead, Brutus asks his servant Lucius to hold his sword while he runs onto it and he dies. Finally, Antony and Octavius arrive as victors after the war, lamenting the fall of Brutus and noting that, despite his crime against Caesar, his intentions were the most honourable of all the conspirators. The play closes with Octavius promising to give Brutus a respectable funeral. ∎

 I love the name of honour more than I fear death.
Brutus
Act 1, Scene 2

IN CONTEXT

THEMES
Power, ambition, rebellion, civil war

SETTING
Ancient Rome

SOURCES
1579 Sir Thomas North's translation of Plutarch's *Lives of the Noble Grecians and Romans*.

The first of Shakespeare's Roman plays, *Julius Caesar* is a tale of ambition, political manipulation, and duty. The true tragic figure of the play is Brutus, whose actions proceed from a noble desire to serve Rome. Brutus's struggle between love for Caesar and fear of his despotism make him a sympathetic and honourable tragic figure.

Following the events laid out in Plutarch's history, the play charts the events leading up to Caesar's assassination and the civil war that breaks out thereafter. The senators' concerns about Caesar's leadership echoed anxieties about the aged and heirless Queen Elizabeth in 1599, when the play was first performed. Her inheritance and legacy were not to be discussed, let alone satirized, but could be approached sideways via history.

Shakespeare brings an acute sense of humanity to the story. His historical figures are not simply biographical documentations of the lives of noble Romans. Rather, the characters experience hardship and anxiety, which makes them more morally ambiguous than Plutarch's counterparts. For instance, it is not clear whether Caesar would have mutated into the tyrant that Brutus fears before his assassination, nor that Cassius is a categorically self-interested man, nor even that Ocatvius will make a suitable successor to his adopted father. Such ambiguity has led the American historian Garry Wills to argue that the play has no villains and is, therefore, unique among Shakespeare's tragedies.

Seductive rhetoric

Power in this play does not come from strength, honour, or military prowess. Instead, power is linked to manipulative and calculated rhetoric. Without the support of the people, the senators cannot avoid civil unrest, and how to convince, placate, and organize the civilians in Rome is a major preoccupation of the leaders. It is this that motivates Brutus's address to the people after Caesar's death and Antony's speech about Caesar's reputation.

Antony's oft-quoted speech beginning "Friends, Romans, countrymen" (3.2.74) is a carefully crafted piece of rhetoric calculated to inspire suspicion of Brutus and respect for the late Caesar. Antony accuses the public who so recently celebrated Caesar's triumph at the Lupercal of being "brutish beasts", an echo of Brutus's name. Antony suggests that his enemy is a liar, simultaneously touting Caesar as a peerless hero. With this speech, and with his reading of Caesar's will, Antony gains the support of the civilians, thereby exploiting their new hatred of Caesar's murderers to justify civil war.

With this support, Antony unleashes havoc in the streets. Rebellions and rioting lead to the assassination of Cinna, the poet. There is no accountability for such violent crimes because the civilians act out of anger and fear. Antony understands this, but chooses to spur on the people's distrust of the conspirators to further his own interests. With persuasive rhetorical flourishes, the senators also manipulate one another. In the same way that Antony persuades the people that the conspirators are treasonous murderers, so too Cassius convinces Brutus »

A 1953 film adaptation by director Joseph Mankiewicz starred Marlon Brando as Antony. Brando received coaching in declaiming Shakespearean verse from co-star John Gielgud.

that Caesar must be removed from office. The most potent piece of rhetoric is the cry made by the conspirators after Caesar's death: "Liberty! Freedom! Tyranny is dead!" (3.1.77). Intangible ideals are cleverly used to justify the horror of Caesar's assassination. Rhetoric and persuasion are integral to the political tacticians in Rome, so it is with a scathing voice that Cassius declares, "For who so firm that cannot be seduced?" (1.2.312).

Women unheeded

The women in this masculine political Rome are presented as supportive, stoic wives. Both Brutus's wife Portia and Caesar's wife Calpurnia exist to temper the passions, albeit unsuccessfully, of their husbands. Neither politician shares his misgivings with his wife, nor does either one heed the wifely warnings of danger.

Calpurnia appeals to Caesar's regard for reputation and honour to ask him to remain at home on the ides of March. By contrast, Portia wounds her own thigh, proving herself an equal to her husband through noble suffering. She takes her own life by swallowing hot coals, setting the bar of honour very high for Brutus's death.

Like the men in this world, the women craft their speech. Portia urges her husband to reveal his anxieties in a series of questions using the rule of listing in threes: "Is Brutus sick? and is it physical / To walk unbracèd and suck up the humours / Of the dank morning? What, is Brutus sick? / And will he steal out of his wholesome bed / To dare the vile contagion of the night, / And tempt the rheumy and unpurgèd air / To add unto his sickness? No, my Brutus, / You have some sick offence within your mind, / Which by the right and virtue of my place / I ought to know of." (2.1.260–269).

Although Brutus promises to be more open with his wife, she remains ignorant of the plot against Caesar. This echoes Calpurnia's lack of influence over Caesar.

Masters of fate?

For the conspirators at the start of the play, time and opportunity work in their favour. Caesar is not yet an emperor, nor has he morphed into a tyrant. Before he can become either, Brutus believes it is in the interests of the people and state to dispatch him:"There is a tide in the affairs of men / Which, taken at the flood, leads on to fortune; / Omitted, all the voyage of their life / Is bound in shallows and in miseries. / On such a full sea are we now afloat, / And we must take the current when it serves, / Or lose our ventures" (4.2.270–276).

When he speaks of riding the tide of opportunity, Brutus suggests that fate has a degree of flexibility to it and that to make the most of opportunities leads on to fortune. This is a theory he takes from Cassius who argues that autonomy is the route to success: "Men at sometime were masters of their fates. / The fault, dear Brutus, is not in our stars, / But in ourselves, that we are underlings." (1.2.140–142).

Contemporary twist

The director Gregory Doran staged a politically provocative adaptation of the play in 2012. With a black cast and set in an unspecified African country, this production of Julius Caesar drew inspiration from contemporary political tyranny in its depiction of a nation familiar with despots, civil war, superstition, poverty, and disease. The actions of 20th-century dictators such as Idi Amin and Bokassa, and, more recently, Robert Mugabe, together with the unfolding of the Arab Spring in 2010, collectively informed this interpretation.

Ray Fearon's Antony was a charismatic, manipulative man whose speech to the citizens was delivered on a raised platform over the bloodied body of Caesar, played by Jeffery Kissoon. Brutus was played as a fiercely honourable but naive man by Patterson Joseph. Caesar's own tyranny was skilfully echoed by a giant statue of the leader, designed by Michael Vale, resembling icons of dictatorship in the 20th century. The production was adapted for the screen later that year.

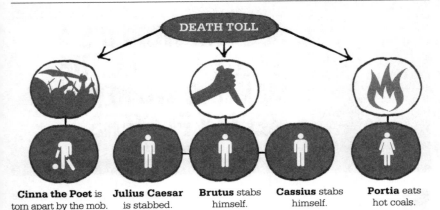

DEATH TOLL

Cinna the Poet is torn apart by the mob.

Julius Caesar is stabbed.

Brutus stabs himself.

Cassius stabs himself.

Portia eats hot coals.

Brutus's belief in destiny explains his willingness to accept his defeat at Philippi. Although he took the opportunity to remove Caesar, it is the ghost and retribution of that same enemy that brings about Brutus's fall. In other words, fate intervenes to punish the conspirators. If fate leads these men to their inevitable ends, how can there be, and what is the purpose of, free will? This question consumes Brutus and Cassius, as well as proving fatal to Caesar. Although Shakespeare does not provide a resolution to the conflict between fate and free will, there is an overwhelming sense of destiny throughout the play, specifically with the many omens that appear during the action.

Ominous portents
Casca expounds on the unnatural events that led up to the ides of March during an equally ominous thunderstorm. Fire drops from the sky, men walk around the streets in flames, lions stalk the Roman roads, and nightingales sing at midday. Casca claims "I believe they are portentous things" (1.3.31).

The signs of doom, as Cassius and Brutus choose to interpret them, echo the Soothsayer's warning to Caesar to "Beware the ides of March" (1.2.25). Caesar ignores the omen by dismissing the Soothsayer, while the conspirators take the omens as a sign to attack Caesar, rather than a warning about impending turmoil should they proceed. Both Caesar and Brutus

misinterpret such signs and go on to make decisions with tragic consequences. It is no accident that, when Casca expostulates about portents, the senator Cicero responds with a statement that rings true for every individual in this tragedy: "Indeed it is a strange-disposèd time; / But men may construe things after their fashion, / Clean from the purpose of the things themselves" (1.3.33–35). There is, in other words, a greater force at work fore-warning these men of their destinies, but the power to interpret and act on those warnings lies with the individual. Ultimately, Brutus takes advantage of chances thrown his way, and yet still ends in defeat. Octavius and Mark Antony will overcome Brutus, just as Brutus took advantage of Caesar's decision to ignore caution on the ides of March.

The intricacies of fate aside, the play makes clear the respect that these men have for one another. Brutus's love for Caesar prevents him from overcoming his guilt at Phillippi; Caesar's trust in Brutus prompts him to exclaim *"et tu, Bruté?"* [you, too, Brutus?] (3.1.77) upon his murder; Cassius is loyal to Brutus despite taking advantage of his integrity; and Antony respects Brutus who, in his opinion, "was the noblest Roman of them all" (5.5.67). They recognize nobility in one another. This is what separates this tragedy from others, including *King Lear*, *Hamlet*, and *Macbeth*, because every character is capable and deserving of redemption. ∎

ALL THE WORLD'S A STAGE AND ALL THE MEN AND WOMEN MERELY PLAYERS

AS YOU LIKE IT (1599–1600)

Since their father's death, Orlando has been kept at home and denied education by his older brother Oliver. When Oliver hears that Orlando plans to fight Charles the wrestler, Oliver tells Charles to kill him. At court, Rosalind laments her father, Duke Senior's, banishment. With her cousin Celia, she watches the wrestling match and both are taken with Orlando, who surprisingly beats Charles. Orlando falls in love with Rosalind, but has to escape to the forest with old Adam, pursued by Oliver. Celia's father, Duke Frederick, feels threatened by Rosalind's popularity and exiles her. Rosalind dresses as the boy Ganymede and flees to the forest with Celia and Touchstone, the fool. In the forest, Duke Senior and his lords, including the gloomy Jaques, enjoy the simple life.

Duke Frederick organizes a pursuit of Rosalind and Celia. In the forest, Rosalind and Celia witness Silvius telling the old shepherd Corin of his unrequited love for Phoebe. Faint with hunger, Orlando meets Duke Senior's men and draws his sword. They offer him supper and he joins their band. Orlando, pining for Rosalind, hangs poems to her on the trees. Touchstone and Corin compare lifestyles. Rosalind finds Orlando's poems and when he appears, she, still disguised as Ganymede, teaches him how to woo her as Rosalind. Rosalind as Ganymede and Celia as Aliena come across Phoebe. Rosalind/Ganymede suggests Phoebe should be thankful for Silvius's love; but instead Phoebe falls for Ganymede.

Rosalind/Ganymede pretending to be Rosalind goes through a mock wedding with Orlando presided over by Aliena as the vicar. Orlando leaves promising to return in the afternoon. He fails to return but Rosalind is distracted by an anguished love letter from Phoebe to Ganymede. Oliver suddenly arrives with a blood-stained cloth. It seems that Orlando found him under a tree about to be attacked by wild beasts and saved his life, only to be injured by a lioness. Oliver is now reconciled with Orlando, and the cloth is a message from Orlando to Rosalind. Rosalind swoons. Touchstone scares off William, his rival for Audrey's affections. Oliver and Aliena decide to marry. Orlando is impatient to be with the real Rosalind and Ganymede promises he will make Rosalind appear by magic so they can be married. He also promises Silvius that he will marry Phoebe.

On the big day, Ganymede and Aliena slip out to return with Hymen as Rosalind and Celia. Four wedding ceremonies are performed by Hyman. News arrives that Duke Frederick has become a hermit, leaving the dukedom to Duke Senior. The actor playing Rosalind bids adieu to the audience. ■

As You Like It is one of Shakespeare's most enduringly popular plays. It forays into the beautiful Forest of Arden for an interlude full of light romance and wit, philosophical speculation, and broad comedy. In the clever, ardent, playful Rosalind, who spends her time in Arden dressed as the boy Ganymede, it has an engaging central character.

Strangely, though, very little happens in *As You Like It*. Two young people, Rosalind and Orlando, run away to the Forest of Arden to escape difficult relatives – Rosalind fleeing her uncle Duke Frederick, who usurped the power of her father (who's already fled to the forest), and Orlando from his brother Oliver, who connives to have him killed, form a rather paper-thin plot. In the forest, Rosalind, dressed as Ganymede, teaches Orlando the ways of love and meets various folk. After a few misunderstandings, Rosalind and Orlando get married, along with three

In 1950, Hollywood star Katharine Hepburn took on the part of Rosalind. She said of the role that it is "one of the great tests of how good an actress you are, and I wanted to find out".

Hugh Thomson's 1915 illustration of Act 1, Scene 3, in which Celia and Rosalind contemplate leaving the court, hints at the move to the idyllic forest in the finery of the peacocks' feathers.

other couples who also found romance in the forest, and all family differences are resolved. And this is all that happens.

Romantic nonsense?

The Irish playwright George Bernard Shaw thought the play so flimsy that he dismissed it as a silly crowd-pleaser. The title "As You Like It", Shaw suggested, was just Shakespeare throwing back at the audience their taste for such romantic nonsense. But although *As You Like It* has had a chequered historical reception, most critics now agree that Shaw missed the point. It is really a clever, sophisticated play. While it is more wholeheartedly entertaining perhaps than any other of Shakespeare's plays, it is still packed full of ideas and insights into life and love. The title, far from being a throwaway, is perhaps both a celebration of the joy of theatre, and an invitation to be open-minded. As the Royal Shakespeare Company put it, "Gender roles, nature, and politics are confused in a play that reflects on how bewildering yet utterly pleasurable life can be." »

There may not be much plot, but there is a feast of romance and comedy – poems and songs, wit and banter, all spilling from characters' lips with continual invention. It is an intellectual and poetic picnic to which the audience is invited to spend a couple of hours for their pleasure and mental stimulation. Nothing much happens because nothing is meant to happen. Just as time is briefly suspended for the characters in Arden – "There's / no clock in the forest," (3.2.294–295) says Orlando – so it is also for the audience watching the play as they go on a holiday in the theatre. It's a chance to mentally recharge and rethink – to "fleet the / time carelessly" (1.1.112–113) – away from the pressures of ordinary life.

Country vs city

As You Like It is structured in three parts. It begins in the court or city, where unsolvable problems arise; it journeys into nature or a fantasy world, where the problems are untangled; and then returns to the court, the real world at the end with the problems resolved. In fact, *As You Like It* ends before the final return to court, but with Duke Frederick's sudden change of heart offstage at the end, it's clear only Jaques will stay in the forest.

It is the nature section, in the Forest of Arden, that dominates most of the play: for this reason, it is often described as a "pastoral comedy". Pastoral literature was very much in vogue at the time – British critic Frank Kermode described

Music is a key part of the pastoral merriment of *As You Like It*, as in this production at the Delacorte Theater, New York (2012). There are more songs in the play than any other of Shakespeare's.

As You Like It as "the most topical of the comedies", because it is most engaged with the intellectual interests of the age. The word "pastoral" refers literally to the shepherd's life. It is not about real shepherds but an idealization – a harmonious "Arcadia". Shepherds don't look after sheep in pastoral literature; instead they are poets, philosophers, and singers. The pastoral world is an imaginary golden age or Garden of Eden, a peaceful and uncorrupted place where harmony can be rediscovered away from the strife and pressures of everyday reality.

Pastoral literature in Shakespeare's time was very highbrow. It was prose and poetry, full of lovelorn shepherds and disdainful girls, and characters with fancy classical names who were quite clearly courtiers on holiday rather than real country folk. Despite its focus on the simple life, it was nothing much to do with real nature. In *As You Like It*, Shakespeare turns the pastoral into popular entertainment for the stage. He continually subverts the form, letting realism bleed into its idealized world and gently satirizing the genre's conventions. In one scene, for instance, Orlando is seen pinning poems to trees in true poet-shepherd style; in the very next scene, the real old shepherd Corin is talking about his hands filthy with sheep grease.

The countryside continually interweaves the ideal and the real, the classical with the native England. Even the name of the forest, Arden, has this ambiguity. In Shakespeare's original source, Thomas Lodge's novel *Rosalynde* (1590), the setting was the Ardennes, a hilly region bordering France and Belgium. In some editions of the play, the Belgian spelling "Ardenne" is kept – and Shakespeare retains French names for characters such as Jaques and Amiens – but in other editions the forest is called Arden. Arden was a real woodland near Shakespeare's childhood home in Warwickshire, and it is also the family name of his grandmother, Mary Arden. Aptly, whether by coincidence or design, the name "Arden" also echoes both Ar-cadia and E-den.

Ambiguous Rosalind

At the very heart of the play's ambiguity is the character of Rosalind. In the forest,

Rosalind dresses as a boy and takes the very classical name, Ganymede – the name of a beautiful Trojan boy in Greek myth. On the Elizabethan stage, she would have been played by a boy actor, and the play has fun with her constantly switching gender identities. At one point, Rosalind, disguised as Ganymede, pretends to be "Rosalind" to teach Orlando how to love. So at this moment on stage, there would have been a boy actor playing a girl who is playing a boy playing a girl! Meanwhile, Orlando is in love not with the pretend Rosalind played by Ganymede but the "real" Rosalind who is at that moment playing Ganymede playing Rosalind. And Phoebe – a girl's role also played by a boy actor – is in love with Ganymede, mistakenly thinking her a boy, when "he" is in fact a girl played by a boy! Much of the entertainment in the play comes from seeing how adeptly it manages these confusions and, at the end, resolves them.

Critics have talked a great deal about gender issues in *As You Like It* and the undercurrents of homoeroticism in, for instance, Phoebe's love for Ganymede/Rosalind, Celia's for Rosalind, and Orlando's flirtation with Ganymede. Indeed, the Ganymede of Greek myth was a beautiful boy who became Zeus's lover and was a byword for erotic

The idyllic countryside setting in Shakespeare's source novel Rosalynde was the Ardennes in Belgium (below). Shakespeare's forest may also be partly inspired by the Arden forest in England.

relationships between men and young boys. In the play's epilogue, "Rosalind" has fun with the ambiguity of her gender. She partly steps out of her role, and as a boy actor toys with the audience, offering a kiss to "as many of you as had beards that pleased". Shakespeare's play is a celebration of all kinds of love and sexual possibilities, as the title implies.

True love
Beneath the role-playing and gender-switching, a portrait of the reality of love appears. When Orlando says he will die for love, Rosalind as Ganymede at once »

A shepherd's life

The origins of pastoral literature date back to writers such as the Greeks Hesiod (c.750–650 BCE) and Theocritus (c.270 BCE) and, most

famously, the Roman poet Virgil (70–19 BCE) in his *Eclogues*. They all wrote of golden ages and rural idylls. The genre was rediscovered in Europe during the Renaissance, and in Elizabethan England, the idea of the pastoral became popular among intellectuals and poets. A key work was Edmund Spenser's much-imitated *The Shephearde's Calender*, first published in 1579. Others include Sir Philip Sidney's long prose work Arcadia and Christopher Marlowe's romantic

poem *The Passionate Shepherd to His Love*, published in 1599.

Pastoral literature often contained subversive messages, and was intended to be held up as a mirror to the contemporary world. At the time As You Like It was written, satire had recently been banned by the Church. The play may contain reference to this ban in Celia's line: "since the little wit / that fools have silenced, the little foolery that /wise men have makes a great show." (1.2.84–86)

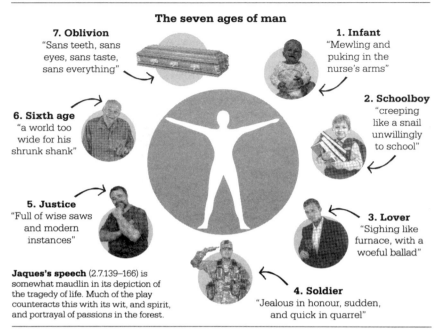

The seven ages of man

7. Oblivion
"Sans teeth, sans eyes, sans taste, sans everything"

1. Infant
"Mewling and puking in the nurse's arms"

2. Schoolboy
"creeping like a snail unwillingly to school"

6. Sixth age
"a world too wide for his shrunk shank"

5. Justice
"Full of wise saws and modern instances"

3. Lover
"Sighing like furnace, with a woeful ballad"

Jaques's speech (2.7.139–166) is somewhat maudlin in its depiction of the tragedy of life. Much of the play counteracts this with its wit, and spirit, and portrayal of passions in the forest.

4. Soldier
"Jealous in honour, sudden, and quick in quarrel"

points out the flaws in this romantic nonsense. "Men have died from time to time for love, and worms have eaten them," she says in her somewhat down-to-earth fashion, "but not for love" (4.1.99–101).

But Rosalind is not a cynic like Jaques, who doesn't believe in love. At this very moment, she is "fathom deep" in love with Orlando (4.1.196) and "cannot be out / of the sight" of him (4.1.205–206). Indeed, she is more in love with him at this moment than he is with her, despite his protestations and poems. At this moment, Orlando is more in love with love than with Rosalind, and she must remain as Ganymede to teach him how to love her for real. She is high-spirited, insightful, witty, and passionate – but she can only stop playing Ganymede when Orlando stops playing at love.

Love is dressed in many guises in the play. Curmudgeonly Touchstone suddenly finds his heart with Audrey. The once-mean brother Oliver falls in love at first sight with Celia. Even Silvius's absurd poems and declarations bear fruit with Phoebe. Yet beneath it all, love is shown to be real and important.

The world's a stage
The best known speech in *As You Like It* is Jaques's speech, which begins: "All the world's a stage, / And all the men and women merely players. / They have their exits and their entrances, / And one man in his time plays many parts" (2.7.139–142).

The speech suggests that we are all merely playing parts, and describes the seven stages of life, from infancy to decrepit old age. This simple metaphor for life is often quoted out of context, and taken as Shakespeare's theme for the whole play and its theatricality. Its message about the pointless artificiality of life seems strangely bleak, though. Indeed, it's not so different from desolate Macbeth's view when he says, "Life's but a walking shadow, a poor player / That struts and frets his hour upon the stage / And then is heard no more. It is a tale / Told by an idiot, full of sound and fury, / Signifying nothing." (*Macbeth* 5.5.23–27).

But of course the speaker is Jaques, whose name, as the jester Touchstone slyly reminds us in dubbing him "Monsieur What-ye-call't" (3.3.66), is pronounced "jakes", Elizabethan slang for toilet. It's a reminder that Jaques might well be talking "crap". In fact, in the character of Jaques, Shakespeare is making fun of a stereotype of Elizabethan times – the melancholy young philosopher with his fashionably jaded outlook on life. In his meandering observations, Jaques is perhaps missing the point just as much as Orlando with his poems on trees. At the very instant Jaques finishes his speech with his bleak summary of old age as "second childishness and mere oblivion", on comes old Adam, carried on Orlando's back, decrepit old age personified. It's a funny moment, and a clear sign we shouldn't take Jaques too seriously. In some ways, neither does Jaques himself, for he relishes the bite of his own sardonic wit too much to be truly gloomy. For all his cynicism, he seems to positively enjoy being miserable. This is his life choice – as valid, perhaps, as any other. When the couples wed, and all is forgiven, the glut of happiness and "dancing measures" are too much for Jaques. Instead, despite entreaties, he chooses to go into exile once more, joining Duke Frederick in a hermit's cave.

It is Rosalind who has the final word, stepping forward to erase the boundary between character and actor, stage and audience, offering an invitation to leave this theatrical diversion, "as you like it": "I am sure, as many as have good beards, or good faces, or sweet breaths will for my kind offer, when I make curtsy, bid me farewell" (Epilogue). ■

James Thomas Watts, a Victorian landscape artist, captured a forest idyll in his painting of Celia, Rosalind, and Touchstone in the forest. Country idylls were popular subjects in Victorian art.

Playing Rosalind

After its initial success at the Globe in 1599, *As You Like* It fell almost entirely out of fashion in the 17th century, and it was not until 1740 that the play was properly performed again by Charles Macklin at Drury Lane in London. In Macklin's production, Hannah Pritchard was unaffectedly lively as Rosalind and the role has been a favourite ever since.

Actors who have played Rosalind include Edith Evans, Katherine Hepburn, Vanessa Redgrave (pictured), Maggie Smith, and Fiona Shaw. Theatre company Cheek by Jowl's 1991 production had an all-male cast, with Adrian Lester as Rosalind.

There have been three major films of the play, each very different. Paul Czinner's whimsical 1936 version, with German Elisabeth Bergner as Rosalind, was an early sound film of the Shakespeare play. Christine Edzard's edgy 1992 version dressed Rosalind in jeans and hoodie in London's "cardboard city" for down and outs. Kenneth Branagh's lush 2007 film was set in 19th-century Japan and starred Romola Garai.

THE SLINGS AND ARROWS OF OUTRAGEOUS FORTUNE
HAMLET (1599–1601)

In Elsinore castle in Denmark, King Claudius grieves for the death of the former king, his brother. He hastily marries Gertrude, the dead king's widow, and sends messengers to Norway, Denmark's feuding neighbour, to prevent an invasion by the Norwegian Prince Fortinbras. Gertrude's son, Hamlet, is also grieving for the king, his father. Horatio, a companion, informs Hamlet that the ghost of his father has appeared on the battlements at night, and takes him to see for himself. The ghost tells Hamlet that Hamlet's father was murdered by his uncle. Hamlet swears to avenge his father. However, unsure if he can believe the ghost, Hamlet feigns madness to distract his peers while he discovers the truth.

The courtier Polonius interprets Hamlet's strange behaviour as a symptom of love for Ophelia. After informing the King of this, they use Ophelia to spy on Hamlet. Hamlet guesses what she is doing and cruelly denies any affection for her.

To help assuage Hamlet's grief the King and Queen send for Rosencrantz and Guildenstern, his old college friends, whom he now distrusts. Instead, he focuses on the arrival at court of travelling players, and orders them to perform a play in which a king is murdered by his brother. Hamlet sees that King Claudius is affected by the play, and takes this as proof of guilt.

On his way to Gertrude's chamber, Hamlet overhears the King in prayer, confessing to the murder. Meanwhile, Polonius hides behind an arras (a tapestry) in Gertrude's chamber to spy on Hamlet. Hamlet berates his mother for remarrying. Polonius calls for help and Hamlet, believing the voice to be the King's, stabs at the tapestry and kills Polonius.

The King punishes Hamlet by sending him to England with Rosencrantz and Guildenstern with the intention of having him killed on arrival. On the journey, they are attacked by pirates. Hamlet escapes and returns to Denmark.

Laertes arrives in Elsinore and demands vengeance for the murder of Polonius. Grief-stricken by the murder, Ophelia loses her mind and drowns in a brook, spurring on Laertes's hatred for Hamlet. Horatio and Hamlet witness Ophelia's burial. Hamlet reveals himself to the mourners and challenges Laertes to a duel. Laertes injures Hamlet with a poisoned blade, after which he is himself mortally wounded with the same blade. Gertrude drinks poisoned wine intended for Hamlet and dies, causing Laertes to accuse Claudius of murder. Hamlet stabs the King and forces the remaining poisoned wine down his throat before himself dying in the arms of Horatio. Fortinbras and his troops arrive to bear away the bodies. ∎

IN CONTEXT

THEMES
Revenge, betrayal, honour, mortality

SETTING
Elsinore in Denmark

SOURCES
c.1185 "Amleth", by Danish historian Saxo Grammaticus is the story of a legendary Danish prince whose uncle killed the king and married the queen.

1580 French poet François de Belleforest retells the story in his *Histories Tragiques*, translated into English in 1608.

Hamlet is Shakespeare's longest play, with perhaps the most challenging lead role. It is also his most enduringly popular tragedy. The play is a story of kingship, war, madness, and revenge. It is also a story that centres on a troubled man whose responsibilities to his father and to his kingdom are diametrically opposed to his instincts and temperament. Unlike its source text about the legendary Danish king Amleth, which is described as a romance, Hamlet is undeniably a tragedy – *The Tragedy of Hamlet, the Prince of Denmark*, as it is listed in the First Folio. Shakespeare retains the details about Amleth's feigned madness and need for revenge, but adds new information, such as naming the ghost – also called Hamlet – and adding a companion for the hero in the form of Horatio. Shakespeare also adds two other sons seeking revenge for their fathers' deaths: Laertes and Fortinbras. *Hamlet* has been read as the story of an ill-fated hero, a victim of fate and "outrageous fortune", as well as one about a mentally unstable, indecisive young man. In both readings, the character and the world he inhabits are overwhelmed by melancholy and corruption.

Prince of Denmark

Hamlet is a man of 30; he is a son, a nephew, a lover, a courtier, and a university student of Wittenberg. As the only male heir to the former king, Hamlet should have ascended immediately to the throne. That his uncle, Claudius, takes the crown is largely because of Gertrude's "o'er-hasty" (2.2.57) marriage, as the character herself describes it. The result is that, when the audience first meets Hamlet, he has been robbed of his father, all trust in his mother, and the throne to which he is entitled. It is not surprising, therefore, that he should be quiet, resentful, and moody in his first appearance.

Claudius calls his subjects together to discuss Fortinbras, Laertes, and Hamlet, respectively. His priorities, in order of significance, are relations political, social, and domestic. Although this may seem justifiable, prioritizing Laertes and his wish to travel abroad above Hamlet's obvious grief seems irresponsible and callous in Hamlet's eyes. This explains the bitterness of his opening words in the play, which are a response to Claudius calling him "son": "A little more than kin and less than kind" (1.2.65).

Despite his dark mood and sombre appearance, Hamlet commands love and respect from his peers. He is the first »

A 2000 film adaptation starring Ethan Hawke sets *Hamlet* in New York City. The ghost is an apparition on CCTV, and the play-within-the-play takes the form of a video game.

Elsinore castle, the setting for the play, is in fact Kronborg, an ancient fortress on the Danish island of Zealand. It was rebuilt in the 1580s and appears here as it did in Shakespeare's day.

The play's the thing

The ghost has informed Hamlet that his father was murdered with a poison administered into his ear while asleep in his orchard. This very same scenario is played out in The Mousetrap, the play Hamlet chooses to stage before the King and Queen. The Player King's brother emerges from the shadows of an orchard to pour poison into the Player King's ear. Hamlet has chosen drama as the medium through which to test the truth of the ghost's story. First, he explains to the players that the function of plays and acting is, "to hold, as 'twere, the mirror up to nature, to show virtue her own feature, scorn her own image, and the very age and body of the time his form and pressure" (3.2.21–24). Drama is, in Hamlet's view, a way of revealing truths about real life. It is with this logic that he claims that a play will "catch the conscience of the King" (2.2.607). The power of drama to move individuals to tears, guilt, and happiness is powerfully explored both here and in the scene in which the chief player delivers a speech to Hamlet about the fall of Troy. This monologue focuses on the intensity of the grief of Hecuba, whose husband, Priam, has been slaughtered by the Greek enemy. Hamlet is clearly moved by the extent of Hecuba's sorrow and by the actor's ability to engage emotionally with the speech. He considers both himself and his mother inadequate in comparison, because Gertrude fails to mourn for her husband's death, and Hamlet struggles to motivate himself to seek revenge.

Mother complex

It is no accident, then, that Hamlet's Mousetrap is not entirely motivated by the

person Horatio thinks to tell about the appearance of the ghost, and it is Hamlet, not the king, whom the players first greet at court. In the play's closing scene, Horatio states that Hamlet has "a noble heart" (5.2.311), echoing Ophelia's early claim that he has "a noble mind" (3.1.153). In fact, Ophelia speaks of Hamlet as though he is a symbol of hope, calling him "Th'expectancy and rose of the fair state, / The glass of fashion and the mould of form, / Th'observed of all observers" (3.1.155–157).

Unstable Hamlet

Hamlet is also described in less positive terms. He is full of "turbulent and dangerous lunacy" (3.1.4), "melancholy" and "unmanly grief", with "A heart unfortified, a mind impatient" (1.2.96). He is, in other words, unstable and rash.

Although Hamlet elicits respect for his nobility and receives censure for his attitude, he has a distinctive need to offer other people advice. He tells Ophelia to choose a nunnery over marriage; he advises the players on their acting techniques, and he reprimands Laertes for weeping at Ophelia's funeral. What makes Hamlet think he has more right to mourn than Laertes, her brother? From what experience, and with what authority does he lecture the actors on stagecraft? And from what motive does he send Ophelia off to a convent?

discovery of Claudius's guilt. He is also using the play to test his mother's conscience. Indeed, much of Hamlet's melancholy stems from anger with his mother, whose marriage to Claudius he thinks incestuous. The Player Queen makes a speech about fidelity, in which she swears never to remarry in the event of her husband's death: "The instances that second marriage move / Are base respects of thrift, but none of love. / A second time I kill my husband dead / When second husband kisses me in bed" (3.2.173–176).

With this play-within-the-play, Hamlet seizes control of events by taking up arms against his troubles in a way that is otherwise rare in the course of the action of the play proper, during which he is often paralysed by indecision, a character flaw that proves fatal.

Outrageous fortune?

Hamlet is not a man in a good position. He has left university at the age of 30 and returned to live at home; his father has died and he cannot reconcile with his mother after her remarriage; and he is forced to take on the responsibility of avenging his father's murder in secret. Although Hamlet's famous question is "to be or not to be" (3.1.58), it is the question he asks immediately after that haunts him more than anything: "Whether 'tis nobler in the mind to suffer / The slings and arrows of outrageous fortune, / Or to take arms against a sea of troubles, / And, by opposing, end them" (3.1.59–62). »

Hamlet (right, Ladi Emeruwa) fights with Claudius (left, John Dougall) in a production by the Globe Theatre that was set to play in 205 countries during a world tour between 2014 and 2016.

Prayer scene

During the 19th century, scholars and actors went to great lengths to excuse Hamlet of wickedness in his pursuit of vengeance. The prayer scene, in which Claudius confesses his guilt and Hamlet stalls his vengeance, was removed from the play until the 1880s. At this moment, Hamlet begins to speak in violent and disturbing terms of damnation, a topic of great debate both in the 16th and 19th centuries. Wishing to damn someone to eternal hellfire is not a Christian sentiment, and whether or not such an attitude might be thought justifiable in Hamlet's search for vengeance, Victorian audiences did not wish to hear these words spoken on the stage.

Notable modern performances of the scene include David Tennant's Hamlet (2009, above). This hit stage production was filmed for a special TV version by the BBC. Hovering his dagger above the head of Patrick Stewart's Claudius, in the film version, he delivers the speech as a voiceover rather than directly to the audience.

Hamlet chooses to suffer the outrageous fortune that he believes is an external attack rather than an internal conflict. Assuming the position of a self-confessed victim of fate, much like Romeo, Hamlet shakes off responsibility for his actions, namely delaying revenge, murdering Polonius, rejecting Ophelia, and having Rosencrantz and Guildenstern executed. In the play's final act, Hamlet speaks of providence and the inevitability of his defeating the King. If, however, the so-called outrageous fortune is removed from the equation, what is left is a series of bad decisions that have ill consequences.

The tragedy spirals out of control because the characters within the world of Denmark make poor choices that lead to a catalogue of even worse outcomes. Not only does Hamlet defer taking revenge on Claudius, but he accidentally stabs Polonius, which leads Laertes to seek vengeance against him. He rejects Ophelia in such a humiliating and devastating way that, when she learns of her father's murder at the hands of her former lover, she loses her sanity and, potentially, her dignity. Polonius, too, is no blameless character. He exhibits poor judgement when he dispatches a spy to France to trail his son, when he convinces Ophelia to trap Hamlet, and especially when he proposes hiding behind the arras in order to eavesdrop on Gertrude's conversation with her son. Add to these tragic events Ophelia's accidental drowning, Claudius's poisoning of the wine goblet, Gertrude accidentally drinking it, and Laertes being wounded by his own poisoned blade, and this tragic world is riddled with fateful accidents. Both the characters' choices and their fortunes do indeed seem outrageous.

Revenge

First and foremost, Hamlet is a tale of revenge. The revenge motif repeats throughout the play, not just in having three avengers all seeking the same thing, but in the terrible cycle of destruction and grief that proceeds from any desire to exact vengeance on an enemy.

As a revenge story, *Hamlet* follows conventions established by the English playwright Thomas Kyd in *The Spanish Tragedy* (1587), which was one of the most popular revenge tragedies of the period. Shakespeare includes a ghost, a play-within-a-play, and a deathly object in the form of Yorick's skull, to echo the revenge tradition. The hero is forced to compromise his own conscience in order to carry out an attack on the original criminal, in this case Claudius.

Poor Yorick

One subject that is inseparable from the play concerns the nature of existence. Perhaps the most iconic image in Shakespearian tragedy is that of Hamlet admiring Yorick's skull. This is the moment when Hamlet recognizes the reality of death. He contemplates the difference between the living head of his father's jester, with its lips, tongue and wit, and the grotesque remnants of his body.

Yorick's skull is given to Hamlet by a gravedigger, who is able to see humour in the tragedy. He speaks in a pragmatic way about whether Ophelia (an alleged suicide case) merits a Christian burial, and casually digs up bones from graves to clear space. In a play in which all is contemplated by Hamlet, the gravedigger is a welcome voice that trivializes the otherwise overwhelming subject of death.

In 1930, G Wilson Knight argued that Hamlet's fixation with death poisons everyone around him, and that it is he who triggers the entire tragedy. Though Hamlet claims to be a victim of fortune, it can be argued that he is ultimately responsible for his own fate.

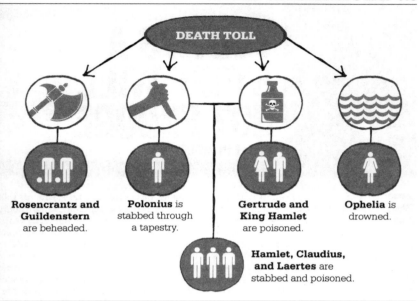

DEATH TOLL

Rosencrantz and Guildenstern are beheaded.

Polonius is stabbed through a tapestry.

Gertrude and King Hamlet are poisoned.

Ophelia is drowned.

Hamlet, Claudius, and Laertes are stabbed and poisoned.

As well as their brutality, revenge ragedies were known for their meta-theatrical jokes, which Shakespeare incorporates into his play when the ghost calls out to Horatio and Marcellus. Hamlet refers to the ghost as "old mole" and "this fellow in the cellarage" (1.5.153), which draws a knowing audience's attention to the actor calling from beneath the stage floor, rather than any disembodied, spectral voice. However, Hamlet is no simple revenge hero: he is torn between hatred for his uncle, love

This haunting depiction of Ophelia's death was painted by British artist John Everett Millais in 1852. The floating flowers correspond to the play's description of her garland.

for his father, disgust for his mother, and distrust of the ghost. He deliberately delays his attack on Claudius, choosing instead to ruminate on his actions and on his existence. Hamlet's approach places him in direct contrast with Laertes and Fortinbras, who also seek revenge against their fathers' murderers. When news of Polonius's death reaches Laertes, he flies in the face of all custom and duty in order to challenge the king, risking his own reputation by committing treason. Unlike Hamlet, Laertes does not delay and even swears to "dare damnation" (4.5.131) in order to have revenge on Polonius's murderer. Although his behaviour is rash and is exploited by the king, who also wishes Hamlet dead, Laertes's motivation and intent are not dissimilar to those of Hamlet. The third avenger is Fortinbras, whose own father was murdered by Hamlet's father, the former king. Whereas Hamlet delays and Laertes rushes in, Fortinbras tactfully assembles his army and plans to invade Denmark, making his vengeance political rather than personal. Laertes and Fortinbras lack Hamlet's tragic flaw – the doubt and indecision that lead Hamlet inexorably to his fate. ■

YOUTH'S A STUFF WILL NOT ENDURE

TWELFTH NIGHT (1601)

Spurned by the beautiful Olivia, Orsino of Illyria begs for sad music to reflect his lovelorn state. Viola is shipwrecked on the shores of Illyria. Convinced her twin brother Sebastian has drowned and that she is alone, she decides to dress as a boy and join Orsino's service. Meanwhile, Olivia's reprobate cousin Sir Toby and her maidservant Maria persuade rich but dim Sir Andrew to pay court to Olivia. Orsino sends Viola (as Cesario) to Olivia as a messenger of his love. But Viola is already in love with Orsino herself.

Feste the clown tries to cajole Olivia out of her mourning, but is rebuked by her puritanical steward Malvolio. They are interrupted by the arrival of Cesario. But Cesario's ingenious pleading of Orsino's case, falls on deaf ears as Olivia is smitten by Cesario. When Cesario goes, Olivia sends Malvolio after to tell him he has left a ring behind.

Viola's twin Sebastian arrives in Illyria, saved by his companion Antonio. Thinking Viola dead, Sebastian resolves to try Orsino's court. When Malvolio gives Viola Olivia's ring, she realizes Olivia has fallen for Cesario. Sir Toby and his friends are partying when the killjoy Malvolio complains about the noise. As he leaves, they plot their revenge on him, forging love letters from Olivia to Malvolio, which he discovers and believes are genuine.

At Orsino's request, Viola dressed as Cesario returns to Olivia, who tells Cesario she loves him. Sir Toby works on Sir Andrew to challenge Cesario to a duel. Antonio tells Sebastian he has enemies at Orsino's court so they decide to part. Convinced by Maria that Olivia wants him to dress colourfully Malvolio changes his normally drab clothes for yellow stockings. Sir Andrew delivers a challenge to Cesario. Just as the two draw swords, Antonio intervenes to rescue Cesario, thinking him to be Sebastian but Cesario denies knowing him.

Thinking him to be Cesario, Sir Toby attacks Sebastian, but he is rescued by Olivia, who also thinks him to be Cesario. Olivia proposes marriage to Sebastian, thinking him Cesario, and Sebastian, already in love with Olivia accepts. Hauled before Orsino as a pirate Antonio is deeply hurt that Cesario, who he thinks is Sebastian, denies their friendship. Olivia arrives and claims Cesario as hers. To Olivia's shock, Cesario aligns herself with Orsino, so Olivia summons the priest to verify they are married. Suddenly, Sebastian arrives and greets Antonio with passionate relief, as everyone else stands amazed by his likeness to Cesario.

All is revealed. Orsino acknowledges his love for Cesario and proposes marriage. The trick on Malvolio is revealed, and Malvolio pledges his revenge. ■

IN CONTEXT

THEMES
Mistaken identity, gender swapping, love

SETTING
Illyria, the name for a province on the Adriatic (present-day Croatia and Slovenia) in Roman times

SOURCES
1531 A risqué Italian play called *Gl'ingannati* (The Deceived Ones).

1581 English author Barnabe Rich's *Farewell to the Military Profession*.

Twelfth Night, or What You Will is a comedy in which genders are swapped and identities mistaken. It has an appealing heroine, Viola, the shipwrecked girl who finds true love dressed as a boy, but there is also a dark side in the tormenting of the puritanical steward Malvolio.

An unruly night
The first half of the play's full title refers to the eve of the 12th Day of Christmas, 5 January. This is the Feast of the Epiphany, when, according to tradition, the Magi, the three wise men, arrived with their gifts for the infant Christ. In Elizabethan England, Twelfth Night was the last day of the Christmas holidays, and its associations were as much pagan as Christian. It was one last riot of feasting, drinking, games, and theater masques, before returning to work. It was a time of "misrule" when normal rules were briefly subverted: masters became servants and servants became masters; and, in the tradition of the Roman winter feast of Saturnalia, men dressed as girls and vice versa. Often, a large cake was made. Whoever got the slice with a bean or coin in it became the Lord of Misrule for the night.

It is thought that Shakespeare's play was written to be performed as Twelfth Night entertainment. The first recorded performance took place in private at Middle Temple Hall, one of the law school Inns of Court, on February 2, 1602. But the play is full of allusions to Twelfth Night. In this topsy-turvy world, servants get above themselves, girls dress as boys, and identities are mixed up. Viola, presumably in a nod to the Roman Saturnalia, calls herself Cesario when she dresses as a boy. And throughout the play, Feste the clown, whose very name suggests a feast, refers often to wise men and fools. Indeed, he is in some ways the only sane one in the play.

A sad place
There is something of the fairy tale in *Twelfth Night*. The play begins with a girl shipwrecked and alone in a strange country, Illyria, after a terrible storm. (We only find much later that her name is Viola.) It is a country sunk, absurdly, in gloom. The Duke of Illyria wallows in the melancholy of his love for the beautiful Olivia, a fashionable affliction in Elizabethan England. He morbidly pleads for such an excess of music that it will spoil his taste for it: "If music be the food of love, play on, / Give me excess of it that, surfeiting, / The appetite may sicken and so die. / That strain again! it had a dying fall" (1.1.1–4).

Meanwhile, the Countess Olivia, the object of his affections, is even more gloomy. She is deep in mourning for her brother, and has pledged to remain veiled for seven years. She has given her household to the charge of her cheerless steward Malvolio, who sees it as his task to ensure that nobody has any fun. Both Orsino and Olivia have locked themselves away in their dark places of melancholy – just as, ironically, Malvolio will be locked in a dark cell when the prank played on him goes all too well.

This melancholy is in some ways a madness that has engulfed Illyria. Olivia and Orsino are both foolish in the theatrical excess of their sadness, as Feste shows:
"Feste: Good madonna, why mournest thou?
Olivia: Good fool, for my brother's death.
Feste: I think his soul is in hell, madonna.
Olivia: I know his soul is in heaven, fool.
Feste: The more fool, madonna, to mourn for your brother's soul being in heaven" (1.5.62–67). »

Lovers and suitors

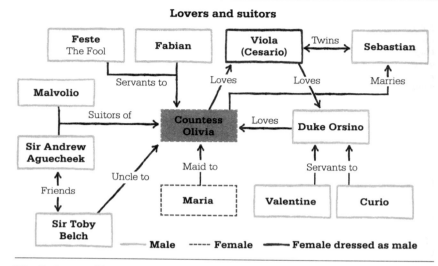

The diagram shows:
- **Feste** The Fool and **Fabian** — Servants to Countess Olivia
- **Viola (Cesario)** — Twins with **Sebastian**; Loves Duke Orsino
- **Sebastian** — Marries Countess Olivia
- **Malvolio** and **Sir Andrew Aguecheek** — Suitors of Countess Olivia
- **Sir Toby Belch** — Friends with Sir Andrew Aguecheek; Uncle to Countess Olivia
- **Countess Olivia** — Loves Viola (Cesario)
- **Duke Orsino** — Loves Countess Olivia
- **Maria** — Maid to Countess Olivia
- **Valentine** and **Curio** — Servants to Duke Orsino

——— Male   - - - - - Female   ▬▬▬ Female dressed as male

The bringer of joy

Viola's role is to break this spell of melancholy and bring joy and true love back into this world, just like the revel spirit of Twelfth Night. At the time, many puritans frowned upon the festivities of Christmas (they succeeded in banning it in 1647) and railed against the riotous excess of the theater, so there may have been a political message here.

Viola, of course, has her own bereavement to contend with. When she comes ashore in Illyria, she is convinced that her brother has drowned and that she is entirely alone in the world. Her reaction is not to go into mourning like Olivia, but to take action.

Viola's choice to dress up to look like her brother is a strange one, but it leads to comic and romantic possibilities. It allows Viola close to her beloved Orsino, yet prevents her from revealing her love. It also opens the way for the chaos caused by mistaken identities as her brother Sebastian turns up.

In a comic subplot, which ultimately turns a little dark, Shakespeare adds two foolish suitors: the roguish Sir Toby Belch and the rather silly Sir Andrew Aguecheek, who, along with the feisty Maria, plot to humiliate Malvolio.

A woman's part

From the start, Orsino is strangely drawn to his young serving boy. He puts it down to Cesario's youth: "they shall yet belie thy happy years / That say thou art a man. Diana's lip / Is not more smooth and rubious; thy small pipe / Is as the maiden's organ, shrill and sound, / And all is semblative a woman's part" (1.4.30–34). To Orsino, locked in his self-love, Cesario simply looks and sounds like a woman – but the lingering over physical details and the innuendo suggest there is a more ambiguous attraction. And of course the gender boundaries are blurred even more as Viola was originally played by a boy actor. Viola's situation becomes even more tricky when she visits Olivia as Cesario. Olivia soon lowers her veil for the young "boy." After just one meeting, she is so eager for him to return that she sends Malvolio after him with a ring that she pretends Cesario has dropped. On the face of it, she thinks Cesario's effeminate looks must be because he is a gentleman. But like Orsino, she lingers just a little too long on Cesario's attractions: "Thy tongue, thy face, thy limbs, actions, and spirit / Do give thee five-fold blazon" (1.5.282–284). Her desperation comes across as comic after her mourning reticence, but it seems more like lust than love.

Untying the knot

Meanwhile, Viola has fallen in love with Orsino, and the situation has become impossible. She describes herself as a "monster," neither man nor woman: "As I am man, / My state is desperate for my master's love. / As I am woman, now, alas the day, / What thriftless sighs shall poor Olivia breathe" (2.2.36–39).

Viola laments that it has become "too hard a knot for me t'untie" (2.2.41). But we have just seen exactly how the knot will be loosened, for Viola's twin Sebastian has turned up, not drowned after all. While Viola's genuine distress becomes ever more poignant, the play becomes a comedy for us, because we know how it will all work out. We laugh as Sebastian is mistaken for Cesario and Cesario for Sebastian, causing comic confusion.

All seems about to turn dark, however, when Olivia, soon after marrying Sebastian believing him to be Cesario, comes to Orsino – only to find that Cesario, in what seems a terrible betrayal, denies all knowledge of the wedding and pledges allegiance to the baffled Orsino. Within moments, all is revealed as Sebastian and Cesario appear together, and everyone stands in wonder as their remarkable likeness appears: "One face, one voice, one habit, and two persons, / A natural perspective, that is and is not" (5.1.213–214).

The solution is simple. Olivia stays married to Sebastian, and Viola can reveal herself as a woman and marry her love Orsino. It is neat, but the ambiguities of gender haven't quite vanished. As Sebastian says to Olivia, "You are betrothed to a maid and a man" (5.1.261), while as Orsino and Viola leave the stage together at the end of the play to be married, Viola is still dressed as a boy, described by Orsino as his "master's mistress."

Gender bending

It is perhaps not surprising that many critics have explored *Twelfth Night* for homoeroticism. Indeed, because Sebastian and Antonio express their love for each other so ardently, many modern theater productions have played theirs as a homosexual relationship, and looked for similar undertones in Olivia's relationship with Cesario.

Yet notions of sexuality were different in Shakespeare's time. Close relationships between two men could be considered the ideal of friendship. Shakespeare may be exploring our double nature: the elements of "man" and "woman" in all of us. As Orsino says: "Cesario, come – / For so you shall be while you are a man; / But when in other habits you are seen, / Orsino's mistress, and his fancy's queen" (5.1.381–384). The play's subtitle, "What You Will," may be a message for us all to embrace love wherever we may find it. ∎

Malvolio

Malvolio is a dark shadow version of the story of *Twelfth* Night, his name a twisted part anagram of both Olivia and Viola's names, meaning in Italian "evil" (mal) and "I desire" (volio). Malvolio's inner world turns ever bleaker as the outer world wakes up to pleasure, and this puritan who believes everyone else is foolish is shown to be the real fool.

Sir Toby, Maria, and their friends conspire to trick Malvolio into believing that Olivia is in love with him – and he, pompous and self-deluding, all too easily falls prey to their games. They fool this sombre puritan into dressing up in garish jesterlike clothes (including yellow cross garters) and smiling inanely at Olivia, who employed him because of his seriousness. He foolishly thinks the letter's words, "Some are born great, some achieve greatness, and some have greatness thrust upon 'em" (2.5.140–141) must be for him. Yet the joke can begin to seem cruel – and in his final humiliation, when the trick is exposed, we almost sympathize with his parting words, "I'll be revenged on the whole pack of you" (5.1.374).

WAR AND LECHERY CONFOUND ALL

TROILUS AND CRESSIDA (1602)

A prologue announces that the story begins seven years into the Trojan War. Troilus, son of King Priam of Troy, the younger brother of Hector and Paris, is in love with Cressida, the daughter of a traitor. He employs her uncle, Pandarus, to woo her for him. Cressida appears dismissive of Troilus, but secretly admits to being attracted to him.

Outside the Trojan walls, the Greek camp is disorderly. Achilles refuses to fight, and Menelaus, their leader, lacks credibility as a warrior. Meanwhile, in Troy, courtiers debate the purpose and expense of the long war with the Greek army. Hector concedes that Helen, whose abduction started the war, must not be returned to the Greeks.

Hector sends a message to the Greek army challenging any warrior to a duel. Ulysses uses the challenge to humiliate Achilles by announcing that the dull-witted Ajax should fight Hector. Ajax is related to the Trojan princes by his mother, who is the sister of Priam.

Back in Troy, Troilus successfully woos Cressida in Pandarus's home, where they spend an evening together. During the night, Calchas makes a deal with the Greek leader Agamemnon to exchange a Trojan prisoner of war, Antenor, for his daughter, allowing Cressida to join her father at the Greek camp. A messenger, Diomedes, brings news of the exchange to Troilus who is forced to hand over Cressida.

When she is returned, Cressida is greeted, not unwillingly, with kisses by the Greek army. This prompts Ulysses to conclude that she is a flirtatious, dangerous woman.

On the day of the duel, Ajax and Hector fight, reaching an amicable draw. Achilles takes a dislike to Hector and swears to kill him. At night, after the fight, Troilus follows Ulysses to Cressida's tent, where she is also overheard by Thersites. Before Troilus can reveal himself, he spots Cressida and Diomedes becoming intimate. Cressida offers Diomedes a sleeve, which was a token of love given to her by Troilus. Heartbroken and disillusioned, Troilus swears vengeance on Diomedes and denounces Cressida as false and unfaithful.

The next morning, in spite of the warnings of his wife and sister, Hector fights Achilles. He wins the battle, and the defeat wounds Achilles's pride, prompting him to murder Hector with the Myrmidons, his gang of Greek soldiers. Troy is forced to watch as Achilles drags Hector's body around the battlefield, and Troilus resigns himself to seek revenge for his brother's murder. The play ends as Pandarus is rejected by Troilus, and is left a cynical old man who promises to bequeath nothing but diseases to future generations. ∎

IN CONTEXT

THEMES
Lust, war, betrayal, honour, heroism

SETTING
Troy, 12th century BCE

SOURCES
1598 *The Iliad*, Homer's epic poem of the Trojan Wars, translated into English by George Chapman.

1385–86 *Troilus and Criseyde* by English poet Geoffrey Chaucer.

1460–1500 *The Testament of Cresseid* by Scottish poet Robert Henryson, an imagined sequel to Chaucer's tale.

In a 2009 production at the Globe, London, Laura Pyper played Cressida as a teenager in the process of discovering herself and working out how to survive in a world of men and war.

T roilus and Cressida is a play about war and lust. Thought of as a problem play with an intellectual one, it is challenging to read and to perform. In the 17th century, English poet John Dryden claimed that the play was a "heap of rubbish", while modern responses tend to focus on the bitterness of the characters. Critic A D Nuttall called it a "sick, clever play".

The play is based on an epic tale of legendary men including Achilles, Hector, Ajax, Ulysses, Paris, and Menelaus. Shakespeare, however, challenges the reputations of these figures by deconstructing the idea of a "hero". Paris is a vain and selfish youth, Achilles a love-sick rebel, Ajax a witless brute, and Menelaus a cuckold and a laughing stock. Troilus, a great warrior, is a melancholy lover, motivated entirely by his infatuation with Cressida. The only symbol of heroism is Hector, who longs to face a worthy hero. However, Hector is murdered by Achilles's men while unarmed. With these amorous, pathetic, and dishonourable soldiers, Shakespeare satirizes heroism in war.

To add to this dearth of honour, the original cause of the crisis is a woman who barely seems worth the effort. The characters spend three acts debating

Helen's virtue and the purpose of keeping her in Troy at the expense of soldiers' lives. When Helen appears finally in Act 3, she speaks little and makes exclamations about love-sickness: "Let thy song be love. 'This love will undo us all.' / O Cupid, Cupid, Cupid!" (3.1.106–107).

These are not the words of a woman for whom thousands of Trojans and Greeks have sacrificed their lives. Helen and Paris represent the lecherous, selfish nature of love in this corrupt Troy. Helen's infidelity to her husband and decadent behaviour with Paris also mirror Cressida's disloyalty to Troilus. As Thersites reminds the audience, the world is filled with nothing but "Lechery, lechery, still / wars and lechery!" (5.2.196–197).

The nature of value

During a debate about Helen, the Trojans – Paris, Hector, and Troilus – discuss her in terms of worth:
"**Hector**: Brother, she is not worth what she doth cost / The holding.
Troilus: What's aught but as 'tis valued?
Hector: But value dwells not in particular will. / It holds his estimate and dignity / As well wherein 'tis precious of itself / As in the prizer" (2.2.50–55).

Troilus argues that something becomes valuable when its cost is high. Cressida understands that Troilus thinks this way, so she refuses his advances in order to seem more valuable in his eyes. However, Hector claims that something has to have an intrinsic value in order to be prized. It is only Paris's obsession with Helen that makes her worthy of Troy's allegiance, »

Trojans v Greeks

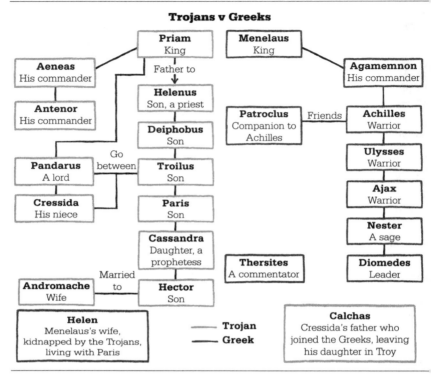

Priam
King

Father to

Helenus
Son, a priest

Deiphobus
Son

Troilus
Son

Paris
Son

Cassandra
Daughter, a prophetess

Hector
Son

Aeneas
His commander

Antenor
His commander

Pandarus
A lord

Cressida
His niece

Go between

Andromache
Wife

Married to

Helen
Menelaus's wife, kidnapped by the Trojans, living with Paris

Menelaus
King

Agamemnon
His commander

Patroclus
Companion to Achilles

Friends

Achilles
Warrior

Ulysses
Warrior

Ajax
Warrior

Nester
A sage

Thersites
A commentator

Diomedes
Leader

—— **Trojan**
—— **Greek**

Calchas
Cressida's father who joined the Greeks, leaving his daughter in Troy

rather than any inherent worth in herself. This sobering fact makes the trauma of warfare in this play seem entirely pointless. This is doubly true for the Greek army, which has no respect for its leader, Menelaus, and his motivation for seeking vengeance on Troy.

Despite Hector's belief that Helen is a disproportionately expensive commodity, it is in the interest of Troy to protect her honour, and that of the men whose lives were lost in her name. The economics may be askew in this city, but in Hector's ideal world, value and worth must be earned. It is this that makes his death at the hands of Achilles, whose heroic worth is entirely unmerited, especially tragic. Both Troilus and Hector, who hold idealistic views about love and war, respectively, are disillusioned by the play's end. Neither Helen nor Cressida turns out to be "worth" anything beyond the tears and

pain they cause to others, and Hector's own value is desecrated by Achilles.

In the politically and morally ugly world that Shakespeare shows, the realist is the vulgar, illegitimate, and deformed commentator, Thersites, who understands the real value and cost of war. He cuts through the high rhetoric of honour, and degree used by the Greek generals with one fundamental truth: "All the argument is a whore and a cuckold. / A good quarrel to draw emulous factions and bleed to death upon" (2.3.71–73). Again, "value" and "worth" are skewed and corrupted by lust and a hunger for war and glory.

The lovers and their go-between, Pandarus, predict their own reputations in posterity, in the same way that the war itself has become a legendary quarrel about Helen of Troy. Familiarity with the story makes the scene in which the lovers pledge eternal faithfulness a moment of ironic foresight.

Troilus swears to be so constant to his love that the analogy "as True as Troilus" shall be coined. In turn, Cressida vows that, should she break her promise, she will inspire future generations to cry "as false as Cressid". Pandarus seals the vow by exclaiming: "[...] let all pitiful /goers-between be called to the world's end after my / name: call them all panders. Let all constant men be / Troiluses, all false women Cressids, and all brokers- / between panders. Say 'Amen'" (3.2.196–200).

Although these outcomes are inevitable, Shakespeare offers the characters the chance to change their fates. Pandarus deliberately involves himself in the affairs of his niece and Troilus, even when they wish him gone. At no point is he forced or cajoled into becoming their go-between. Troilus chooses to hand over Cressida to Diomedes: something he does not have to do. As a warrior and prince, he ought to be more concerned about his kingdom than his lover, like Hector who actively chooses battle over the pleas of his wife, Andromache. Cressida seemingly embraces her move to the Greek camp, allowing the generals and soldiers to kiss her in a way that prompts Ulysses to doubt her virtue. Although Cressida struggles with guilt about betraying Troilus, she fails to reject Diomedes; she encourages him. These decisions are made freely, and imply that the characters, rather than fate or destiny, are responsible for their own tragedies.

Which genre?

When it first appeared in print in 1609, the play was announced as *The Historie of Troylus and Cresseida*. An introduction by the publisher claimed that the play was a comedy. To further complicate matters, the First Folio lists the play under the tragedies.

However, the only character to die during the play's action is the heroic Hector. The play is cynical in tone but, with its subversive depiction of legendary warriors and of the character of Helen, it seems to have a mischievous, darkly comic heart.

While there is humour in the situations these characters find themselves in, the play is riddled with despair and disappointment. Ulysses discusses the importance of order in the army and attempts to teach Achilles about honour and reputation, but all in vain. Achilles would prefer to cheat his way to glory by murdering Hector like a coward, rather than fight battles. Shakespeare forces the audience to experience Troilus's pain as he witnesses Cressida offer her new lover the very token that he gave to her in exchange for her fidelity. At that moment Troilus loses faith in love and loyalty. There is nothing comical about this sentiment.

In the late 19th century, the British scholar Frederick Boas re-categorized the text as a "problem play", meaning that it is comic in structure but tragic in tone and subject matter. Irish playwright George Bernard Shaw sparked scholarly interest in the play in 1884 when he argued that the subject matter "starts at the twentieth century". In other words, it is a modern play expressing the concerns of a new age. It is self-consciously cynical, and it refuses to provide the audience with characters and events that satisfy our sense of justice. As such, it is seen as one of Shakespeare's most bitter and disillusioned plays. ∎

For their 2012 production, the Ngakao Toa theater company moved the action to the tribal Maori wars of pre-European New Zealand. The play starts with a *haka*, or war dance.

124

'I SCORN TO CHANGE MY STATE WITH KINGS'
SHAKESPEARE'S SONNETS (1593–1603)

IN CONTEXT

THEMES
Romantic love, platonic love, jealousy, religion, sex

SOURCES
14th century Italian poet Francesco Petrarch writes some of the first sonnets, expressing unrequited love for an unavailable muse.

The word sonnet comes from the Italian *sonetto*, meaning a little sound. In Shakespeare's time, it could be used to refer to any short poem, but now it is limited to poems of 14 lines with a particular rhyme scheme.

Structure of a sonnet
A typical Shakespearean sonnet has 14 lines, and each line is an iambic pentameter – that is, it has 10 syllables made up of five units (known as feet) in each of which an unstressed syllable is followed by a stressed one, as in "And **look** up**on** my**self** and **curse** my **fate**" (Sonnet 29). The lines have the following rhyming pattern: a b a b a b c d c d e f e f g g.

Using Sonnet 29 (see box below) as a typical example,

close examination shows that the poem does not follow the pattern exactly. For instance, it would be natural to stress the first, not the second syllable of the first line, and in the third line it is natural to stress both "deaf" and the first syllable of "heaven". The second and fourth lines fit the regular pattern. Variations like these enable the poet to avoid a simple jog-trot rhythm and to draw a reader's attention to especially significant words or phrases.

This sonnet has a clear structure, which is created partly by its rhyme scheme. The first four lines (known as a quatrain) establish a situation: the poet is unhappy. The next four lines elaborate on this by giving reasons for his unhappiness. It is common for sonnets to change direction in the ninth line; this is known as the volta (Italian for "turn"). Here, the poet thinks of his friend, or lover ("thee"), which cheers

Sonnet 29

When, in disgrace with fortune and men's eyes,
I all alone beweep my outcast state,
And trouble deaf heaven with my bootless cries,
And look upon myself and curse my fate,
Wishing me like to one more rich in hope,
Featured like him, like him with friends possessed,
Desiring this man's art and that man's scope,
With what I most enjoy contented least:
Yet in these thoughts myself almost despising,
Haply I think on thee, and then my state,
Like to the lark at break of day arising
From sullen earth, sings hymns at heaven's gate;
    For thy sweet love remembered such wealth brings
    That then I scorn to change my state with kings'.

him up, and his happiness is conveyed partly by the image of the lark rising from earth to heaven and singing as it goes; line 11 has an extra syllable in "arising", which leads with no pause to the next line (an effect known as enjambement, a running over of the sense from one line to the next). The poet's new happiness is conveyed partly by the emphatic rhythm of "sings hymns at heaven's gate", where it is natural to stress both "sings" and "hymns". Then the new situation is summed up in the final couplet, with stresses on both syllables in "sweet love" and "such wealth", and the poem comes to a triumphant conclusion with the emphatic rhythms of its last line and the contrast between the poet's new state of happiness in love with that even of kings.

Not all the sonnets have as clear a structure as this one.

Italian sonnets

The first sonnets came from medieval Italy, most famously written by Francesco Petrarch (1304–74). Typically they express hopeless love for an inaccessible and idealized beloved. Shakespeare refers to Petrarch in Romeo and Juliet when Mercutio, thinking that Romeo is still in love with Rosaline, says "Now is he for the numbers [verse rhythms] that Petrarch flowed in" (2.3.36–37).

The first English sonnets were written by Sir Thomas Wyatt and the Earl of Surrey in the middle of the 16th century. Their poems were included in a popular book known as *Tottel's Miscellany*, also called *Songs and Sonnets*, first published in 1557. Shakespeare refers to this in *The Merry Wives of Windsor*, in which a bashful young man, Abraham Slender, wishes he had a copy of it to hand to help him in his wooing of Mistress Anne Page. He says "I had rather than forty shillings I had my book of songs and sonnets here" (1.1.181–182).

What are sonnets about?

Typically, sonnets are poems of romantic love, often directly addressed to an object of love, but over the centuries poets have used the sonnet form for many different purposes. It has also been common to write

The Italian poet Francesco Petrarca (commonly known in English as Petrarch) wrote a series of sonnets addressed to a woman named Laura, whom Petrarch admired from afar.

a collection or sequence of interconnected sonnets all addressed to the same real or imagined person. For example, English poet and soldier Sir Philip Sidney wrote poems addressed to his beloved calling himself "Astrophil" and her "Stella". Sidney's collection was published as *Astrophil and Stella* in 1591, five years after his death, and many other poets imitated it in a spate of sonnets from 1591 to 1597.

In later Elizabethan times, the sonnet form came frequently to be used for religious verse – love poems addressed to God, as it were. Shakespeare's contemporary, poet and cleric John Donne (1572–1631) wrote a number of Holy Sonnets, and one of Shakespeare's sonnets, No 146, is a religious poem.

Sonnet form in the plays

Few of Shakespeare's sonnets appeared in print until 1609, but he had often used the sonnet form before this date. Parts of his plays, especially but not only in the early part of his career, are written in the form » of a sonnet. An obvious example is the Prologue to Romeo and Juliet. Shakespeare also uses sonnet form within the dialogue of that play, most conspicuously in the first lines that Romeo and Juliet speak to each other (see box, below).

The first reference to the sonnets comes in 1598, when Francis Meres, in a book on contemporary and other writers called *Palladis Tamia*, or *Wit's Treasury*, cryptically mentions "Shakespeare's sonnets among his private friends", implying that he had written poems of love or friendship that came to be known about at least within a circle of intimates. The following year, versions of two sonnets – Nos 138 and 144 – made it into print without his permission in a book called *The Passionate Pilgrim*, which also includes three extracts from *Love's Labour's Lost* and other short poems that may or may not be by Shakespeare.

In 1609, a collection of 154 sonnets called *Shakespeare's Sonnets* appeared in print. The 154 sonnets are followed by a longer poem, "A Lover's Complaint" (p.224). It is not clear whether Shakespeare himself intended the collection to be published, and there are a number of strange features about it. The title page reads not, as might have been expected, "Sonnets, by William Shakespeare", but "Shakespeare's Sonnets, never before imprinted", which seems to imply both that someone else was publishing them on his behalf and that people had known of their existence, and looked forward to their publication, for some time.

"Mr W. H."

Even stranger is the fact that the book's dedication appears not over the author's name, as is the case with the poems *Venus and Adonis* and *The Rape of Lucrece*, but over the initials "T. T." of its publisher, Thomas Thorpe. The dedication, laid out in the manner of a tombstone, is puzzling in other ways, notably in that the dedicatee is also identified only by his initials. It reads: "To the onlie begetter of these insuing sonnets Mr W. H. all happinesse and that eternity promised by our ever-living poet wisheth the well-wishing adventurer in setting forth."

The question of who is meant by "Mr W. H." is a long-standing mystery in literary history. Some of the sonnets are clearly addressed to a man, or boy ("sweet boy", No 108, "my lovely boy", No 126), and it has often been supposed that Thorpe is thinking of this person as the "begetter" of the sonnets. Two candidates are Henry Wriothesley, Earl of Southampton, dedicatee of the narrative poems, and William Herbert, Earl of Pembroke, dedicatee of the First Folio of 1623. But neither man was properly addressed as "Mr" and Southampton's initials are "H. W.", not "W. H.". Also, "begetter" might simply mean the person who supplied the manuscript. Nobody really knows what Thorpe meant – and trying to work it out now is, according to poet W H Auden, "an idiot's job". There is good reason to believe that Shakespeare wrote his sonnets, sometimes singly, sometimes in interrelated batches, over a long period of time. Probably the first sonnet he wrote – maybe even his first

---

Romeo and Juliet's first words

Romeo
If I profane with my unworthiest hand
This holy shrine, the gentler sin is this:
My lips, two blushing pilgrims, ready stand
To smooth that rough touch with a tender kiss.
Juliet
Good pilgrim, you do wrong your hand too much,
Which mannerly devotion shows in this.
For saints have hands that pilgrims' hands do touch,
And palm to palm is holy palmers' kiss.
Romeo
Have not saints lips, and holy palmers, too?
Juliet
Ay, pilgrim, lips that they must use in prayer.
Romeo
O, then, dear saint, let lips do what hands do:
They pray; grant thou, lest faith turn to despair.
Juliet
Saints do not move, though grant for prayers' sake.
Romeo
Then move not while my prayer's effect I take.
[*He kisses her.*]

attempt at verse – is No 145 (see p.220 for the full poem), irregular in that it is written in octosyllabics, that is, eight-syllabled lines instead of the usual ten. The reason it is believed to have been written so early is partly that it is light in tone and not very sophisticated in technique, but mainly that in the last two lines the words "hate" and "away" pun on the name of the woman he married when he was 18, Anne Hathaway. It is a wooing poem.

It looks as if Shakespeare himself put the poems into the order in which they are printed. Some stand alone as independent poems, but others are related to one another in subject matter and fall naturally into groups of varying length.

The first 17 appear to be addressed to a young man who is very dear to the writer but whom he is encouraging to marry and to have children. Other poems up to No 126 also relate to one or more young men with whom the poet has a close and loving, though not necessarily sexual, relationship. Many other poems in this group could equally well relate to a man or a woman.

Sonnet 145 may have been written by a young Shakespeare as he courted his future wife, Anne Hathaway. She came from a prosperous family and lived in this home outside Stratford-upon-Avon.

The Dark Lady

The last 26 poems include all those that are clearly addressed to a woman, with whom the poet clearly has a difficult sexual relationship. Some of these sonnets indicate that she is dark in colouring, and even in character, that she is a rival »

 Let not my love be called idolatry, Nor my belovèd as an idol show, Since all alike my songs and praises be To one, of one, still such, and ever so.
Sonnet 105

Henry Wriothesley, 3rd Earl of Southampton, painted here in his teens around 1590, has been proposed as the unnamed young man to whom Sonnets 1–126 are addressed.

of the poet in his love for his friend, and that the poet loves her against his better judgement. For this reason, they have come to be known as the Dark Lady sonnets, and many fruitless attempts have been made to identify a woman of the period who might fit the bill.

Sonnet 145

Those lips that love's own hand did make
Breathed forth the sound that said "I hate"
To me that languished for her sake;
But when she saw my woeful state,
Straight in her heart did mercy come,
Chiding that tongue that ever sweet
Was used in giving gentle doom,
And taught it thus anew to greet:
"I hate" she altered with an end
That followed it as gentle day
Doth follow night, who like a fiend,
From heaven to hell is flown away.
   "I hate" from hate away she threw,
   And saved my life, saying "not you."

 When my love swears that she is made of truth I do believe her though I know she lies, That she might think me some untutored youth Unlearnéd in the world's false subtleties.
Sonnet 138

All aspects of love

Although all the sonnets are written in the same form, with only minor variations, they are extremely varied in style and ease of understanding. The poems also run the whole gamut of love, from romantic idealism to brutal sexual realism. For this reason, it is difficult to read them in one sitting.

They include some of the most beautiful and popular love poems in English, some of which might equally be addressed to a male or a female, young or not so young. They tell of the power of love and of friendship to convey happiness, to transcend time, to confer a kind of immortality on the loved one. "Shall I compare thee to a summer's day? / Thou art more lovely and more temperate", says the poet in No 18, while No 116 is a great hymn to love (see p.221, opposite).

Other poems are very different in tone and the emotion they inspire in the reader. Some speak of rivalry: "Two loves I have, of comfort and despair, / Which like two spirits do suggest me still. / The better angel is a man right fair, / The worser spirit a woman coloured ill." (No 144). Some poems tell of disillusionment and self-deception in love: "When my love swears that she is made of truth / I do believe her though I know she lies." (No 138).

No 147 makes the point bluntly: "For I have sworn thee fair, and thought thee bright, / Who art as black as hell, as dark as night."

Sonnet 116

Let me not to the marriage of true minds
Admit impediments. Love is not love
Which alters when it alteration finds,
Or bends with the remover to remove.
O no, it is an ever-fixèd mark
That looks on tempests and is never shaken;
It is the star to every wand'ring barque,
Whose worth's unknown, although his height be taken.
Love's not time's fool, though rosy lips and cheeks
Within his bending sickle's compass come;
Love alters not with his brief hours and weeks,
But bears it out even to the edge of doom.
    If this be error and upon me proved,
    I never writ, nor no man ever loved.

The poet's complicated relationship with love is explored in the sonnets. In No 149, the poet abases himself before the beloved: "Canst thou, O cruel, say I love thee not / When I against myself with thee partake?" In No 147, he writes with self-disgust of his enthralment to someone he feels is unworthy of him: "My love is as a fever, longing still / For that which longer nurseth the disease." No 129 expresses shame at having yielded to lustful desire: "Th'expense of spirit in a waste of shame / Is lust in action".

However, there is also celebration of bodily desires. In No 146, the poet writes that the soul can be enriched by bodily decay: "Then, soul, live thou upon thy servant's loss, / Buy terms divine in selling hours of dross." In No 151, he says with exultant obscenity that: "thou betraying me, I do betray / My nobler part to my gross body's treason. / My soul doth tell my body that he may / Triumph in love; flesh stays no farther reason, / But rising at thy name doth point out thee / As his triumphant prize." In the closing lines of No 151, the poet leaves no doubt about what part of the body he means by "flesh": "Proud of this prize, / He is contented thy poor drudge to be, / To stand in thy affairs, fall by thy side. / No want of conscience hold »

In 2009, American director Robert Wilson and Canadian songwriter Rufus Wainwright produced a pop-opera, setting 25 of Shakespeare's sonnets (in German) to a variety of musical styles.

it that I call / Her 'love' for whose dear love I rise and fall."

Reputation

Unlike the narrative poems *Venus and Adonis* and *The Rape of Lucrece*, the sonnets were not a publishing success, and the 1609 edition was not reprinted. The sonnets (like the other poems) were not included in the First Folio of 1623. They did not appear in print again until

Painted between 1595 and 1610, the Cobbe Portrait is believed to be the only image of Shakespeare drawn from life. It was probably commissioned by his patron and muse Henry Wriothesley.

1640, in a book published by John Benson that omits eight of them, changes their order, alters pronouns in three of them so that they appear to refer to a woman rather than to a boy or a man, mangles others, gives some of them titles such as "An Invitation to Marriage" and "The Picture of True Love", and adds poems by other writers. After this, the sonnets were largely ignored for close on 150 years, with the result that critics such as John Dryden, Alexander Pope, and Samuel Johnson have nothing to say about them.

Only in the late 18th century did the sonnets come back into circulation. The English Romantic poet-critics John Keats and William Wordsworth both took the sonnets seriously and were influenced by them in their own work. Keats is said to have kept a bust of Shakespeare next to his desk for inspiration. In a letter to the painter Benjamin Robert Haydon, dated 10 May 1817, Keats wrote: "I remember your saying that you had notions of a good Genius presiding over you. I have of late had the same thought – for things which I do half at Random are afterwards confirmed by my judgment in a dozen features of Propriety. Is it too daring to fancy Shakespeare this Presider?"

Wordsworth, who was critical of certain aspects of the poetry in Shakespeare's plays, famously wrote of the sonnet form that "with this key / Shakespeare unlocked his heart". If so, responded fellow poet Robert Browning "the less Shakespeare he." Commenting on this exchange, Auden held that the artist is always both unlocking his heart and dramatic.

Victorian disapproval

Especially but not only in the Victorian period, the poems' reputation has suffered from homophobic distaste for the fact that some of them are love poems from one male person to another. This has also made some readers prefer to think that in them Shakespeare is writing of imagined situations rather than from personal experience. Nevertheless, the most obviously romantic of them have exerted strong appeal. They have frequently appeared in poetic anthologies.

Adapting the sonnets

Many attempts, all unsuccessful, have been made to rearrange the poems into an order that appears to be more meaningful than the original. The density of style of many of the poems makes them difficult to set to music, but there have been successful settings of a few of them in a variety of musical styles by musicians as diverse as the classical composer Benjamin Britten, the jazz arranger Johnny Dankworth, and the singer-songwriter Rufus Wainwright. ∎

Love is not love /
Which alters when it
alteration finds (116)

But my five wits nor
my five senses can /
Dissuade one foolish
heart from serving
thee (141)

Shakespeare's love poems still strike a chord with lovers across the world. Sonnets 116 and 141, in particular, are often read at marriages and civil partnership ceremonies.

Religion and merit

The religious references in Shakespeare's sonnets reflect both sides of a central doctrinal dispute of his time. The reformist Martin Luther (above) held that the key to salvation lay in faith alone. This contrasted with Catholic doctrine, which held that good works, prayers, pilgrimages, or the purchase of indulgences could increase an individual's chances of salvation. The poet takes from both traditions when dealing with the value of individual merit.

Sonnet 88 opens with the lines "When thou shalt be disposed to set me light / And place my merit in the eye of scorn." Here, he appears to take the reformist line, holding that his merit is worthless.

However, in No. 108, merit is raised in a different way: "What's new to speak, what now to register, / That may express my love or thy dear merit?" Here, the poet seems to think merit far from worthless. Moreover, he follows with "Nothing, sweet boy; but yet like prayers divine / I must each day say o'er the very same," alluding to the Catholic practice of repeating the same prayers daily.

THAT FALSE FIRE WHICH IN HIS CHEEK SO GLOWED
A LOVER'S COMPLAINT (1609)

IN CONTEXT

THEMES
Love, betrayal

In the 1609 volume *Shakespeare's Sonnets*, the final item was printed with a separate heading saying that it too is by Shakespeare. It is a 329-line poem called "A Lover's Complaint", written, like *The Rape of Lucrece*, in the seven-line stanza form known as rhyme royal. It was not uncommon for collections of sonnets to conclude with a complaint, or lament, of a woman forsaken by her lover. Here, a nameless young woman, abandoned by her irresistibly attractive but faithless young man, also unnamed, bemoans her plight.

The poem is very different from the sonnets. It is written in a self-consciously old-fashioned and artificial style and employs a series of distancing perspectives. A narrator merely sets the scene. After saying that he has seen a love-lorn lass "Tearing of papers, breaking riwain, / Storming her world with sorrow's winds and rain", he departs to let her tell her story to "A reverend man that grazed his cattle nigh". But this man also fades out of sight as the girl tells a story of seduction and abandonment. Her complaint contains within itself another long complaint, her lover's ultimately successful speech of seduction ending with the tears of desire that brought about her downfall: "O father, what a hell of witchcraft lies / In the small orb of one particular tear!"

She fell, she says, and she would fall again in the face of such eloquent persuasion: "O that infected moisture of his eye, / O that false fire which in his cheek so glowed, / O that forced thunder from his heart did fly, / O that sad breath his spongy lungs bestowed, / O all that borrowed motion seeming owed / Would yet again betray the fore-betrayed, / And new pervert a reconcilèd maid." ∎

 What a hell of witchcraft lies
In the small orb of one
particular tear!
A Lover's Complaint 〞

TRUTH AND BEAUTY BURIED BE

THE PHOENIX AND TURTLE (1601)

IN CONTEXT

THEME
The death of ideal love

I n 1601, in a book by Robert Chester called *Love's Martyr: or Rosalind's Complaint*, appeared a poem by Shakespeare called "The Phoenix and Turtle".

The poem falls into three parts of mounting intensity. First, it summons a convocation of benevolent birds, with a swan as priest, to celebrate the funeral rites of a phoenix and a dove who have fled "In a mutual flame from hence". ("Turtle" here means a turtledove.) The birds sing an anthem in which the death of the lovers is seen as marking the death of "love and constancy": "So they loved as love in twain / Had the essence but in one, / Two distincts, division none. / Number there in love was slain. Their mutual love was such that "either was the other's mine". In the third section, Love makes a funeral song: "'To the phoenix and the dove, / Co-supremes and stars of love, / As chorus to their tragic scene."

The funeral song, known as a threnos, or threnody, is written in an even more incantatory style than what has gone before. Its five stanzas have three rhyming lines, whose tone is grave simplicity: "Beauty, truth, and rarity, / Grace in all simplicity, / Here enclosed in cinders lie. / Death is now the phoenix' nest, / And the turtle's loyal breast / To eternity doth rest. / Leaving no posterity / 'Twas not their infirmity, / It was married chastity. / Truth may seem but cannot be, / Beauty brag, but 'tis not she. / Truth and beauty buried be. / To this urn let these repair / That are either true or fair. / For these dead birds sigh a prayer."

This strange, mystically beautiful poem probably had meanings for its original readers that are lost to us. Many unsuccessful attempts have been made to interpret it as a religious allegory or a celebration of the love of a real married couple. ■

> ❝ Truth may seem
> but cannot be,
> Beauty brag, but 'tis not she.
> **The Phoenix
> and Turtle** ❞

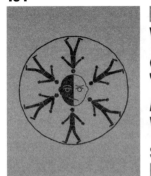

WITH SELFSAME HAND, SELF REASONS, AND SELF RIGHT, WOULD SHARK ON YOU
SIR THOMAS MORE (1603–1604)

IN CONTEXT

THEMES
Justice, religion, moral fortitude

SETTING
London

SOURCES
c.1575 Nicholas Harpsfield's biography of More, *The life and death of Sir Thomas Moore.*

1587 Holinshed's *Chronicles of England, Scotland, and Ireland.*

I n 1753, the British Museum acquired a remarkable bequest from the bookseller John Murray. It was a manuscript called "The Booke of Sir Thomas Moore" and is a working draft of the play *Sir Thomas More* dating from around 1600. The manuscript contains the only known examples of writing in Shakespeare's hand, aside from a handful of signatures.

The manuscript is believed to show revisions to the text for a play originally written by Anthony Munday and, maybe, Henry Chettle, after it had been submitted to the official censor Edmund Tilney. The manuscript shows both Tilney's interventions and the hands of at least four writers, including Chettle, Thomas Heywood, Thomas Dekker, and Shakespeare, not to mention an editor, known simply as Hand C.

 The fool of flesh must with her frail flesh die
More
Scene 17

The power of the censor

The subject of the play was a sensitive one: the Catholic martyr Sir Thomas More (1478–1535). More rose from comparatively humble beginnings to become King Henry VIII's chancellor. He was an opponent of the Protestant Reformation and strongly against Henry's split from the Catholic church. In 1535, he was executed for treason for his quiet refusal to go along with the annulment of Henry's marriage to Catherine of Aragon and his subsequent marriage to Anne Boleyn.

Anne Boleyn was the mother of the reigning queen, Elizabeth I, so a play that was favourable to More would be seen as undermining Elizabeth's legitimacy. This made More a bold choice of subject matter, and it is not surprising that the play was probably never performed in the queen's lifetime. The writers are careful to steer around the issue of Anne's marriage, and Henry VIII is never mentioned by name. The brunt of Tilney's demands for cuts came in the first third of the play where Londoners riot against foreigners. He appears to have been most concerned over public order.

The German artist Hans
Holbein captured More's
intelligence and dignity in this
extraordinarily vivid portrait of
1527, painted when More was a
rising star at Henry's court.

An unwieldy play

The play's failure to reach the
stage may have been due to
practical as well as political
reasons. It has 59 speaking
parts, which would have
severely taxed any theatre
company, with many actors
playing three or more roles.
Probably only the roles of Sir
Thomas More and perhaps
the Earls of Shrewsbury and
Surrey, could have been
played by actors with no
other parts.

More's life is split into
three parts – his rise, his
chancellorship, and his fall.
The early part of the play
shows More as Sheriff of
London, and stresses his
wisdom and moderation.
When a group of Londoners rise in rebellion
against foreigners in their midst, More
ends the riot with quiet persuasion.

It is thought that the key scene in
this part of the play was written
by Shakespeare. It seems likely that
Shakespeare had not seen the rest of
the play and was simply given a brief
by the editor, since there are characters
he just names as "other" or even "o",
and the entry of More is confused. But
what he writes stands out in a generally
mediocre play.

Tolerance for foreigners

In Shakespeare's script, More calmly
stands before the rioters in St Martin's
Gate. He makes a passionate plea for the
tolerance of refugees. Painting a poignant
picture of the foreigners (strangers) bullied
out by the rioters, More tells them that
this brings only the idea that bullying
prevails:"Imagine that you see the
wretched strangers, / Their babies at their
backs, with their poor luggage, / Plodding
to th' ports and coasts for transportation, /
And that you sit as kings in your desires…
What had you got? I'll tell you: you had
taught / How insolence and strong hand
should prevail." (6.84–87, 90–91).

More asks what will stop bullies preying
on them. "With selfsame hand, self reasons,
and self right, / Would shark on you, and
men like ravenous fishes / Would feed on
one another." (6.95–97).

Moreover, More goes on, if the
king is driven to banish the rioters
themselves, surely they would expect
to be treated decently abroad: "Would
you be pleased / To find a nation of
such barbarous temper" (6.145–146).

More carries his constancy through
to his own death. He cannot change his
mind and sign the articles that recognize
Anne Boleyn and her heirs as legitimate.
Yet he calmly accepts his fate. "No eye
salute my trunk with a sad tear", More
says to end the play as the axeman
prepares to behead him, "Our birth to
heaven should be thus: void of fear."■

THE KING

1603–1613

On 24 March 1603, Queen Elizabeth I died after 45 years on the throne. She was succeeded by her cousin James VI of Scotland, son of Mary Queen of Scots, whom Elizabeth had beheaded 16 years earlier. One of James's first acts on becoming king was to give Shakespeare's company a royal patent to make them the King's Men.

By royal command

This was a financial boost for the troupe, but it also added pressure. Now they not only had to please the general public; they had to please the king and his courtiers, too. In the 13 years between James becoming king and Shakespeare's death, the King's Men performed for the court 187 times – more than once a month.

Around this time, Shakespeare's style changed. He moved away from the crowd-pleasing comedies, romances, and histories of the later years of Elizabeth's reign. Now he wrote fewer plays, but they were grander and darker. In the first three years of James's reign, he wrote just six plays, five of which were ambitious tragedies – *Othello*, *King Lear*, *Macbeth*, *Antony and Cleopatra*, and the uncompleted

Timon of Athens. Even *Measure for Measure* was intense and morally challenging. While Shakespeare was writing these great works, the company had his impressive back-catalogue to keep the theatres full.

Escape to Stratford?

Nobody knows quite how Shakespeare spent his time during these years. One of the few things we do know is that, by 1604, he was renting a room in the house of a Huguenot called Christopher Mountjoy. We know this because Mountjoy got into a bitter lawsuit with his son-in-law and Shakespeare is mentioned in the legal documents.

Living perpetually in rented accommodation clearly brought its stresses. So it may be that Shakespeare, not under as much pressure as in his younger days, took every chance to go home to Stratford and write in a calmer environment. He may also have had to leave London when the plague returned.

On 5 November 1605, a very distant relative of Shakespeare, Robert Catesby, was involved in the most infamous Catholic attempt to bring down England's Protestant government, the Gunpowder Plot. The plot was foiled when a Catholic lord was given a secret warning and tipped off the authorities. They were told to search under the Houses of Parliament, and there they found Guido (Guy) Fawkes sitting on 36 barrels of gunpowder. Had Fawkes set them off, it would not only have blown up the Parliament buildings but the nearby Whitehall Palace and the royal family too. Practising Catholics were already in a minority by this time, and the clampdown on Catholics that followed effectively ended the Catholic challenge to government in England.

The last plays

The King's Men continued to prosper, and in 1608 were able to acquire a second theatre, the Blackfriars. This new theatre was very different from the Globe – indoors and much smaller, so performances were almost entirely by candlelight. The company continued to perform at the Globe in summer, then they could play right through winter in the Blackfriars.

Shakespeare began to write plays suited to the more intimate space of the Blackfriars and its facility for spectacular theatrical effects, such as the storm and the flying spirits in *The Tempest* and the statue coming to life in *The Winter's Tale*. He was also collaborating with other writers again – Thomas Middleton (1580–1627) on *Timon of Athens* in 1606, George Wilkins (1576–1618) on *Pericles* in 1607, and John Fletcher (1579–1625) on the lost play *Cardenio*, *All Is True* (*Henry VIII*), and *The Two Noble Kinsmen* in 1613.

The collaborations with Fletcher were Shakespeare's last plays. On 29 June 1613, the Globe Theatre caught fire during a performance of *Henry VIII* when a theatrical cannon misfired and set the roof thatch alight. Everybody escaped unhurt, but the theatre burned down. The Globe was rebuilt ready for the following summer, but it appears that it reopened without Shakespeare. All we know about his life from that point on is that he wrote nothing more and died just three years later at home in Stratford on 23 April 1616, within a month of signing a document saying he was in "perfect health". He was 52 years old. ∎

MAN, PROUD MAN DRESSED IN A LITTLE BRIEF AUTHORITY
MEASURE FOR MEASURE (1603–1604)

Duke Vincentio hands power to his deputy Angelo and announces that he is leaving the country on business. During the 14 years the Duke has been in government, Vienna has become a lawless city, where pimps and prostitutes thrive. The Duke secretly plans to observe how the puritanical Angelo governs in his absence. He assumes the disguise of a friar in order to move around the city unrecognized.

Once in power, Angelo enforces forgotten laws. Claudio is arrested for getting his wife-to-be Juliet pregnant, and the pimps and bawds fear that they too will soon suffer. On hearing of Claudio's death sentence, his sister Isabella leaves the nunnery she was about to join to plead with Angelo to spare her brother's life.

Isabella is escorted by Lucio who encourages her to argue her brother's case. Angelo remains unmoved by Isabella's argument, but he asks her to return the next day. She comes unaccompanied and Angelo presents her with a chilling ultimatum: he will spare her brother's life on the condition that she sleeps with him. Isabella is distraught, but Angelo reminds her that no-one would believe her were she to report his proposal.

Isabella visits her brother in prison and tells him of Angelo's behaviour. Though Claudio is appalled, he questions her commitment to her chastity when his life is at stake. The disguised Duke overhears their conversation and ministers to each of them. He tells Isabella that all is not lost, and suggests a cunning solution. He will arrange for Mariana, Angelo's ex-fiancée, to sleep with him under the cover of darkness, so that Angelo will believe he has slept with Isabella and spare Claudio.

The Duke's plan is successful but Angelo is still resolved to execute Claudio. The disguised Duke intervenes by having the head of a condemned prisoner sent to Angelo in place of Claudio's. The Duke does not share his plan with Isabella, leading her to believe that her brother has been beheaded.

Vincentio stages his return to Vienna and praises Angelo for his good government. Isabella accuses Angelo of corruption; she has no idea that the Duke has observed everything while in disguise. When Mariana confirms that it was she who slept with Angelo, the Duke, who has returned disguised as a friar once more, supports her story. The Duke is unmasked by Lucio and Angelo begs for execution; he is surprised when Mariana pleads to spare his life, and Isabella joins Mariana in her plea. The Duke grants their wish on the condition that Angelo marry Mariana. Having reunited Isabella with her brother, the Duke asks for her hand in marriage – twice! ∎

IN CONTEXT

THEMES
Justice, morality, power, sex

SETTING
Vienna

SOURCES
1565 Shakespeare may have been familiar with Giraldi Cinthio's Italian novella *Hecatommithi*. However, he introduced Mariana and the "bedtrick". In the source material, the Isabella figure sleeps with the Angelo character, and marries him.

1578 Shakespeare made use of George Whetstone's English tragicomedy *Promos and Cassandra*.

I n the opening scene, Duke Vincentio reveals to Escalus his plan to leave Vienna, lending Angelo "all the organs / Of our power" (1.1.20–21) to rule in his absence. He is keen to hear Escalus's opinion of his plan: "What think you of it?" (1.1.21). He is also eager to know his companion's estimation of Angelo himself: "What figure of us think you he will bear?" (1.1.15–16). In asking so many questions, the dramatist is readying his audience to observe, evaluate, and pass judgement upon Angelo's behaviour. Angelo's reaction to being "Dressed in a little brief authority" (2.2.121) will be a concern throughout the drama.

Early 17th-century Vienna, shown in this engraving, is described as a lawless and immoderate city in need of a firm hand. The neglectful Duke chooses exacting Angelo for the task.

Shakespeare builds a sense of anticipation around Angelo's arrival. By the time Vincentio announces "Look where he comes" (1.1.24), the audience is sure to be curious about this mysterious figure with whom the Duke seems somewhat obsessed. Angelo shows respectful reticence at first to taking control of "Morality and mercy in Vienna" (1.1.44); he asks that "there be some more test made of [his] metal" (1.1.48) before he assumes this powerful role. Little does he realize that the Duke will be testing him throughout the rest of the drama.

Testing times

Angelo's job will not be easy, for law and order have all but disappeared in Vienna. Having passed responsibility to Angelo, the Duke confides in a friar that: "We have strict statutes and most biting laws, / The needful bits and curbs to headstrong weeds, / Which for this fourteen years we have let slip… / And Liberty plucks Justice by the nose, / The baby beats the nurse, and quite athwart / Goes all decorum." (1.3.19–31).

During the Duke's time, Vienna has become a city where criminality and prostitution are rife; and slanderous allegations are even made about the Duke's own behaviour: "Ere he would have hanged a man for the getting a hundred bastards, he would have paid for the nursing a thousand" (3.1.380–383). The puritanical Angelo would seem a prime candidate for restoring moral order in a city that has become diseased. The Duke recognizes that having, neglected his »

The virtuous character of Isabella is played here by Flora Robson in a production in 1933. In Whetstone's tale, she is a chaste maid; in Shakespeare's play, she is about to enter a nunnery.

This early 19th-century engraving depicts the moment in Act 5, Scene 1 when Mariana takes off her veil: "My husband bids me; now I will unmask." Unveiled, she denounces "cruel Angelo."

authority for so long, he would prove a tyrant were he to try to enforce order a new; far better, he thinks, to have Angelo "in th'ambush of [his] name strike home" (1.3.41). While Angelo will in time prove to be a hypocrite, the Duke will prove a Machiavellian operator.

Abuse of power

Various characters pass comment on Angelo's character during the course of the play. The Duke notes that Angelo is "precise" (1.3.50), and that he "Stands at a guard with envy, scarce confesses / That his blood flows, or that his appetite / Is more to bread than stone." (1.3.51–53). The gossipy and salacious Lucio presents an image of Angelo that drains him of every drop of blood and compassion: Lucio professes that "Some report a sea-maid spawned him, some that he was begot between two stockfishes. But it is certain that when he makes water his urine is congealed ice; that I know to be true." (3.1.372–375).

While Angelo may not be the monstrous figure of Lucio's imagination, he proves to have little in the way of compassion when he sentences Claudio to death for having had sex with his wife-to-be outside of wedlock: "'Tis one thing to be tempted… / Another thing to fall" (2.1.17–18). His conviction would remain steadfast were it not for the sudden entrance of the virtuous Isabella into his life. Like Angelo, Isabella has a reputation for "stricture and firm abstinence" (1.3.12). Her first exchange with a nun expresses both her moral

fortitude and her readiness to live by a strict set of rules; she is surprised to hear, for example, that the votarists of Saint Clare do not live by "a more strict restraint" (1.4.4). In different circumstances, Angelo and Isabella might find that they have much in common, but the context in which they first meet is crucial in defining the dynamic of their relationship. Isabella finds herself before a figure of immense authority, and faces the challenge of persuading him to overturn the death sentence he has placed on her brother. Two strictly principled individuals must find it within themselves to forgive a sinful act. Shakespeare lends Isabella a powerfully persuasive voice. Her speeches suggest a keen intellect and a compassionate heart. She finds ways to prick Angelo's conscience, to unearth doubts and anxiety. "If he had been as you and you as he, / You would have slipped like him, but he, like you, / Would not have been so stern." (2.2.66–68). At other times her speeches remind Angelo of his shared humanity: "Go to your bosom; / Knock there, and ask your heart what it doth know / That's like my brother's fault?" (2.2.140–142). Ultimately, her words have the desired effect – to shame Angelo into reconsideration: "O, it is excellent / To have a giant's strength, but it is tyrannous / To use it like a giant." (2.2.109–111).

Persuasive power

The question for readers and audiences is whether it is Isabella's words alone, or also her physical appearance that affect Angelo? With Lucio and the Provost present, Angelo maintains his image of the stern authoritarian, but his behaviour alters dramatically when Isabella returns as instructed for their second meeting, in private. When she returns, Isabella promises

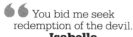

You bid me seek
redemption of the devil.
Isabella
Act 5, Scene 1

to "bribe" (2.2.149) Angelo, but as she goes on to explain "Not with fond shekels of the tested gold, / Or stones, whose rate are either rich or poor / As fancy values them; but with true prayers, / That shall be up at heaven and enter there / Ere sunrise" (2.2.153–157). Is Isabella's "bribe" completely innocent, or is there a sense in which she manipulates her womanliness as Lucio has instructed her to? Her brother had confidence in his chances of getting his death sentence overturned because he believed that "in her youth / There is a prone and speechless dialect / Such as move men" (1.2.170–172).

Whether Isabella "moves" Angelo, or whether he discovers unknown passions within is a matter of debate. Either way, Angelo moves from being a law enforcer to a corrupt abuser of power: "I have begun, / And now I give my sensual race the rein. / Fit thy consent to my sharp appetite. / …Redeem thy brother / By yielding up thy body to my will, / Or else he must not only die the death, / But thy unkindness shall his death draw out / To ling'ring sufferance." (2.4.159–167). Having been indecently propositioned by Angelo, Isabella retorts: "I will proclaim thee, Angelo; look for't. / Sign me a present pardon for my brother, / Or with an outstretched throat I'll tell the world aloud / What man thou art." (2.4.151–154). However, she is in a vulnerable position – Angelo is a powerful man and she has no witnesses on whom to draw.

Power corrupts

Angelo's response is chilling. He replies: "Who will believe thee, Isabel? / My unsoiled name, th'austereness of my life, / My vouch against you, and my place i'th'state, / Will so your accusation overweigh." (2.4.154–157). Angelo calculates that his power makes Isabella powerless. She knows that she is in the right, but to whom should she complain? Isabella is trapped. In the story from which Shakespeare borrowed for his play, the Isabella character does, in fact, sleep with the deputy, but Shakespeare's incarnation says "Then Isabel live chaste, and brother die." (2.4.184). Shakespeare provides her a way out of this situation through the comic device of the "bedtrick", by which Angelo sleeps with his ex-fiancée, believing it to be Isabella.

Having escaped Angelo's bed, Isabella now finds herself the subject of the Duke's desires when he recovers power. The Duke offers her his hand in marriage on two separate occasions at the close of the play: "Dear Isabel, / I have a motion much imports your good, / Whereto, if you'll a willing ear incline, / What's mine is yours, and what is yours is mine." (5.1.533–536). There is no response from Isabella. ∎

Problem play

Shakespeare does not have Isabella respond to the Duke. Is it to be assumed that Isabella is speechless and overcome with joy at the prospect of marrying this high ranking official, who has returned to Vienna and exercised his authority by helping to reveal Angelo's abuse of power? Or does Isabella's silence convey her distrust of men? Her brother hoped that she would lose her virginity to save his life; Angelo made her the focus of his lust; and the Duke allowed her to grieve over her brother's death when he knew him still to be alive. Opinion remains divided over whether Isabella should or should not take the Duke's hand at the close; her silence will always invite various interpretations.

Measure for Measure is often referred to today as being one of Shakespeare's "problem plays". Though the play ends with the prospect of three marriages, the atmosphere of the final scene, and the play in general, is far from buoyant and uplifting. This a dark comedy, shaped by Shakespeare to shock rather than enchant.

BEWARE MY LORD OF JEALOUSY IT IS THE GREEN-EY'D MONSTER
OTHELLO (1603–1604)

With the help of the love-sick gentleman Roderigo, the soldier Iago plots to thwart the Moorish general of the Venetian army, Othello. Iago tells Brabanzio that his daughter, Desdemona, has eloped with Othello. Brabanzio demands justice from the Venetian court. After hearing Desdemona's defence, the law favours Othello, who must now speed to Cyprus to prevent a Turkish invasion. Desdemona insists upon meeting Othello in Cyprus once he has defeated the Turks.

Iago plagues Othello with suspicions about Desdemona's relationship with Cassio. In the meantime, Iago persuades Roderigo, who is in love with Desdemona, to challenge Cassio to a fight. Their brawl wakes Othello, who dismisses Cassio from the army. Cassio pleads with Desdemona to persuade Othello to forgive him, causing the Moor to suspect his wife of infidelity.

Iago has his wife Emilia steal a handkerchief that was given to Desdemona by Othello. He plants it in Cassio's bedchamber and weaves a plot to make Othello believe that Desdemona gave it to Cassio as a token of love.

Iago continues to weave his web of deceit around Othello, telling him that Cassio has admitted committing adultery with Desdemona. Othello is consumed by jealousy, refusing to speak with Desdemona. Othello suffers an epileptic fit, after which he resolves to kill Cassio and Desdemona.

When Desdemona's cousin, Lodovico, arrives as an ambassador from Venice, he sees Othello strike Desdemona in public. Roderigo grows restless at his lack of progress in wooing Desdemona. Iago persuades him to kill Cassio. During their struggle, Cassio fatally wounds Roderigo, who confesses his part in Iago's plot.

At the same time, Othello wakes Desdemona from her sleep. He asks her to pray for forgiveness for what she has done. He can then murder her with a clear conscience. Desdemona swears her innocence, but he smothers her with a pillow, whereupon Emilia enters and accuses Othello of murder. Desdemona revives briefly, falsely telling Emilia that she has killed herself. When the others enter the chamber to inform Othello of Roderigo's death, they discover Desdemona's body and demand an explanation. Emilia admits taking the handkerchief. Iago stabs Emilia to stop her betraying him further, whereupon Othello immediately repents of his actions. He asks forgiveness of all present, and out of rage drives his dagger into Iago who, although wounded, is not killed. Othello stabs himself and dies by Desdemona's side, leaving Cassio in control of the Venetian army. ■

 Yet she must die, else she'll betray more men.
Othello
Act 5, Scene 2

IN CONTEXT

THEMES
Jealousy, loyalty, betrayal, love

SETTING
16th-century Venice and Cyprus

SOURCES
1565 *Un Capitano Moro* (A Moorish Captain), a tale by the Italian author Giraldi Cinthio, which Shakespeare may have read in Italian, or in a French translation from 1583.

c.1600 Arrival of a Moorish delegation at the Elizabethan court to promote an Anglo-Moroccan alliance.

1603 The 1570 Turkish attack on Cyprus, documented in *The History of the Turks* by English historian Richard Knolles.

U nlike the original story of "A Moorish Captain", which rarely mentions it, Shakespeare makes Othello extremely conscious of his race. Black characters in Elizabethan drama are often devilish, cruel individuals, like Aaron in *Titus Andronicus*. Othello is the first sympathetic black character on the Elizabethan stage. The audience sympathizes with his plight, and Desdemona clings desperately to her love for "the Moor".

Othello the Moor

Iago and Roderigo are openly vicious in their racial attacks on Othello. Othello is introduced to the audience through the eyes of Iago in crude racial and sexual terms. He is described as a "black ram" mounting Brabanzio's "white ewe" (1.1.88–89). When Shakespeare wrote the play, darkness of skin, along with physical deformity and non-Christian heritage, were popularly associated with immorality and savagery. Othello himself refers frequently to his black heritage, which he blames for making him quick to anger and to experience jealousy. Othello belies the stereotype in all his conduct except for his rage and suspicious nature, which prompt Emilia to accuse him of being "the blacker devil" (5.2.140).

Othello the military hero

Not everyone characterizes Othello in racial terms. He is often judged by his military prowess. Before he is called before it by Brabanzio's complaint, the court is in discussion about choosing Othello to lead the attack on the Turks off the coast of Cyprus. Shakespeare makes it clear that Othello's merit speaks for itself within the Venetian hierarchy. His calm level-headedness is evident when he defends himself against Brabanzio's accusations that he kidnapped Desdemona.

Othello's tone and experience, compared with Desdemona's rebelliousness and the fact that she still resides with her father, suggest a significant age gap between the couple. Nevertheless, Othello's love for Desdemona is sincere, and it is this sincerity that makes him vulnerable to Iago's machinations. Othello is brought down from a justified position of strength and respect to a savage, unjustified, and bitter end all because he could not control his jealousy. The respect and love with which the Venetians regard Othello is made clear by their shock when he is discovered with Desdemona's body at the end. This was not a man they imagined succumbing to anxiety, paranoia, and murder.

"Honest" Iago

Manipulative, cruel, and motivated by hatred and jealousy, Iago uses Roderigo's unrequited love for Desdemona as a way of extorting money and extra hands to support his scheme to undermine Othello. Roderigo compulsively follows Iago's instructions in the hope that it will bring him closer to »

Nineteenth-century Irish painter Daniel Maclise captures a troubled marriage. Othello broods while Desdemona looks up at him pleadingly, clutching the cursed handkerchief.

Desdemona. Iago also manipulates the audience by divulging his scheme in soliloquies. He justifies his contempt for Othello with two uncorroborated arguments: that Othello has slept with his wife, Emilia, and that Cassio has stolen his promotion to captain. Curiously, Iago's warning to Othello about the "green-eyed monster" is one that he cannot heed himself. It is a cruel irony that both Othello and Cassio hold Iago in the highest of esteem, bestowing on him the title "honest".

It is Iago who convinces Othello that Desdemona is false and Iago who suggests that Othello "strangle her in bed, even the bed she hath contaminated" (4.1.202–203).

Jealous Iago

When Othello swears to take vengeance on Cassio, he makes a vow that has a ritualistic flavour to it. He speaks in terms of oceans and the heavens, while Iago calls on the stars to witness his commitment to serving his master. The nature of this exchange, and the fact that Othello calls it a "sacred vow" (3.3.463), has led critics to characterize it as a sinister echo of the wedding ceremony between Othello and Desdemona, which the audience is not invited to see. As well as making Iago his accomplice in Cassio's murder, Othello promotes him to the position of lieutenant. Now Iago has replaced Desdemona, figuratively, and Cassio, literally, in Othello's life.

In spite of Iago's villainy, the character receives as much attention as Othello. Historically, actors have competed for audience acclaim when performing these roles. Othello's dependence on and vulnerability to Iago's deceit, coupled with Iago's ambiguous motivation and manipulative skill, make them a dynamic and even disturbing couple, who drag one another down into a pit of psychological

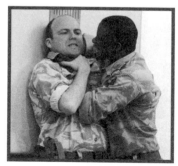

Set in a modern army, the award-winning 2013 National Theatre production in London imagined Iago (Rory Kinnear) and Othello (Adrian Lester) as long-time comrades.

Ira Aldridge

In 1825, American actor Ira Aldridge became the first black person to play Othello on a London stage. Born in New York in 1807, Aldridge moved to Europe when he found acting opportunities hard to come by in his native country. He was just 18 years old when he first took the role of the Moor. Aldridge received favourable reviews for his performance, although the praise was tinged with racist assumptions. One critic wrote that he "delivers the most difficult passages with a degree of correctness that surprises the beholder", suggesting that the critic had been sceptical of a black actor's ability to perform such a feat.

Aldridge went on to play the title roles of *King Lear* and *Richard III* in a long career on the European stage. In an inversion of the usual practice with Othello, Aldridge would sometimes take on roles as white men, using make-up to "white up". Although he never returned to the US, Aldridge was seen as an inspirational figure among black American actors. He died in 1867 while on tour in Poland.

horror because neither one can control his jealousy. From the 18th century on, leading actors performing the play began to double up and alternate the roles of Othello and Iago. In a famous example from the Victorian era, English actor Henry Irving and American actor Edwin Booth alternated roles in a production at the Lyceum Theatre in London.

A husband's jealousy

Strip away the Venetian court, the social hierarchy, and the military setting, and at the heart of this play is a story about a husband and wife separated by a malicious conman. With its grand opening scenes in the political world of law and warfare, the play's domestic focus may seem strikingly incongruous. Shakespeare narrows his focus gradually through the action so that the final scene takes place in a bedchamber. That the Venetian army, politicians, and lords spill into this same room reminds the audience how vulnerable the private life of a public figure like Othello truly is. To acknowledge that this tragedy is triggered by jealousy is to admit something fundamentally insecure about human trust and, most disturbingly, about love.

Where does this jealousy come from? After hearing her defence, Brabanzio disowns Desdemona and warns Othello that, having deceived her own father, she is likely also to be false to her husband. The seeds of suspicion are sown in Othello's imagination from the first act of the play. However, it is really Iago who baits and encourages Othello's mistrust of Desdemona. Iago's four most powerful words are "look to your wife" (3.3.201).

Jealousy and envy eat away at the core of this play. Brabanzio, Cassio, and Roderigo all experience some kind of envy that reflects and orbits the central jealousy between Iago and Othello. The image of a bright-eyed monster feeding and slowly growing fat is sickly and disturbing. The monster is a demonic entity that possesses its host and takes over its life. Iago plants a small suspicion in his general's mind, feeding it slowly until Othello is physically incapacitated by an obsession with his wife's infidelity. Throughout the play,

The American actor and singer Paul Robeson played Othello on the London stage in 1930, opposite Peggy Ashcroft as Desdemona. At the time, it was still rare for black actors to play the role.

jealousy is described as wicked, a plague, and as something damned.

Othello's fervid imagination is tainted by carnal images, which manifest themselves in his use of bodily rhetoric. He speaks of Desdemona's flesh rotting and perishing, of other men "tast[ing] her sweet body" (3.3.351), and of Cassio stealing her lips so that she is "stolen". Othello accuses Desdemona of being a strumpet and whore. This preoccupation with carnal imagery culminates in an analogy in which he compares his wife's genitals to the gates of hell.

Many Shakespearean tragedies revolve around a character's central and unfixable flaw. In this case, the tragedy comes from green-eyed jealousy that was born, nursed, and nurtured in Othello's own imagination. The jealous "nature" that he argues was inherited from his Moorish ancestors becomes, by this logic, Othello's tragic flaw. The evil seeds that Iago sows thrive so virulently in Othello's mind and body that in the end there is nowhere else for them to grow but to reach out and destroy Desdemona.

This very specific tragic flaw has not always been considered a satisfying topic for a great tragedy. In the early 20th » century, the British Shakespeare scholar A C Bradley complained that the tragic aspects of the play were overshadowed by its subject matter: a man who is sexually jealous of his wife. This, in Bradley's view, was something profoundly objectionable and morally repulsive.

Faithful wives

Both Emilia and Desdemona are depicted as women who loyally follow and obey their husbands. Desdemona's loyalty to Othello is clear in her submissiveness to his will. She follows him to Cyprus, tends to him when he appears to be ill, apologizes for being the object of his scorn even after he strikes her in public, and finally dies when he wishes her to. In a similar fashion, Emilia obeys Iago's will when she steals Desdemona's handkerchief at his bidding.

The difference between the women becomes apparent at the play's close when Desdemona refuses to name her murderer, and Emilia denounces Iago. But the result is the same – they are both murdered by their husbands and their faithfulness goes unrewarded. Desdemona's helplessness in the face of Othello's accusations and Iago's manipulation is counteracted by Emilia, whose love for her companion emboldens her to speak out against Othello and to accuse her husband of villainy even when

Iago holds a dagger to her throat. It is Emilia who travels with Desdemona, comforts and supports her when she is abandoned by her father and, later, her husband. Emilia also encourages Desdemona to consider herself an equal to Othello. She asks "have not we affections, / Desires for sport, and frailty, as men have?" (4.3.99–100). In contrast to her husband's relationship with Othello, Emilia is fiercely loyal to Desdemona, and her dying words are spent in defence of her companion.

While the women display loyalty to their men, the men themselves are far more concerned with appearances, which are a major driver in their actions. Cassio and Othello are both preoccupied with their reputations. Cassio's name is tainted by his late-night brawl with Roderigo, for which he is dismissed from his service under Othello. Cassio's lament for his reputation early in the play's action foreshadows Othello's far more sinister concern over his honour.

While the military men grow fearful over their honour, the women suffer attacks on their sexual reputations. Iago's accusations against Desdemona are sufficient to cast her entire character into doubt. This is echoed in Cassio's comments to Bianca. He calls her a "bauble", implying that her moral laxity makes her unworthy to be his bride.

Portraying Othello

Critics have famously disagreed in their responses to the character of Othello. In 1937, the critic F R Leavis argued that the

character is inherently savage, and only barely manages to cover his uncivilized nature until he gives in to instinct. On the other hand, romanticized readings of Othello characterize him as an honorable man rather than an unprincipled savage. In the 1870s and 80s, the Italian actor Tommaso Salvini interpreted the Moor as a hot-blooded and passionate but noble hero. He performed Othello's suicide by slitting his throat and dying with fierce bodily convulsions.

Salvini performed the part in Italian, even on occasions when the rest of the cast spoke English, which led to him being known as the Italian Moor.

Prior to the late 20th century, Othello was played by white actors such as Orson Welles (pictured) wearing dark make-up, a practice now obsolete. An exception was in a racially inverted production in 1997 in Washington DC, when Patrick Stewart played a white Othello in a black nation.

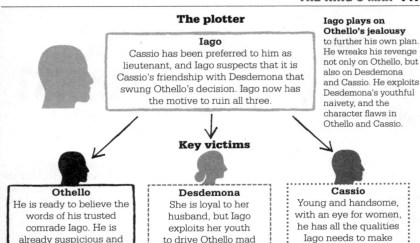

The plotter

Iago
Cassio has been preferred to him as lieutenant, and Iago suspects that it is Cassio's friendship with Desdemona that swung Othello's decision. Iago now has the motive to ruin all three.

Iago plays on Othello's jealousy to further his own plan. He wreaks his revenge not only on Othello, but also on Desdemona and Cassio. He exploits Desdemona's youthful naivety, and the character flaws in Othello and Cassio.

Key victims

Othello
He is ready to believe the words of his trusted comrade Iago. He is already suspicious and insecure by nature.

Desdemona
She is loyal to her husband, but Iago exploits her youth to drive Othello mad with jealousy.

Cassio
Young and handsome, with an eye for women, he has all the qualities Iago needs to make Othello jealous of him.

——— Control   ■■■■■ Jealousy   ---- Naivety   ······· Lechery

Damnation

What does it mean to be damned? And what constitutes a damnable sin? These are questions that Shakespeare has his characters struggle with throughout the action of the play.

Othello frequently uses the word "damn" in reference to Desdemona, and even tells her that she is "double-damned" (4.2.38) by her deceit. Damnation is associated with hellfire and eternal punishment, which is suited to the Catholic characters of the play. Because of the dishonour and sinfulness of Desdemona's alleged infidelity, Othello considers it his duty to murder her "else she'll betray more men" (5.2.6). Her infidelity is what he calls "the cause" that spurs him on to seek her death. He requests that she pray so that he can preserve her immortal soul despite killing her body. This suggests that the murder is, in Othello's mind at least, an honour killing rather than a vengeful killing.

Honour is a word that creeps into the world of the characters. How can Othello be honourable if he is also a murderer? When the truth is eventually known to Othello, he calls for his own damnation, claiming that Desdemona is a "heavenly sight" while he is a "cursèd, cursèd slave" (5.2.283). The question on everyone's lips at the close of the play relates to Iago. What will happen to him now? Othello accuses him of being a "demi-devil" (5.2.307) and Lodovico calls him a "hellish villain" (5.2.378). Iago might have survived this tragedy, but his torment will begin now, first through earthly torture and then in everlasting hellfire. Survival may be his punishment.

The handkerchief

Othello's handkerchief, which is embroidered with strawberries, is a key instrument of his marital downfall. By attaching emotional significance to this small object, Othello makes himself vulnerable to Iago's scheming, and readily accepts the theory that Desdemona handed over this treasured gift to her "lover". The fact that Desdemona lies about misplacing it affirms her husband's suspicions about her infidelity.

This tiny prop comes to represent the tension and mistrust in Othello and Desdemona's marriage. So weighted is this object that, in 1693, the historian Thomas Rymer argued that the play ought to be called "The Tragedy of the Handkerchief". ∎

A MAN MORE SINNED AGAINST THAN SINNING
KING LEAR (1605–1606)

King Lear renounces his throne and divides the kingdom among his three daughters. He asks each to profess her love for him, so that he may decide who will gain the larger share. Goneril and Regan play along, but Cordelia refuses to flatter. She is banished, along with the Earl of Kent. The King of France offers marriage to Cordelia, and they depart for France. Kent adopts the disguise of the servant Caius.

Shortly after Cordelia's banishment, the Earl of Gloucester is estranged from his elder son, Edgar. In a plot contrived by the illegitimate Edmond to steal his brother Edgar's inheritance, Gloucester is tricked into thinking that Edgar seeks to kill him and seize his land. Edgar is pursued by the law, but disguises himself as the beggar Poor Tom.

Lear takes up residence at the court of his eldest daughter, Goneril, and her husband, Albany, but she accuses her father of rowdy behaviour. Lear curses her with barrenness and leaves for Regan's house, only to find that she and her husband, Cornwall, are away from home, and that they have put Kent in the stocks. After a furious confrontation with both daughters, Lear rushes into a thunderstorm. Deranged with fury and grief, he and his Fool befriend Poor Tom.

Goneril and Regan plot to have their father killed, but Gloucester has the king secretly conveyed to safety at Dover, in the knowledge that Cordelia is returning with a French army to avenge her father. When Gloucester's actions are discovered, he has both his eyes plucked out by Cornwall (who is fatally wounded by his own servant). Edgar leads the blinded Gloucester to what he pretends to be the edge of Dover Cliff so that he may end his life. When Gloucester falls forward onto level ground, Edgar convinces him that he has miraculously survived the jump.

Cordelia takes Lear into her protection. A battle ensues. Lear and Cordelia are defeated and imprisoned. Disguised as a knight, Edgar challenges Edmond to single combat. When Edmond is fatally wounded, Edgar reveals his identity. The jealousy between Goneril and Regan over Edmond erupts into murder and suicide – Goneril poisons her sister, and then stabs herself. Edmond urges Albany to rescue Lear and Cordelia, but it is too late. Lear enters, carrying the dead Cordelia in his arms. Broken with grief, the King slips back into madness, failing to recognize Kent when he finally reveals his true identity. Just at the moment when Lear thinks that Cordelia might still be alive, he dies. Albany offers to divide the kingdom between Kent and Edgar, but Kent says that he will follow his master, leaving the crown to Edgar. ∎

IN CONTEXT

THEMES
Love, betrayal, bereavement, and death

SETTING
Ancient Britain, approximately 800 BCE

SOURCES
12th century Geoffrey of Monmouth's *Historia Regum Britanniae (History of British Kings).*

1587 Raphael Holinshed's *Chronicles of England, Scotland, and Ireland.*

While *King Lear* is often considered the height of Shakespeare's achievement in tragedy, it also undermines many of the assumptions upon which his other tragedies were built. It lays waste to our ideals, producing a vision of nihilistic despair not unlike the plays of 20th-century Irish playwright Samuel Beckett. In this way, *King Lear* is both ancient (it is set in 800 BCE) and remarkably modern.

From the start, Shakespeare conceived of Lear in a mould that is significantly different from his other tragic heroes. Where

the sources give the King's age as in his sixties, Shakespeare emphasizes Lear's decrepitude, insisting that he is more than 80 years of age and ready to "crawl toward death" (1.1.41). Modern productions often cast a significantly younger actor in the role. In 2014, a 53-year-old Simon Russell Beale played Lear as a dangerously volatile figure, tyrannizing his daughters in the initial love test, and later stabbing the Fool to death in a frenzied attack. But neither in this production nor in the play as written is there any sense of how Lear's physical strength or rhetorical power might ever have served his subjects' interests, or indeed how he might once have inspired admiration and love. Goneril and Regan suggest that his lack of judgment in banishing Cordelia is not a single tragic error, associated with "the infirmity of his age", but a personality trait: "he hath ever but slenderly known himself" (1.1.292–293). Without any sense of Lear's former greatness, his descent into madness loses something of the grandeur and sense of waste that it might have possessed in another Shakespearean tragedy. »

Lear divides his kingdom between his three daughters. In this production at the Bad Hersfeld Festival, Germany (2012), Volker Lechtenbrink plays Lear and Kristin Hoelck is Cordelia.

Lear is accompanied by his Fool during the storm, illustrated here by Scottish artist William Dyce (1806–64). The Fool is the only character allowed to speak the truth to the king.

Lear as tragic hero

Lear's description of himself as "a man / More sinned against than sinning" (3.2.59–60) hints at his passivity in the play. By comparison with Edmond, who plots his father's death and orders the deaths of Lear and Cordelia, Goneril, who will use her lover to kill her husband and who poisons her sister, and Cornwall, who plucks out Gloucester's eyes, Lear's acts of banishment (though they constitute a kind of social death) will come to seem relatively mild. Throughout acts three and four, when Hamlet or Macbeth are acting furiously to bring about their own destruction, Lear exists on the margins of the plot, in the liminal space of the heath. In his mental confusion, he identifies the behaviour of a mad beggar as the pattern for his own paternal betrayal, and muses on the dangers of female sexuality and the hypocrisy of the powerful. In this respect, *King Lear* is a remarkably philosophical tragedy, in which the plot pauses whenever it encounters the protagonist. Nothing that Lear does after the opening scene has any real impact on the action.

> 66 I have no way, and therefore want no eyes. I stumbled when I saw
> **Earl of Gloucester**
> Act 4, Scene 1 99

Sins of the father

So what "sins" might Lear be blamed for in that opening scene? For Shakespeare's audience, his act of "unburdening" himself by giving up his throne would have been deeply suspect. In a society with no expectation of retirement, the voluntary renunciation of power would have seemed to undermine the respect for age and male authority that was so deeply embedded in the culture. Kingship was also believed to be divinely appointed – hence it was an act of sacrilege to attempt to sever king from crown. Also potentially damaging is Lear's decision to divide the kingdom. Myths abounded about the catastrophic consequences of such division, leading to bloody civil war and fratricide, and Shakespeare was writing during the reign of James I, a king seeking to strengthen ties between his two hostile kingdoms, England and Scotland.

Ultimately, however, it is Lear's disavowal of Cordelia that brings the King to his knees. Lear estranges himself from the one daughter whose love and reverence will be unaffected by his loss of status, unlike Goneril and Regan whose respect for their father exists only while he has power. If the kingdom had been divided in three, Cordelia might have served as a buffer between her two elder and ambitious sisters. Furthermore, banishment results in her becoming Queen of France, which leads her to seek to depose the rightful rulers of Britain with French troops. Though Shakespeare makes clear that her motive is "love, dear love, and our aged father's right" (4.3.28) rather than ambition, the fact remains that Lear has made his kingdom vulnerable. It can certainly be argued that Lear's actions in the first scene set a destructive precedent. By failing to value the genuine love of Cordelia over the insincere flattery of her sisters, Lear encourages a character like Edmond to pursue his inheritance by faking filial love, and by slandering his brother. As though Lear's blindness were infectious, Gloucester fails to see through the deception and fatally places his trust in the wrong son. But in a larger sense, the tragedy sees suffering as something that exists outside any simple process of cause and effect, and as a fundamental part of the human condition. To be "a man / More sinned against than sinning" is not some kind of cosmic injustice, but the norm. »

The blind Gloucester (right, Geoffrey Freshwater) meets with the now-mad Lear (left, Greg Hicks). Without his sight, Gloucester finally realizes his previous blindness toward Edmond.

Paul Scofield

In a 2004 poll of RSC actors, Paul Scofield's Lear was voted the greatest Shakespearean performance of all time. Then aged 40, Scofield appeared in Peter Brook's 1962 staging of *King Lear*. Critic Kenneth Tynan described Brook's production as revolutionary in its depiction of Lear not as "the booming, righteously indignant Titan of old, but an edgy, capricious old man, intensely difficult to live with." Scofield's Lear was a very human depiction of the king, for whom our pity is not automatically to be granted.

In 1971, Scofield played Lear in Brook's film adaptation of the play, and in 2002, having himself reached the age of 80, he starred in an acclaimed radio version.

Lear was one of many Shakespearean roles that Scofield took on in a career that spanned 65 years. He appeared infrequently on screen, despite many approaches from Hollywood, preferring the relative anonymity of the stage and radio, but won an Academy Award for his portrayal of Sir Thomas More in the 1966 film *A Man for All Seasons*.

The basest beggar

Where *Hamlet* only pretends to consider "What a piece of work is a man", *King Lear* offers a profound meditation on this subject, and its conclusions are as melancholy as Hamlet might have wished them. Blinded Gloucester describes the mad Lear as a "ruined piece of nature", and when he tries to kiss Lear's hand, the King advises: "Here, wipe it first; it smells of mortality" (4.5.128–130). The play relentlessly confronts man's physical needs. Lear's madness coincides with the assault upon his body of extreme cold, wind, and rain. It is no coincidence that his wits are only restored once he has been brought into shelter, given fresh clothes, and allowed to sleep. Earlier on in the play, Lear had appeared to glimpse the troubling physical similarities that define all men, if they are deprived of the external trappings of class and wealth. When his daughters try to take away his knightly retinue, he counters: "O, reason not the need! Our basest beggars / Are in the poorest thing superfluous. / Allow not nature more than nature needs, / Man's life is cheap as beast's." (2.2.438–441).

But King Lear at this point has no idea what the life of the basest beggar might be, and it is with a kind of redemptive sadism that Shakespeare casts him out into the wilderness to encounter one. Poor Tom represents a misery that Lear has never imagined – a vagrant, tormented by demonic voices, clothed only in a blanket, and drinking from puddles mixed with horse urine. Lear's response, which is to take off his own clothes, signifies his final descent into madness. He now conspires in the destruction of his familial and social identity. But there is also a sense of fellowship in the discovery that in his nakedness he is no more than "such a poor, bare, forked animal, as thou art" (3.4.101–102). In this respect, *King Lear* has often been seen as a socialist play, in that it forces the king to acknowledge his similarity to the lowest social class (even though Edgar is actually an earl's son) and, more importantly, to acknowledge his own responsibility for Poor Tom's condition: "O, I have ta'en / Too little care of this" (3.4.32–33). In a radical challenge to contemporary politics, the play features both a king and an earl calling for a redistribution of wealth, "So distribution should undo excess, / And each man have enough" (4.1.64–65).

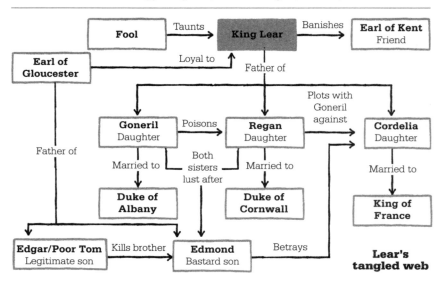

Lear's tangled web

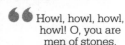

> Howl, howl, howl,
> howl! O, you are
> men of stones.
> **King Lear**
> Act 5, Scene 3

More's the pity

If the play is initially driven by the need to strip man down to his bare essentials, as anticipated by Cordelia's destructive use of the term "Nothing", it then begins to move towards the "something" upon which humanity is founded. This "something" is the capacity to feel pity. The play's most virtuous characters, Edgar and Cordelia, repeatedly tell us of their emotional reaction to other people's suffering. Edgar wonders at both Gloucester and Lear: "O thou side-piercing sight" (4.5.85); "my heart breaks at it" (138); while Cordelia repeatedly voices her pity for the father who wronged her. Both characters also attest to the efficacy of pity, with Edgar being driven to rescue his father from despair, and Cordelia using her tears to gain an army, before using the same restorative drops to bring Lear back to his senses.

By contrast, evil is defined in the play as the absence of pity, which leads in turn to an absence of pitiful action. Goneril and Regan allow Lear to wander on the heath in a thunderstorm, drawing forth language that defines pity as that which separates man from beast. Thus, Cordelia observes, "Mine enemy's dog, though he had bit me, should have stood / That night against my fire" (4.6.30–31).

That the play has limits to its own capacity for pity, however, is something critics have recently pointed out with regard to the treatment of Goneril and Regan. But perhaps the most violent reaction against the play has focused on the way in which its supposedly redemptive experience of suffering, and the value it places on pity, comes to nothing.

When Shakespeare's audience went to see *King Lear*, they were expecting, at worst, to endure the grief of his daughters'

ingratitude and the physical deprivations of his homelessness. Gloucester's blinding was an added turn of the screw, derived from Sir Philip Sidney's prose romance, *The Countess of Pembroke's Arcadia* (1593). However, in all the other versions of the Lear story, including an earlier play *The True Chronicle Historie of King Leir* (c.1594), in which Shakespeare may even have acted, good triumphs over evil in the final battle and Lear is restored to his throne. He dies of old age and is succeeded by Cordelia. Audience reactions must certainly have echoed Kent's sentiments "Is this the promised end?" (5.3.238), when not only do Lear and Cordelia lose the battle, but Cordelia is murdered, causing her father to die of grief.

A problematic end?

Subsequent critics, including Samuel Johnson, put on record their dismay with the play's ending. The 17th-century Poet Laureate Nahum Tate felt compelled to draft a new ending in which Cordelia survives. In Tate's version, a love story develops between Cordelia and Edgar, to whom she is betrothed at the end. It was this version of the tragedy that would be performed for nearly 150 years, to the detriment of Shakespeare's original version.

Tate was partly responding to the fact that much of the structure of *King Lear* is comic. The double plot is a feature of comedy, usually allowing a broader perspective and the exploration of alternative themes – though the similarity of Gloucester's plight to that of Lear only serves to render the play more claustrophobic. The combat between the older and the younger generation, »

> Unaccommodated
> man is no more but
> such a poor, bare,
> forked animal
> as thou art.
> **King Lear**
> Act 3, Scene 4

with the latter attempting to free itself from parental oppression particularly in matters of the heart, is also the stuff of comedy. The movement of exiled characters into a green world where they discover a truer relationship to nature and to their own humanity, before returning to civilization, is also a staple of the pastoral genre. Even the Fool naturally belongs in a play like *As You Like It* rather than a tragedy.

Agony of grief

But these romantic, comic expectations endure only to be smashed to pieces. When Lear enters, carrying dead Cordelia, some fantasy about how the world works is finally destroyed. It is not just the futility of it – after all their suffering, Lear and Gloucester cannot make use of anything they have learned, and are denied the chance to make amends to their children – it is rather that the play confronts the unavoidable destiny of bereavement and death, with no offer of consolation.

At the end of a Shakespearean tragedy, the hero's demise is usually carefully stage-managed, offering him artistic control so that he may leave a final impression of greatness, but Lear dies in the middle of a thought – and not about himself but about Cordelia, whose death is so painful as to be incomprehensible: "Why should a dog, a horse, a rat have life, / And thou no breath

In Jean-François Sivadier's 2007 production, the play was translated into tough, contemporary French. A physical production, its action was as uncompromising as its language.

at all? Thou'lt come no more. / Never, never, never, never, never." (5.3.282–284). Pity is revealed to be something that no one feels enough ("O, you are men of stones" (232)), and that cannot rescue Lear from his agony of grief. No other play by Shakespeare offers such a bleak perspective on the tragic fact of human mortality.

Shakespeare's society was deeply Christian, with a system of religious practices a part of everyday life. Yet no one can comfort Lear, other than to will that he be spared further pain by not feeling. It is in this respect that *King Lear* remains perhaps Shakespeare's most devastating play. ∎

A feminist reading

In 1817, the English literary critic William Hazlitt argued that "that which aggravates the sense of sympathy in the reader, and of uncontrollable anguish in the swol'n heart of Lear, is the petrifying indifference, the cold, calculating, obdurate selfishness of his daughters." Since the late 20th century, however, feminist critics have taken issue with this reading, arguing that the childless Goneril at least has plenty of motivation to act as she does against her father. Lear's curse of sterility upon her in 1.4 has allowed actors to give greater psychological depth to her character, and to make her an object of pity.

Similarly, the incestuous intensity that defines Lear's possessiveness over Cordelia at the start of the play was a theme explored by the US writer Jane Smiley in her novel *A Thousand Acres* (1991). This retells the story from the perspective of Goneril. Ginny (Goneril) suffers flashbacks that reveal how her relationship with her father has been shaped by the sexual abuse she and her sister Rose (Regan) experienced from him in childhood.

THE MIDDLE OF HUMANITY THOU NEVER KNEW'ST, BUT THE EXTREMITY OF BOTH ENDS

TIMON OF ATHENS (1606)

A rtists and merchants gather at Timon's home to present him with gifts and seek his patronage. Timon is well known for his extravagant generosity. A poet at the gathering has written a fable in which a patron like Timon falls from fortune to find himself destitute. Timon receives the poet's work gladly, and pays bail to release one of his friends from prison, but will not accept any favours in return.

The satirist Apemantus tries to warn Timon that his "friends" are simply feeding off his generosity. Flavius, a servant, reveals privately that Timon's wealth has been spent, and that he is running further into debt. Timon remains unperturbed, believing that his friends will come to his financial aid. However, when three of his "friends" are asked to lend money, they all refuse, making elaborate excuses to justify their lack of kindness. Hearing this news, Timon flies into a rage and decides to treat them to a feast. Believing Timon to be wealthy again, his friends are shocked when he serves them stones and warm water and forces them from his home, berating them for their falsity.

Timon leaves Athens for the woods and prays for the city's destruction. A vengeful soldier called Alcibiades enters the woods at the same time, intent upon destroying the city. He has been banished for attempting to save the life of a soldier who has been sentenced to death. When Timon reaches the woods, he digs for roots,

> ❝ That what
> he speaks
> is all in debt,
> he owes
> For every word. ❞
> **Flavius**
> Act 1, Scene 2

but discovers gold, and news soon spreads to Athens that he is rich once again. Hating humankind for the ingratitude he has been shown, Timon rails at his former friends, who now come to seek him (and his gold) in the woods. Timon provides the soldier Alcibiades with money to finance his attack on Athens, and gives money to whores to spread disease among citizens. Both Apemantus and Flavius visit Timon, and the Athenian lord reluctantly acknowledges Flavius's goodness, despite his hatred of humankind. He writes his epitaph and dies by the sea, as Alcibiades enters Athens, spares the city, and promises peace. ∎

IN CONTEXT

THEMES
Love, pride, wealth, vanity, hate, revenge, misanthropy

SETTING
Athens and woods outside the city

SOURCES
c.100 CE Plutarch's *Lives of the Noble Grecians and Romans*.

1566 William Painter's *Palace of Pleasure*.

1602 An anonymous play called *Timon*.

 Th'unkindest beast more kinder than mankind.
Timon
Act 4, Scene 1

Timon is perhaps Shakespeare's most extreme characterization. He swings from being a lover of humankind to hating all of humanity. Timon's companion, the satirist Apemantus, finds it remarkably straightforward to sum up the Athenian lord's experience of life: "The middle of humanity thou never knewest, but the extremity of both ends" (4.3.302–303). Apemantus witnesses Timon's transformation from philanthropist to misanthropist, and provides a satirical commentary on the transition. At first, Apemantus watches as Timon showers the visitors to his home with lavish gifts and banquets, but then sees him hurling stones and gold at the people he had once held so dear.

In choosing to dramatize a life story that had previously been alluded to in the works of Plato, Aristophanes, Lucian, and Plutarch, Shakespeare created a play that focused upon man's relationship with "Yellow, glittering, precious gold" (4.3.26). As a generous gift-giver, Timon is never short of "friends" – "Methinks I could deal kingdoms to my friends, / And ne'er be weary" (1.2.220–221). But once Timon's debts are revealed, none of his friends is prepared to show him the same generosity of spirit.

Blindness and vanity

Timon's story is not simply a tale of riches to rags. It is true to say that the play's structure is schematic, dividing into two contrasting

parts, but Shakespeare's presentation of Timon himself is far from simplistic. The faithful steward Flavius reveals early in the play that Timon's coffers are already empty, and that he "owes" (1.2.198) for every word he speaks. Timon's extreme generosity is puzzling. On the one hand, he makes caring pronouncements, arguing that, "'Tis not enough to help the feeble up / But to support him after" (1.1.109–110). However, he also declares that "there's none / Can truly say he gives if he receives" (1.2.9–10). How can Timon's guests ever repay his generosity if he will not let them do so? Flavius suggests that Timon's "worst sin is he does too much good" (4.2.39), but Apemantus is keenly aware of the glass-faced flatterers who circle around Timon like vultures, and is frustrated by his blindness (and vanity): "It grieves me to see so many dip their meat in one man's blood; and all the madness is, he cheers them up, too" (1.2.39–41).

Retreat from humanity

Having learned that his "fortunes 'mong his friends can sink" (2.2.227), Timon turns his back on society and heads for the woods, where he concludes he will find "Th'unkindest beast more kinder than mankind" (4.1.36). Like King Lear, Timon discards his clothes, in an attempt to be

Here lie I, Timon, who alive
All living men did hate.
Pass by and curse thy fill, but pass
And stay not here thy gait.
Timon's epitaph
Act 5, Scene 5

free from the "disease" of false friendship and sugar-tongued sycophancy. Once outside the Athenian walls, Timon announces that he will bear nothing but nakedness from this detestable town. As a cursing misanthrope, Timon grows in lyrical prowess, spitting forth condemnatory verse, shaped to shock: "This yellow slave / Will knit and break religions, bless th'accursed, / Make the hoar leprosy adored, place thieves, / And give them title, knee, and approbation / With senators on the bench. This is it / That makes the wappered widow wed again. / She whom the spittle-house and ulcerous sores / Would cast the gorge at, this embalms and spices / To th' April day again" (4.3.34–42).

Entrenched firmly at the other extreme of humanity, Timon's pronouncements are as savage and bilious as they had once been naive but well meaning. His hymns to hatred possess a strange music that is both hypnotic and somewhat overwhelming. Having looked to the gods and the mercenary soldier Alcibiades to wreak vengeance on Athens, Timon looks forward only to his own death: "My long sickness / Of health and living now begins to mend, / And nothing brings me all things" (5.2.71–73). Rather than remaining in a "dream of friendship", Timon prefers to rail through his "sickness". He dies at peace with himself, although still at war with humankind.

Few Shakespearean characters embody a nihilistic vision with the same commitment as Timon. This is one of Shakespeare's longest roles, and it provides actors with a challenge: to avoid presenting "the middle of humanity" and concentrate on capturing the "extremity of both ends" while retaining psychological realism for audiences. ∎

Timon the banker

A 2012 production at the National Theatre in London, set *Timon of Athens* in the financial district during the credit crunch. The action is imagined as a meltdown among the financial elite, played out to a backdrop of anti-capitalist protest. Timon's debts are a "liquidity crisis."

Timon, played by British actor Simon Russell Beale, is a vain philanthropist, who is fawned upon while his stock is high. He is a power player in a world where friendship is a commodity with a cash value. This production exemplified Karl Marx's characterization of the play as about the power of money. Timon's scorn is directed toward today's elite: "Your solemn masters are large-handed robbers and filch by law."

When Shakespeare wrote the play, England was going through a political crisis, and Guy Fawkes had recently been executed for his part in the Gunpowder Plot. In Hytner's production, protesters wear the Guy Fawkes masks popularized by the Internet-based Anonymous activist movement, and the play feels as relevant as ever.

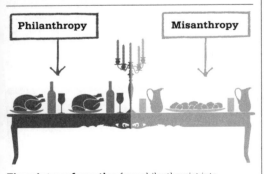

Timon's transformation from philanthropist into misanthropist marks the turning point in the play. Feast becomes famine as food and wine are turned into stones and water.

BLOOD WILL HAVE BLOOD
MACBETH (1606)

Three witches assemble on a heath for an encounter with Macbeth. Returning from victory on the battlefield Macbeth and Banquo meet these "weird sisters," who prophesy that Macbeth will become king and that Banquo's heirs will reign thereafter. Soon after, Macbeth receives word that he has been made Thane (clan chief) of Cawdor, which leads him to give credence to the witches' foresight. He shares his news with his wife, and she begins to plot to murder King Duncan so that Macbeth can become king.

News arrives that Duncan will visit the Macbeths' castle, and Lady Macbeth persuades her husband to kill him that night. She lays plans to drug the king's guards, so that Macbeth may slip into the king's chamber. As he makes his way there Macbeth sees a vision of a floating dagger signalling the way. Having murdered the king, Macbeth returns to his wife with the bloody daggers still in his hands. Terrified that the murder has woken other sleepers, Macbeth begins to panic until his wife calms him. As the couple leaves to wash themselves of the king's blood, a knocking is heard at the gate. The porter ushers in Macduff, who finds the king's body and raises the alarm. Macbeth murders the guards in case they wake. On hearing of their father's murder, the king's sons, Malcolm and Donalbain, leave for England.

Macbeth becomes king, although Banquo harbors secret fears that he murdered King Duncan. Fearing Banquo's suspicions,

Macbeth arranges his murder, but Banquo's son Fleance escapes the killers. Macbeth is terrified when Banquo's ghost appears at a banquet he holds that evening. Lady Macbeth tries to distract their dinner guests from her husband's strange behaviour, especially when he addresses an empty chair.

Macbeth returns to find the witches and is told that his throne is secure until Birnam Wood marches toward Dunsinane. He feels further reassured when told that he cannot be killed by anyone born of woman. On hearing that Macduff has traveled to England to persuade Malcolm to lead a rebel army, Macbeth orders the murder of Macduff's wife and children. This terrible news reaches Macduff in England and strengthens his resolve to be revenged.

Lady Macbeth's guilt for Duncan's death leaks out when she is heard speaking of the murder in her sleep. While Macbeth believes that he can see a forest walking toward his castle, he hears that his wife has died. The moving wood is in fact an army carrying the branches of trees. In the battle that ensues, Macduff reveals that he was ripped from his mother's womb; the prophecy is complete, and Macbeth is killed. ∎

IN CONTEXT

THEMES
Ambition, kingship, fate, the supernatural, betrayal

SETTING
Scotland and England

SOURCES
1587 Raphael Holinshed's *Chronicles* describes the reigns of King Duncan and Macbeth and features a woodcut illustration of the weird sisters.

The Macbeths risk everything to become king and queen of Scotland. In murdering King Duncan they are committing the greatest of sins: regicide. The couple are fully aware that their desire for the crown is criminal and diabolical, and yet they resolve upon this course of action that will bring calamity to them both. Like Richard III, the Macbeths discover to their despair that gaining the throne will not bring them contentment. Macbeth is convinced that he will only rest easy once he knows that he is safely in power: "To be thus is nothing / But to be safely thus" (3.1.49–50). To be "safely thus" would mean that there are no contenders for the throne

Laurence Olivier's *Macbeth* was acclaimed for its "dazzling darkness" in 1955. The glamorous production had Olivier's wife, the film actress Vivien Leigh, as a goading Lady Macbeth.

left alive. The Macbeths find themselves trapped in a cycle of violence, haunted by their deed and the "horrible imaginings" (1.3.137) that ensue: "Blood will have blood" (3.4.121). The killing must continue. »

King James I

Macbeth was written during the reign of James I. When James took to the throne in 1603, he became the patron of

Shakespeare's acting company, honoring them with the title of the King's Men. Shakespeare wrote plays for audiences in London's playhouses, but he was also writing to entertain his king. In the tale of Macbeth, Shakespeare is playing toward some of the king's interests. James I of England had previously sat on the Scottish throne as James VI of Scotland, so the play's Scottish setting would have had royal appeal. James also believed that he was a direct

descendant of Banquo, and Shakespeare's presentation of this figure is duly honorable. He may also have been pandering to one of the king's particular concerns: witchcraft. The king had published a treatise on the subject in 1597 called *Daemonologie*, a fact that would not have gone unnoticed by the playwright. Although *Macbeth's* dramatic ingredients would have entertained the king, they would of course have appealed to a much broader public as well.

English actress Ellen Terry played Lady Macbeth in London, in 1888. Society portraitist John Singer Sargent was in the audience and painted her in a dress made of iridescent beetle wings.

Macbeth is literally and symbolically a dark play. About two-thirds of it takes place at night, lending the drama an eerie intensity. Ghosts walk at night; deadly deeds are committed under the cover of darkness; and night-time brings nightmares for those with a guilty conscience. The audience's relationship with Macbeth also darkens scene by scene as he falls from being a trusted warrior to becoming a Machiavellian murderer.

Traces of humanity are gradually stamped out as the drama progresses. Lady Macbeth calls upon "spirits / That tend on mortal thoughts" (1.5.39–40) to "unsex" her, filling her with "direst cruelty" (1.5.42). In order to fulfil her murderous ambition, she must in effect transform herself into a merciless monster. Shakespeare draws attention to her womanliness in order to emphasise her fierce rejection of her own femininity. Fearing that her husband is "too full o'th' milk of human kindness" (1.5.16), she encourages him to harden his heart and place ambition above consideration for others: "I have given suck, and know / How tender 'tis to love the babe that milks me. / I would, while it was smiling in my face, / Have plucked my nipple from his boneless gums / And dashed the brains out, had I so sworn / As you have done to this." (1.7.54–59).

As the couple settle upon their homicidal plan, their dependency upon one another strengthens, but so, too, does their sense of entrapment and claustrophobia. The couple share a murderous secret that simply cannot be disclosed. The secret ultimately devours them both and serves to put distance between them.

Taunted to murder

Macbeth does not enter blindly into the murder of Duncan, though he does show some unwillingness to commit. Shakespeare complicates our relationship with Macbeth by voicing the character's reluctance to go through with the crime. Having listened to his wife's reaction to the witches' prophecy that he "shalt be king hereafter" (1.3.48), he states firmly that "We will proceed no further in this business" (1.7.31). For a moment it looks as though Macbeth will resist temptation and conquer his "Vaulting ambition" (1.7.27). His wife's stinging taunts, however, make him think again. Lady Macbeth launches into a targeted emotional assault that offends, humiliates, and shocks her husband in equal measure: "Was the hope drunk / Wherein you dressed yourself? Hath it slept since? / And wakes it now to look so green and pale / At what it did so freely? From this time / Such I account thy love. Art thou afeard / To be the same in thine own act and valour / As thou art in desire? Wouldst thou have that / Which thou esteem'st the ornament of life, / And live a coward in thine own esteem, / Letting 'I dare not' wait upon 'I would', / Like the poor cat i'th' adage?" (1.7.35–44).

In the space of just 10 lines, Lady Macbeth questions her husband's masculinity, honour, ambition, courage, and love for her. Macbeth's male pride overpowers his questioning mind, resulting in the defensive riposte "I dare do all that may become a man" (1.7.46). How much did Macbeth actually want the crown for himself, and to what extent does he carry out his part in the murder to confirm and

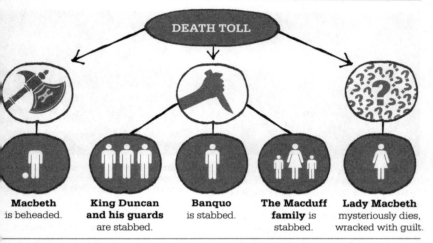

DEATH TOLL

Macbeth
is beheaded.

**King Duncan
and his guards**
are stabbed.

Banquo
is stabbed.

**The Macduff
family** is
stabbed.

Lady Macbeth
mysteriously dies,
wracked with guilt.

maintain his understanding of his own manhood? Typically, Shakespeare does not settle upon a straightforward answer. The audience's responses to Macbeth's actions are further complicated by the role played by the witches throughout the drama. Did Macbeth have a choice? Was his fate always to murder Duncan and become king himself?

Macbeth's "heat-oppressèd brain" (2.1.39) comes to haunt him as much as the witches' prophecies. Paranoia practically paralyses Macbeth, and his imagination proves a constant torment. As he prepares to murder Duncan, he sees a floating dagger sign-posting his way to the king's bedchamber.

Has this dagger been conjured by the weird sisters? Or is it merely, as Macbeth suspects, a "dagger of the mind" engendered through fear and his reluctance to act upon his ambitions? His imagination will not be suppressed. Having murdered the king, Macbeth imagines that he will never sleep again: "Methought I heard a voice cry 'Sleep no more, / Macbeth does murder sleep' – the innocent sleep, / Sleep that knits up the ravelled sleave of care, / The death of each day's life, sore labour's bath, / Balm of hurt minds, great nature's second course, / Chief nourisher in life's feast" (2.2.33–38).

Infected minds

The desire to unburden one's self of problems by telling others is all too human. Shakespeare skilfully depicts the breakdown of a marriage under stress, which leaves Lady Macbeth vulnerable psychologically. Lacking her husband's attention, she ruinously divests herself of her troubles while speaking in her sleep:" Out, damned spot; out, I say. One, two, – why, then 'tis time to do't. Hell is murky. Fie, my lord, fie, a soldier and afeard? What need we fear who knows it when none can call our power to account? Yet who would have thought the old man to have had so much blood in him?" (5.1.33–38).

As the Doctor diagnoses, "infected minds / To their deaf pillows will discharge their secrets" (5.1.69–70). Lady Macbeth's disclosure puts her own life and her husband's at risk. Shakespeare draws a stark contrast between his initial portrait of Lady Macbeth and her final depiction. While she was once strong and controlling, she becomes a pitiful shadow of her former self. Her deadly secret has drained the life from her, and she is left to obsess about death. Her own will follow soon enough.

At moments of extreme crisis or violence, Shakespeare has Macbeth voice some of the playwright's most poetic reflections upon the nature of existence itself. The murder of Duncan prompts thoughts on the soothing qualities of sleep, while Lady Macbeth's »

death encourages a meditation upon the transitory nature of life: "Out, out, brief candle. / Life's but a walking shadow, a poor player / That struts and frets his hour upon the stage, / And then is heard no more. It is a tale / Told by an idiot, full of sound and fury, / Signifying nothing." (5.5.22–27).

Banquo's ghost
Having killed the king, Macbeth faces a future of "restless ecstasy" (3.2.24). His mind is "full of scorpions" (3.2.37) and his every thought is about the fact that he has "scorched the snake, not killed it" (3.2.15). While Banquo lives, Macbeth fears exposure. He is also angered by the witches' prophecy that Banquo's sons will reign after him. Banquo certainly suspects Macbeth of villainy: "Thou hast it now: King, Cawdor, Glamis, all / As the weird women promised; and I fear / Thou played'st most foully for't." (3.1.1–3).Macbeth's decision to have his friend murdered is taken alone; he is keen that his wife "Be innocent of the knowledge" (3.2.46). Banquo's murder creates a rift between husband and wife, and as a result produces one of the play's most thrilling moments: the appearance of Banquo's ghost.

Bloody apparition
As Macbeth attempts to join his guests at the banquet table he cannot see a chair reserved for himself. Though his guests motion towards an empty seat the king recoils in horror and begins to address Banquo's ghostly figure, visible only to himself: "Never shake / Thy gory locks at me" (3.4.49–50). The king's behaviour is sufficiently alarming that it prompts his wife

The witches become a chorus in Guiseppe Verdi's opera *Macbeth*. Here, the San Francisco Opera company performs a production in modern dress in 2007.

to placate the bewildered and discomfited diners: "The fit is momentary. Upon a thought / He will again be well. If much you note him / You shall offend him, and extend his passion. / Feed, and regard him not." (3.4.52–57).

In performance this moment can be played to emphasise the black humour. If the king's "fit" is particularly dramatic then it can prove impossible for the diners to "regard him not". As the king's reactions to the ghost grow more extreme, Lady Macbeth's need to take control of the situation becomes pressing. She takes her husband aside and tries to reason with him, Macbeth's mind is, obsessed with thoughts of blood: "Blood hath been shed ere now, i'th' olden time, / Ere human statute purged the gentle weal; / Ay, and since, too, murders have been performed / Too terrible for the ear. The time has been / That, when the brains were out, the man would die, / And there an end. But now they rise again / With twenty mortal murders on their crowns, / And push us from our stools. This is more strange / Than such a murder is." (3.4.74–82).

Shakespeare is retracing here the dynamic between the Macbeths that he created just after the murder of Duncan. Having killed the king, Macbeth froze with bloody daggers in hand as a wave of nervous thoughts swamped his mind. Fortunately for the Macbeths they were in private, and Lady Macbeth had been able to shake her husband from his terrifying thoughts.

Macbeth's strange behaviour at the banquet is played out in front of the puzzled guests. When the ghost appears before him for a second time, he cannot contain his horror: "It will have blood, they say. Blood will have blood. / Stones have been known to move, and trees to speak, / Augurs and understood relations have / By maggot-pies and choughs and rooks brought forth / The secret'st man of blood." (3.4.121–125).

End of the bloodbath

By the play's close Macbeth's world has come crashing down, and he finds little left in life to delight him: "I have lived long enough" (5.3.24). The witches' improbable prophecies all come to fruition, and Macbeth leaves the stage fighting despite the odds being against him: "Though Birnam Wood be come to Dunsinane, / And thou opposed being of no woman born, / Yet I will try the last. "(5.10.30–32).

It is only through the deaths of this "dread butcher and his fiend-like queen" (5.11.35) that the blood-letting can be brought to a close. "The time is free" (5.11.21), says Macduff, and he hails the new king Malcolm, who can build a future for Scotland, free from tyranny. ■

The witches

In Shakespeare's time, witchcraft was a serious matter. King James himself was a judge in the North Berwick witch trials of 1590–92, at which 70 people were tried and many burned at the stake; witch trials would be held in England and Scotland until the 18th century.

Shakespeare's audience would have known of such events. The presence of the witches in *Macbeth* is intended to be unsettling, and their appearance, as described by Banquo, emphasizes their otherworldliness: "What are these, / So withered, and so wild in their attire, / That look not like th'inhabitants o'th'earth / And yet are on't?" (1.3.37–40).

Shakespeare's description encourages spectators to use their imaginations to see more than is before their eyes – to see supernatural and hideous figures. He also creates an image that troubles both the audience's and Macbeth's minds. Modern-day audiences tend to see Macbeth's psychological state as more important than the witches' curses as a driver of the action.

Dagger – Macbeth's murderous intent.

Heart – the intense relationship between Macbeth and his wife.

Crown – Macbeth's determined ambition.

Sword – Macbeth's prowess as a warrior.

Shakespeare dramatically combines a warrior's courage as he wields the sword, "vaulting ambition" in seeking the crown, the bond of hearts with Lady Macbeth, an evil intent in the form of a dagger, and the power of prophecy to bring Macbeth to commit murder, several times over.

AGE CANNOT WITHER HER NOR CUSTOM STALE HER INFINITE VARIETY
ANTONY AND CLEOPATRA (1606)

Roman soldiers are disgusted with their general, Mark Antony, who has fallen for the charms of the Egyptian queen, Cleopatra. They fear that this love affair has transformed one of the world's most powerful men into a dishonourable fool. When Antony hears that his wife Fulvia has died, he recognizes that he must return to Rome to help Caesar defeat Sextus Pompey. Cleopatra taunts Antony about his love for her; she is jealous of other women, and of Antony's duty to Rome.

Antony returns to Rome while Cleopatra seeks comfort from her companions. Antony meets with Caesar's displeasure on his return. He is criticized for ignoring his responsibilities as a leader, and is encouraged to marry Caesar's sister Octavia, as a sign of his commitment to Rome. Antony agrees to the political marriage. When Cleopatra hears of Antony's marriage she is enraged.

Caesar and Antony meet with the rebellious Sextus Pompey on his boat to prevent civil war. Peace is agreed, although one of Pompey's soldiers tries to persuade his master to murder his guests. Pompey ignores this advice, and spends the evening drinking with his former enemies. Enobarbus says that Antony's allegiance to Cleopatra will remain strong, despite his political reunion with Caesar.

Antony returns to Egypt without his new bride. Caesar is angered by Antony's neglect of Octavia and declares war. Antony's soldiers argue that they should fight Caesar on land, but Cleopatra persuades him to fight at sea.

 Give me some music – music, moody food Of us that trade in love.
Cleopatra
Act 2, Scene 5

She flees the battle, and is followed closely by Antony, bringing dishonour to his soldiers and his own reputation.

Antony's soldiers begin to lose faith in their general, and his loyal companion Enobarbus defects to Caesar's side. Antony is defeated for a second time and blames Cleopatra for the loss. Fearing for her safety, she sends Antony news that she has died, not anticipating that Antony will respond by seeking to commit suicide himself. He fails to kill himself, and his soldier Eros takes his own life rather than aid his master's death. News arrives that Cleopatra had feigned her death and is sheltering in a monument. Antony asks to be taken to her and warns her against Caesar before he dies.

Cleopatra discovers Caesar's plan to parade her through Rome. She determines to take her own life, and calls for a poisonous snake to be brought to her. She dresses in her majestic robes before placing the snake to her breast, and dies in the company of one of her maids. Caesar arrives to find Cleopatra dead, and orders that she and Antony be buried together. ■

IN CONTEXT

THEMES
Love, power, duty, honor, jealousy, betrayal, death, desire

SETTING
Rome, Alexandria, Athens

SOURCES
1579 Sir Thomas North's translation of Plutarch's *Lives of the Noble Greeks and Romans*. The play compresses events that took place over the space of a decade. Enobarbus speaks words taken directly from the source in his description of Cleopatra sat on her barge.

 I have offended reputation;
A most unnoble swerving.
Antony
Act 3, Scene 11

A ntony and Cleopatra are not young "star-crossed lovers" like Romeo and Juliet. These are mature adults, both past their "salad days" (1.5.72). Antony is married to Fulvia, and yet he is drawn to spending time with his "Egyptian dish" (2.6.126) away from his wife in Rome: 'I'th East my pleasure lies" (2.3.38). Though she is unmarried, Cleopatra has also loved before: "She made great Caesar lay his sword to bed. / He ploughed her, and she cropped." (2.2.234–235). The intensity of Antony and Cleopatra's passion for one another can be overwhelming. Shakespeare expresses their hunger, desire, and dependency upon each other in some of the most beautiful and heightened verse to be found anywhere in the Shakespearean canon. "Age cannot wither" either of them, for in one another's eyes, they are like gods. Even in death, Antony will remain like Mars to Cleopatra; following his suicide she declares that "there is nothing left remarkable / Beneath the visiting Moon" (4.16.69–70). However, their relationship is far from idyllic. As a pair, they are heroic, majestic, and superhuman, but they are also mean, monstrous, cowardly, and drunken. Shakespeare presents these characters, individually and as a pair, in a rich and memorable manner – audiences are shown the good, the bad, and the ugly.

Cleopatra the seductress

Cleopatra is one of Shakespeare's greatest dramatic creations. She can also prove for some people one of his most exhausting and irritating characterizations. Shakespeare went to great lengths to impress upon his audience Cleopatra's charm and vitality. We hear throughout the play of how men have fallen for her charms, and even the priggish Roman, Octavius Caesar, notes that in death she looks "As she would catch another Antony" (5.2.341). Men see her as a powerful seductress, a witch even, who holds them under her spell. She is first described in derogatory terms; she is, according to two of Antony's soldiers, a lusty "strumpet" and "gypsy". Angered by their general's newfound domesticity, the soldiers speak of a woman who can transform a former "pillar of the world" (1.1.12) into a "strumpet's fool" (1.1.13). For them, her allure is intoxicating and dangerous, destroying Antony's sense of duty and commitment to Rome. Other hardened soldiers such as Enobarbus find themselves reaching for the finest poetic »

Husband and wife Laurence Olivier and Vivien Leigh took on the title roles in a 1951 production. Olivier's Antony was reckless, while Leigh played the queen as sensuous yet regally aloof.

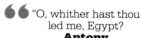

> 66 "O, whither hast thou
> led me, Egypt?
> **Antony**
> Act 3, Scene 11 99

descriptions to communicate her appeal to those who have not been in her presence: "Age cannot wither her, nor custom stale / Her infinite variety. Other women cloy / The appetites they feed, but she makes hungry / Where most she satisfies. For vilest things / Become themselves in her, that the holy priests / Bless her when she is riggish." (2.2.241–246).

Enobarbus's words serve in some respects to justify Antony's obsession with this "lass unparalleled" (5.2.310). How could anyone fail to be intrigued by a woman who encompasses such infinite variety of mood and behaviour? It would seem that everyone, from priests to world leaders, finds something extraordinary about Cleopatra. She does not need to be in a scene, or even on the stage to create a lasting impression. From memory, Enobarbus conjures her stately appearance in one of the play's most richly poetic passages:

"The barge she sat in, like a burnished throne / Burned on the water. The poop was beaten gold; / Purple the sails, and so perfuméd that / The winds were love-sick with them. The oars were silver, / Which to the tune of flutes kept stroke, and made / The water which they beat to follow faster, / As amorous of their strokes. For her own person, / It beggared all description. She did lie / In her pavilion – cloth of gold, of tissue – O'er-picturing that Venus where we see / The fancy outwork nature. On each side her / Stood pretty dimpled boys, like smiling Cupids, / With divers-coloured fans whose wind did seem / To glow the delicate cheeks which they did cool, / And what they undid did" (2.2.198–212).

Enobarbus's speech serves like a hymn to Cleopatra. The imagery must have wooed Shakespeare himself, for this speech owes much to Shakespeare's source, Thomas North's 1579 translation of Plutarch's *Lives of the Noble Grecians and Romans*. Thomas North describes among other things, "the sails of purple", the "pavilion of cloth of gold of tissue", and the "pretty fair boys apparelled as painters do set forth god Cupid, with little fans in their hands, with the which they fanned wind upon her." By adapting his source material, Shakespeare added to the variety of images of Cleopatra, both in print and

Parallel Lives

Shakespeare's main source of knowledge about the ancient world was a translation of Plutarch's *Lives of the Noble Greeks and*

Romans (also known as *Parallel Lives*). Written in the 1st century CE, the work is a collection of biographies of Greek and Roman figures, arranged in pairs. In each pair, a Roman from the recent past is compared to a Greek figure from the remote past. Plutarch paired Antony with Demetrius, a military leader who ruled Macedon from 294–288 BCE. Demetrius died exactly 200 years before the birth of Antony.

Plutarch says of Demetrius and Antony

that both "abandoned themselves to luxury and enjoyment." However, he judges Antony more severely. When preparing for war, Demetrius's "spear was not tipped with ivy, nor did his helmet smell of myrrh." By contrast, Antony was "disarmed by Cleopatra, subdued by her spells, and persuaded to drop from his hands great undertakings and necessary campaigns, only to roam about and play with her on the sea-shores by Canopus and Taphosiris."

26891671

> This foul Egyptian hath
> betrayèd me. My fleet hath
> yielded to the foe, and yonder
> They cast their caps up
> and carouse together
> Like friends long lost.
> Triple-turned whore!
> **Antony**
> Act 4, Scene 13

paint, that have been created since her death in 30 BCE.

In Antony's eyes, Cleopatra is a woman whom "everything becomes" (1.1.51); her magnificence shines through tantrums, laughter, and tears. For Antony she is the personification of the country that she commands; she is an "Egyptian dish" (2.6.126), and a "serpent of old Nile" (1.5.25). She is however also labelled as being a "wrangling queen" (1.1.50), a "triple-turned whore" (4.13.13), and "this false soul of Egypt" (4.13.25). Her temperament is as fluid as the Nile itself: "If you find him sad, / Say I am dancing; if in mirth, report / That I am sudden sick" (1.3.3–5). One moment she wishes to hop around the streets, and the next she wishes to draw blood from a messenger. Cleopatra is predictable only in her changeability.

Love or duty

In their first interaction, Cleopatra badgers Antony to quantify his love for her. His response plays to her taste for hyperbole: "Let Rome in Tiber melt, and the wide arch / Of the ranged empire fall. Here is my space. / Kingdoms are clay. Our dungy earth alike / Feeds beast as man. The nobleness of life / Is to do thus; when such a mutual pair / And such a twain can do't – / in which I bind / On pain of punishment the world to weet – / We stand up peerless." (1.1.35–42).

Antony's words suggest the extent to which he has fashioned himself as a convert to the Egyptians' way of being. The Roman Antony is a builder of empires, one for whom expansion and growth are

key goals and motivations. But in this early speech, which serves to establish Antony's state of mind, his focus is upon contraction and reduction rather than extension. His conquering ambitions have been narrowed to the point at which he can say "Here is my space" (1.1.36) – here being in Egypt, by the side of, or in the arms of Cleopatra. Egypt and its queen have transformed Antony's Roman understanding of honour and nobility, and have changed him from a conquering warrior into a man whose ambition is to be part of a "mutual pair" (1.1.39). Nothing could be more romantic, or more self-centred, depending upon one's point of view.

In order to appreciate Antony's commitment to a life of pleasure, Shakespeare presents its antithesis, in his depiction of Octavius Caesar, and life in Rome. In so doing, Shakespeare structured his play around contrasting worlds, filling his drama with a variety of voices and viewpoints. Caesar's rhetoric is cold and clinical; he speaks with the politician's tongue. Lacking the Egyptian's taste for poetic indulgence, Caesar's speeches tend to be purely functional, short, and succinct in expression. Caesar's sense of rigorous discipline leads him to view Antony's behaviour in Egypt as dishonourable; in Caesar's judgement, Antony simply "fishes, drinks, and wastes / The lamps of night »

Octavius, depicted here in a statue in Rome, stands for Roman martial values in the play. The historical Octavius would go on to be proclaimed emperor of Rome following his defeat of Antony.

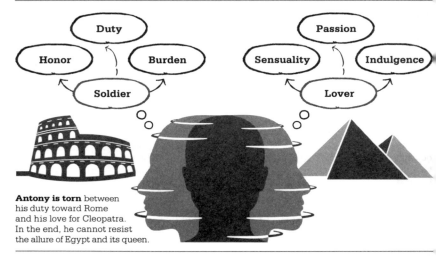

Antony is torn between
his duty toward Rome
and his love for Cleopatra.
In the end, he cannot resist
the allure of Egypt and its queen.

in revel; is not more manlike / Than
Cleopatra" (1.4.4–6). Caesar is too rash in
his judgement of his fellow triumvir: "'tis
better playing with a lion's whelp / Than
with an old one dying" (3.13.94–95). Like
Cleopatra, Antony resists easy labelling;
Shakespeare varies his presentation
throughout the play, so that audiences see
glimpses of the "plated Mars" (1.1.4) as well
as the "strumpet's fool" (1.1.13).

Erotic Egypt
Egypt is characterized as a place of
excessive appetites, where eight wild
roasted boars can be shared between 12
people for breakfast. Caesar's stomach
churns at such extravagance: he would
"rather fast from all, four days, / Than
drink so much in one" (2.7.98–99). The
Egyptians' appetite for sexual pleasure is
also insatiable, but in Rome covetousness
and eroticism are substituted for marriage.
Caesar's sister Octavia functions like a
pawn in a political game when Antony
takes her as his wife. The marriage
symbolizes a reunion between Antony and
Rome, though many presume that "He will
to his Egyptian dish again" (2.6.126).

Did Shakespeare intend his audiences
to side with Antony? Is love more important
than duty? As ever, Shakespeare presents
a variety of questions, but provides few

answers. They are questions for actors to
interpret and audiences to decide. Life in
Egypt has encouraged Antony to celebrate
and feed his appetites, but ultimately his
decision to act against his natural "Roman"
instinct comes at great personal loss. As
his devotion to Cleopatra leads to his defeat
in battle, Antony complains: "Authority
melts from me of late. When I cried 'Ho!', /
Like boys unto a muss kings would start
forth, / And cry "Your will?" (3.13.90–92).

Burden of duty
Like King Lear, Antony wishes to be free
of his duties, but still desires to hold on
to the authority and accolades that such
power brings. He battles with his
conscience, and blames Cleopatra for his
own weakness when he deserts a battle
in pursuit of her: "Egypt, thou knew'st too
well / My heart was to thy rudder tied by
th' strings, / And thou shouldst tow me
after. O'er my spirit / Thy full supremacy
thou knew'st, and that / Thy beck might
from the bidding of the gods / Command
me." (3.11.56–61).

Although Cleopatra does much to
endanger Antony, he remains devoted to her
right up to the end. Having experienced her
infinite variety of moods to the full, he wards
off impending death to lay the "poor last" of
"many thousand kisses" (4.16.21) upon her lips.

Tribute to Antony

Cleopatra is one of Shakespeare's most self-absorbed and self-seeking characters, and thus it can come as something of a surprise to hear her rhapsodize upon someone other than herself. Her emotional tribute to Antony, following his failed suicide, serves to augment her lover's reputation, encouraging a personal rather than political assessment of the man's life.

Through Cleopatra, Shakespeare ensures that our final memory of Antony is not of a strumpet's fool, but of a Herculean god:"His legs bestrid the ocean; his reared arm / Crested the world. His voice was propertied / As all the tunèd spheres, and that to friends; / But when he meant to quail and shake the orb, / He was as rattling thunder. For his bounty, / There was no winter in't; an autumn 'twas, / That grew the more by reaping. His delights / Were dolphin-like; they showed his back above / The element they lived in. In his livery / Walked crowns and crownets. Realms and islands were / As plates dropped from his pocket." (5.2.81–91).

The wonder of Cleopatra's elaborate and rather fanciful tribute should have the effect of wiping all previous remembrances of Antony from one's mind: "The crown o'th, earth doth melt" (4.16.65).

Putting on a show

The Egyptian Queen is a consummate performer, who flows from one mood to another with the ease of an accomplished actress. She wears many faces during the course of the play, expressing a wide range of emotions: love, hate, fear, jealousy, suspicion, and pride. Many of her conversations with Antony are in fact played out in front of an audience of attendants. The most private of conversations are often made public. Having listened to Antony declare his undying love for her, Cleopatra turns to those around her to ask, "Why did he marry Fulvia and not love her?" (1.1.43). Shakespeare perhaps alludes to Antony's distaste for Cleopatra's attention-seeking showiness when he ventures that "Tonight we'll wander through the streets and note / The qualities of people" (1.1.55–56).

There is the slightest of suggestions here that Antony desires Cleopatra's private company, away from the crowds before whom she is constantly performing. Shakespeare also uses this line to make the extraordinary seem familiar. Though Antony and Cleopatra are powerful leaders surrounded by wealth and luxury, they also value love's simple pleasures enjoyed by lovers rich and poor. ■

Death of Cleopatra

Shakespeare saves Cleopatra's greatest performance until the end of the play. She orchestrates her death scene, which is full of theatricality, ritual, and ceremony. The final Act, in which Cleopatra prepares for death, can often prove one of the play's most powerful passages in performance. Shakespeare shrinks the scope of his play. Audiences are no longer invited to imagine movement between continents, but are asked to feel Cleopatra's grief and loneliness.

Cleopatra calls for Charmian and Iras to fetch her best attire, so that she may dress for death. Shakespeare ensures that our final image of Cleopatra is of the queen in all of her greatness. Her language is sexually charged, and in her final moments she makes an ecstasy of death itself. She talks of "immortal longings," and figures that "the stroke of death" is as a "lover's pinch, / Which hurts and is desired" (5.2.290–291). While Antony's botched suicide attempt is awkward and inelegant, Cleopatra remains in control of herself, her image, and her reputation in death as in life.

THE WEB OF OUR LIFE IS OF A MINGLED YARN, GOOD AND ILL TOGETHER
ALL'S WELL THAT ENDS WELL (1606–1607)

Following the death of his father, Bertram must leave for the court. The Countess and Lafeu discuss the King's illness, and wish that the physician Gérard de Narbonne, were still alive to cure him. Narbonne's daughter, Helen, weeps – but for Bertram's departure not for the death of her father. The Countess learns of Helen's passion for her son.

War has broken out between the dukedoms of Florence and Siena. The King of France refuses to send troops, but gives permission for his young noblemen to fight on either side. Lafeu introduces a disguised Helen to the court. She promises that if she fails to cure the King, she will willingly be put to death, but if she succeeds, the King must give her a husband of her choice. The King is restored to health, and presents Helen with four lords as potential husbands. She chooses Bertram, who is disgusted at the idea of being married to a physician's daughter. Bertram capitulates, but he refuses to consummate the marriage. He runs off to the Florentine wars with Paroles. In letters to his mother and Helen, he insists that he will only acknowledge Helen when she has a ring he never removes, and when she has conceived their child. Helen travels to Florence, where she takes lodgings with a Widow. She discovers that Bertram has won favour for his bravery, and has been trying to seduce the Widow's beautiful daughter, Diana.

The other lords in the Florentine army pretend to be enemy soldiers, take Paroles captive, and blindfold him. Paroles reveals everything he knows about his fellow soldiers. When the blindfold is removed, Paroles's reputation is ruined.

Helen reveals her true identity to the Widow. She offers money for help in satisfying the conditions of Bertram's letter. Diana will arrange a sexual liaison with Bertram, but Helen will take her place. Bertram tries again to seduce Diana. He gives her his ancestral ring, and after their assignation, she gives him another ring in return. Bertram is informed that Helen is dead, and leaves for France to be reconciled to the King.

The King forgives Bertram and supports his proposed marriage to Lafeu's daughter. However, when Bertram offers as a betrothal gift the ring Diana gave him, the King recognizes it as belonging to Helen. Bertram is arrested on the charge of murdering his wife. Diana arrives, and accuses Bertram of breaking his promise to marry her. She produces the ring Bertram gave her, which the Countess recognizes as the family heirloom. Diana refuses to explain how she got the ring, and is arrested. She sends for someone to stand bail, and Helen enters. She declares that the conditions Bertram set have been met. Bertram asks for her forgiveness, and promises to love her in the future. ∎

IN CONTEXT

THEMES
Love, betrayal, bereavement and death

SETTING
Roussillon and Paris, France, and Florence, Italy

SOURCES

1353 Italian poet Giovanni Boccaccio's *Decameron* is the main source of the play.

1566–67 Shakespeare probably read Boccaccio's story in English translator William *Painter's Palace of Pleasure*.

T he title of Shakespeare's comedy *All's Well That Ends Well* could arguably end with a question mark. As American author John Jay Chapman wrote in 1915: "Melancholy moulders in the very title of it; for we feel that all is not well, nor ever has been nor can be well again."

The play's "mingled yarn" is one reason for the uncertain reactions it has provoked. Although it makes use of a number of fairytale and folkloric conventions, including the hero who is set a series of impossible tasks and the bedtrick (where one woman substitutes for another to secure a husband), the psychological insight with which the characters are written, and the realistic setting in which they are placed make these elements highly problematic. Indeed, *All's Well* has often

On learning of Helen's passion for her son, the countess (Janie Dee, right, at the Globe, 2011) supports Helen's (Ellie Piercy) plan to prove her worthiness by curing the King.

 T'were all one
That I should love a bright particular star And think to wed it, he is so above me.
Helen
Act 1, Scene 1

been labelled one of Shakespeare's "problem plays", along with *Measure for Measure*, *Troilus and Cressida*, and even sometimes *Hamlet*. This is not a term that Shakespeare would have recognized, as it was invented in the 19th century to describe Norwegian playwright Henrik Ibsen's plays, but it is still a useful way of thinking about *All's Well*. The features of a problem play include the interweaving of fantastic plots with realistic characters, the struggle to resolve an ethical dilemma, and the experience of emotional suffering including grief. *All's Well* fits all of these criteria. Its mingling of comedy and tragedy is beautifully exemplified by Helen when, having been declared dead, she reappears on stage "quick", which means both alive and pregnant. Yet even this joyful conclusion has often been felt to be overshadowed by the darker undercurrents of the play.

Ambivalent virtue

The first problem is Bertram. If we are to delight in Helen's achieving her ambition to marry him, we have to believe that he is worthy – and this is where audiences have struggled. In general, the play sees human beings as deeply ambivalent: "Our virtues would be proud / if our faults whipped them not, and our crimes would / despair if they were not cherished by our virtues" (4.3.75–77). He demonstrates courage and loyalty as a soldier, but at the same time, he is trying to seduce a young virgin with false promises. In the final scene, he expresses remorse for Helen's loss and even claims to love her, but then shows himself to be incapable of telling the truth, slandering Diana, whom he had also professed to love. »

Held up high by his comrades, Bertram (Alex Waldmann in a 2013 RSC production) wins plaudits for his bravery in war. By contrast, the war reveals Paroles to be a coward.

We might defend Bertram on the grounds that he is suffering from the crisis of masculinity that occurs elsewhere in Shakespeare. Like Adonis, who prefers hunting the boar over Venus's seductions in Shakespeare's poem *Venus and Adonis*, Bertram is still young, and in the process of becoming a man. The desire of a woman like Helen threatens to confine him in the feminine domestic space he has only just succeeded in escaping. Bertram also falls foul of the institution of wardship. This was a system, much criticized in Shakespeare's time, that gave an elder guardian control over the young man's marriage, usually to his/her own advantage. In *All's Well*, we might argue that it is unfair on Bertram that he should be married to pay the King's debt, and especially to a woman whom he declares he cannot love. Equally troubling is the emasculation that is built into this process. The King's wards are paraded in front of Helen so that she may "send forth [her] eye" (2.3.53) and choose one. By this means, Helen adopts the traditionally masculine role of wooer, whilst Bertram is placed in the role of passive female. There is even an echo of Capulet in *Romeo and Juliet* in the King's threats to exile and revenge himself upon Bertram, which would place Bertram in the role of Juliet.

This all matters less if we can believe that the marriage of Bertram and Helen will prove a good thing for him as well as for her. But the play struggles to reconcile the forceful and manipulative Helen with contemporary ideals of female modesty and submissiveness. Helen registers what an impossible situation she is in when she has to choose Bertram: "I dare not say I take you, but I give / Me and my service ever whilst I live / Into your guiding power" (2.3.103–105).

If Bertram was not enamoured with Helen before, he certainly will not be now. It is no coincidence that the woman he does actively desire, Diana, is named after the goddess of chastity. She inspires his lust precisely because she seems impervious to love herself. Furthermore, the play implies an unflattering parallel between Helen and Paroles. Both are ambitious, lower-class characters whose designs on Bertram promise to be socially advantageous to them. More specifically, Helen's use of the bedtrick is morally suspect, in that she forces Bertram to have sex with someone against his will, and uses Diana as a public scapegoat for her own desires.

Social mobility

A further ethical debate centres around the meaning and importance of class distinctions. Bertram insists that he will be shamed, and his noble lineage degraded, by uniting with the lower-class Helen. The King argues that all titles were once bestowed for worthy service, and so he can make Helen Bertram's social equal on the basis of her virtue.

Although this sounds very progressive, it is at odds with assumptions elsewhere in the play, and beyond it. One of the few guidelines for wardship was that the ward was not supposed to be married to anyone socially beneath him. Furthermore, the King may

Wars is no strife
To the dark house and
the detested wife.
Bertram
Act 2, Scene 3

argue that everyone's blood is ultimately the same, but he would hardly be in his own position of royal privilege were that the case. What the play tries to do towards the end is to argue that, rather than jeopardizing Bertram's class status, Helen actually preserves it. He carelessly gives away his ancestral ring, but Helen takes it into her own safe-keeping. Equally, Bertram thinks he is wasting his noble seed in an illicit sexual encounter, but Helen takes possession of this, too, and nurtures it into an heir to honour him.

Problematic reconciliation?

The final reconciliation scene can be read and performed in a number of different ways. Bertram may be transfigured by the return of dead Helen, sometimes dressed in white like an avenging angel or the Virgin Mary. He may be filled with gratitude as she releases him from his arrest for murder and exonerates him from any crime against Diana.

Freed from the influence of Paroles and his hyper-masculine ethos, Bertram may give way to an attraction to Helen that he has always secretly felt. Equally, Helen's reaction to Bertram takes on many different hues. A review of the 1992 RSC production, directed by Sir Peter Hall, describes how, "With a pained, dignified 'et cetera' (uttered after a beautifully pointed pause), she spares both of them a full recital, and then determinedly rends the paper in two." We might interpret this action as a fresh start for the couple, or as a long-awaited expression of Helen's rage against her husband.

Ultimately, the understanding that life is like a "mingled yarn, good and ill together" is reserved for the older generation. When she discovers Helen's love, the Countess reflects on her own past lovesickness, and concludes that it is an essential part of being young: "this thorn / Doth to our rose of youth rightly belong" (1.3.125–126). She also questions the value of young love: "Such were our faults – or then we thought them none" (131).

However, it remains to be seen whether Helen's idolatrous passion for Bertram or his "sick desires" for Diana will be assuaged by marriage, and indeed whether they will be able to put these events behind them. Can we imagine Bertram and Helen a few years on, teasing one another about the fact that Bertram was once accused of hating his wife so much he might have killed her? Or is that part of the weave always likely to bring Helen sorrow because Bertram never fulfils his promise to "love her dearly, ever, ever dearly" (5.3.318)? The difficulties that have to be overcome may be too great for the ending to feel anything other than bittersweet. ∎

The braggart soldier

For Shakespeare's audience, Paroles would have been an instantly recognizable comic type. The braggart soldier, whose much vaunted courage on the battlefield turns out to be a sham, had been a popular figure in classical comedy, and appears elsewhere in Shakespeare's plays in the guise of Pistol in *Henry IV Part 2* and Falstaff in *Henry IV* and *Henry V*. The character's popularity in the 17th century was such that King Charles I wrote "Monsieur Paroles" next to the title in his private copy of *All's Well That Ends Well*, and the play was subsequently adapted to expand his part.

For all his shocking betrayal of his friend Bertram and his fellow soldiers, Paroles gains a certain amount of sympathy from his obvious relief at abandoning the pretence: "Simply the thing I am / Shall make me live" (4.3.334–335). In the 2013 RSC production, as played by Jonathan Slinger, Paroles drops the Sandhurst accent that he had used to ingratiate himself, and finally accepts his homosexuality.

THIS WORLD TO ME IS BUT A CEASELESS STORM WHIRRING ME FROM MY FRIENDS
PERICLES, PRINCE OF TYRE (1607)

The medieval poet Gower acts as the narrator relating the story of Pericles, Prince of Tyre. His story begins with King Antiochus whose daughter's suitors must answer a riddle in order to win her hand. Pericles solves the riddle, which exposes Antiochus's incestuous lust and forces Pericles to flee back to Tyre for safety. King Antiochus sends the villainous Thaliart to murder Pericles. Pericles hears of Thaliart's murderous plans and escapes on a ship to Tarsus, leaving his trusted counsellor Helicanus to govern Tyre.

Arriving in Tarsus, Pericles relieves the famine-struck city with corn, earning the gratitude of the governor Cleon and his wife Dioniza. After setting sail again in a storm, Pericles is shipwrecked on the shores of Pentapolis, losing all his possessions except his armour. He is rescued by fishermen and incognito taken to the court of King Simonides, who is celebrating his daughter Thaisa's birthday with a tournament. Pericles wins the jousting competition and the king grants him the hand of Princess Thaisa.

Meanwhile, King Antiochus has died so Pericles is safe to reveal his identity as Prince of Tyre and return home with his now pregnant wife. On the way to Tyre, they encounter a tempest, during which Thaisa appears to die giving birth to a daughter and, at the insistence of the sailors, is buried at sea. Pericles sails to Tarsus where he entrusts his daughter, now named Marina, to the indebted Cleon and Dioniza.

Thaisa's coffin is washed ashore at Ephesus where a physician revives her and sends her to be a priestess at the Temple of Diana.

Gower recounts how 14 years have passed during which time Marina has grown into a virtuous young woman, attracting the envy of Dioniza, who conspires to have her murdered. Marina flees, but is abducted by pirates who sell her to a brothel in Mytilene. Pericles has returned to Tarsus to find Marina but is falsely told that she is dead, causing him to pledge himself to a lifetime of silent mourning sailing the seas.

Marina has steadfastly clung to her chastity, to the annoyance of her bawd (brothel madam), but while she is there she is able to convince the governor Lysimachus, who has visited the brothel in disguise, to help her. When Pericles' ship arrives by chance at Mytilene, Lysimachus tries to cheer the sorrow-drowned Pericles by sending Marina to sing to him.

Hearing Marina's life's story, Pericles joyfully realizes she is his daughter. The goddess Diana appears to Pericles in a dream telling him to visit her temple at Ephesus. Pericles journeys there with Marina and is miraculously reunited with his wife, Thaisa. ∎

IN CONTEXT

THEMES
Life's journey, love, fate, family, endurance, reunion

SETTING
Antioch, Tyre, Tarsus, Pentapolis, Ephesus, Mytilene (Mediterranean)

SOURCES
1390s Shakespeare used John Gower's *Apollonius (Pericles) of Tyre* included in *Confessio Amantis*. Gower expanded on the popular Greek story.

1576 Shakespeare also took some details from Laurence Twine's novella *The Pattern of Painful Adventures*.

S hakespeare shaped his plays to satisfy his audience's expectations. People attending a tragedy would expect to see a tableau of death by the play's close; those attending a romance or comedy anticipated marriages and reunions. *Pericles, Prince of Tyre* is no exception. In this romance, Shakespeare separates his protagonist from his wife and daughter in order to build towards their reunion at the close. Pericles is tossed upon the seas of the Mediterranean from shore to shore and must endure life's "ceaseless storm" (15.71) in order, at the end of the story, to appreciate fully the pleasures of reconciliation.

Believing his wife and daughter to be dead, Pericles slips into a near comatose state. Twenty scenes into the drama Shakespeare asks his audience to imagine that Pericles "for this three months hath not spoken" (21.18). The protagonist is emotionally exhausted. Grief has transformed the voyager; as Helicanus suggests, when he draws back a curtain to reveal Pericles with an overgrown beard, "This was a goodly person / Till the disaster of one mortal night / Drove him to this" (21.29–30). Separated from his wife and daughter, Pericles all but withdraws from society.

Emotional reunion

Shakespeare's presentation of Pericles's reunion with his daughter Marina is a moving moment. The couple's gradual realization that they are father and daughter is developed across the space of some hundred lines. Marina begins by telling Pericles that she has "endured a grief" (21.76) that may equal his own. By this point in the play, audiences will be acutely aware of the misfortunes that have befallen both characters. They will also be aware that Pericles believes his daughter to be dead. Having listened to Marina's opening words, Pericles shares his private thoughts with the audience in an aside that is filled with dramatic irony: "I am great with woe, and shall deliver weeping. / My dearest wife was like this maid, and such / My daughter might have been. My queen's square brows, / Her stature to an inch, as wand-like straight, / As silver-voiced, her eyes as jewel-like, / And cased as richly, in pace another Juno, / Who starves the ears she feeds, and makes them hungry / The more she gives them speech." (21.95–102).

Building tension

Pericles' yearning to see his daughter again is palpable, but Shakespeare delays the revelation, thereby increasing the audience's desire to see this moment.

With every speech the pair edge closer to their »

John Gower, illustrated in this 14th-century manuscript, was a popular poet and storyteller. Shakespeare drew on his retelling of the Greek tale and made Gower the narrator in the play.

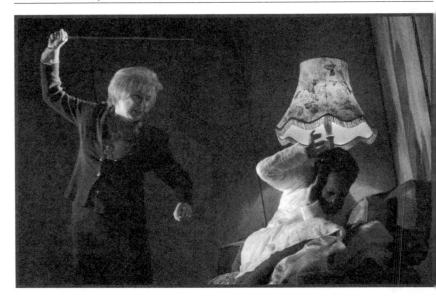

mutual understanding. When Pericles discovers Marina's name, he fears that the gods are mocking him; when he discovers that her mother died at sea while giving birth, he believes he is experiencing "the rarest dream" (21.149). When it eventually comes, the revelation also serves as a plot-reminder for the audience: "The King my father did in Tarsus leave me, / Till cruel Cleon, with his wicked wife, / Did seek to murder me, and wooed a villain / To attempt the deed; who having drawn to do't, / A crew of pirates came and rescued me. / To Myteline they brought me. But, good sir, / What will you of me? Why do you weep? It may be / You think me an impostor. No, good faith, I am the daughter to King Pericles, / If good King Pericles be." (21.158–167). Pericles' tears begin to fall during Marina's speech, though Marina has yet to realize the import of her story. When she confirms that her mother was called Thaisa, her father shares the knowledge he has determined: "Now blessing on thee! Rise. Thou art my child" (21.200). Marina's thoughts about this are not put into words, but her silence is touchingly truthful.

Marina, played here by Ony Uhiaria, defends herself from the bawd, played by Linda Bassett, in this production at Stratford-upon-Avon (2006).

Closing scenes

There are similarities between *Pericles* and *The Winter's Tale*. Rather than staging the reunion between King Leontes and his daughter Perdita, Shakespeare conveys this information through reported speech. Both plays end with another revelation and a reunion. In *The Winter's Tale*, Shakespeare created a moving scene in which Leontes stares at a life-like statue of his wife; and father and daughter are stunned when it begins to move. There is a similar effect in *Pericles*. Pericles finds himself unwittingly before his wife Thaisa at the Temple of Ephesus. She listens as his story unfolds: "I here confess myself the King of Tyre, / Who, frighted from my country, did espouse / The fair Thaisa at Pentapolis. / At sea in childbed died she, but brought forth / A maid child called Marina, who, O goddess, / Wears yet thy silver liv'ry." (22.22–27). As Pericles reunites mother with child, despair is replaced with hope; the "ceaseless storm" (15.71) of ill fortune has been abated. ∎

WHAT IS THE CITY BUT THE PEOPLE?

CORIOLANUS (1608)

I n Rome, a mob of plebeians gather to discuss with each other their grievances with the patricians, who they believe are hoarding grain during a time of famine. Having resolved to kill Caius Martius, thought to be the worst of the patricians because of his pride and arrogance, the plebeians are calmed by Menenius, who suggests that they reconsider.

Caius Martius returns covered in blood from a battle with the Volscian army, and his mother, Volumnia, revels in her son's honour and courage. Caius is rewarded with the title "Coriolanus". Two tribunes, Sicinius and Brutus, fear that he will be promoted into a position of political power. As the tribunes feared, the Senate decides to make Coriolanus a consul, but in order to assume this role he must first receive the plebeians' vote. Coriolanus is reluctant to pander to the people and show them the scars they wish to see, but is persuaded to do so by his mother. Although the people give him their voices, the tribunes Sicinius and Brutus persuade them to change their minds.

Coriolanus is outraged that he must appear before the people once more, and cannot contain his disdain. He gladly leaves the city that has shown him ingratitude and joins the enemy Volscian army. Together with Aufidius, his old enemy, he plots Rome's destruction. Aufidius secretly plans Coriolanus's downfall.

When the people of Rome hear about Coriolanus's intention to burn the city, they send Menenius to discourage him,

> ❝ It is held That valour is the chiefest virtue, and Most dignifies the haver.
> **Cominius**
> Act 2, Scene 2 ❞

but Coriolanus's mind is resolved. In a final attempt to change his mind, Volumnia and Coriolanus's wife and son visit the Volscian camp to plead with the soldier to spare them and the city. Coriolanus is steadfast at first, but his resolve melts when his mother pleads on her knees before her son. In sparing Rome, Coriolanus sacrifices his own life by betraying the Volscian army. While the people of Rome rejoice, Coriolanus's mother acknowledges the sacrifice her son has made. He is brutally murdered by the Volscians, but Aufidius states that he should be given a warrior's burial. ■

IN CONTEXT

THEMES
Class struggle, identity, pride, honour, masculinity, power, politics, family

SETTING
Ancient Rome

SOURCES
1579 Thomas North's English translation of *Plutarch's Lives of the Ancient Greeks and Romans*.

Coriolanus is a play about power, politics, personality, and the fraught relationship between Rome's plebeians and its proud patricians. The play opens with a scene of riotous discontent. The citizens are appalled with a governing class that shows little concern for the people's welfare during a time of famine. Ten lines into the play we hear the first rallying call for the murder of a patrician: "Let us kill him" (1.1.10). The plebeians hate the city's leaders in general for their greed and profligacy, but target Caius Martius as "chief enemy to the people" (1.1.7–8). Of all the patricians who place their own needs above those of the people they govern, Caius Martius (later Coriolanus) is most despicable: "He's a very dog to the commonality" (1.1.27).

Although some of the plebeians recognize that Coriolanus has fought valiantly in battle to protect the city and its people from harm, most resent his "nature", which they perceive to be scornful and self-important. For Coriolanus, the people of Rome represent little more than a

> All the contagion of the south light on you, You shames of Rome! You herd of—boils and plagues
> **Caius Martius**
> Act 1, Scene 5

Control of the city of Rome is a central question in *Coriolanus*. Does the city belong to its people, or do the patricians have a right – and duty – to rule as they see fit?

stinking, cowardly, fickle mob worthy only of disdain – a herd of "boils and plagues" (1.5.2) in his words.

Undeserving people

This play pits an individual against society. Coriolanus's greatest battle is not against invading forces, but against his own people, who are fighting for equality and against injustice. The citizens perceive themselves as being the lifeblood of the city itself, but Coriolanus sees them merely as a blot on the landscape. In his mind they are rioting "To curb the will of the nobility" (3.1.41), rather than, as their appointed tribunes would argue, fighting for their liberties and their human rights. The patrician Menenius presents the ruling class as compassionate and paternal: "most charitable care / Have the patricians of you" (1.1.63–64). He argues that the famine should be blamed on the gods, and discourages accusations of grain-hoarding by the patricians. Coriolanus, however, has no talent as, or desire to be, a political spin-doctor; as Menenius suggests, "His heart's his mouth" (3.1.257). As Coriolanus sees it, the plebeians "Did not deserve corn gratis" (3.1.128) because they performed poorly in

> 66 His sword, death's stamp, Where it did mark, it took. From face to foot He was a thing of blood, whose every motion Was timed with dying cries.
> **Cominius**
> Act 2, Scene 2 99

battle: "Being i'th' war, / Their mutinies and revolts, wherein they showed / Most valour, spoke not for them" (3.1.128–130).

In other words, Coriolanus champions meritocracy (reserved for patricians) and the status quo, while the "tongues o'th' common mouth" (3.1.23) favour democracy.

Opposing views

Coriolanus is structured around argument and debate. Shakespeare introduces alternative perspectives from the outset. While some citizens respect Coriolanus for his valour, others mock him as a mummy's boy who fought only to please his mother. The

divergent opinions voiced by Shakespeare's mob complicates the audience's experience of the play. Should our sympathies lie with this rioting throng intent on violent acts? Is the mob's murderous intent justifiable and based on accurate information?

Over the centuries, readers and audiences have also been inclined to interpret the play in a wide variety of ways, producing a string of alternative and often politically divergent readings. Coriolanus has been interpreted as both the hero and the villain of this drama, and the plebeians have been accused of being dangerously fickle, as well as morally justified in their behaviour. The mob also proves a dangerous force, threatening to turn their fury on their own tribunes by the close.

Bad politician

Diplomacy is not a quality for which Coriolanus is renowned. This character makes enemies very easily, and it is perhaps surprising that he avoids assassination for as long as he does. He is at once one of Shakespeare's most »

An 18th-century print depicts Coriolanus with his mother, Volumnia. She is a key influence, first persuading him to run for the Senate, and later to abandon plans to destroy Rome.

unattractive and most compelling characterizations. The patrician soldier is courageous and awe-inspiring on the battlefield, but has little success when he enters the world of politics, for which he requires the citizens' approval.

Coriolanus is larger than life, a killing machine; he would always prove a misfit in public life. "Rather say I play / the man I am." (3.2.13–14) he declares when his mother urges him to play the role of the diplomat in receiving the citizen's voices of election. He cannot dissemble; he can only speak as he feels. Ultimately, Coriolanus's stinging and unbridled tongue, combined with the machinations of two power-hungry tribunes, will lead to his banishment from Rome. Though the citizens view this as a victory, their safety is no longer assured. In a typical act of arrogant defiance Coriolanus "banishes" Rome, and looks to revenge the people's ingratitude.

Firm voice

Though there are many citizens' voices to be heard in this play, it is Coriolanus's distinctive tone that will remain in the audience's ears. Coriolanus carries with him both the charisma of a celebrity and the terror of a mythological monster. There is crispness and bite in the phrasing of his angry dismissal of the Roman mob: "You common cry of curs, whose breath I hate / As reek o'th' rotten fens, whose loves I prize

Let me have war, say I. It exceeds peace as far as day does night. It's sprightly, walking, audible and full of vent. Peace is a very apoplexy, lethargy; mulled, deaf, sleepy, insensible; a getter of more bastard children than war's a destroyer of men.

First servingman
Act 4, Scene 5

/ As the dead carcasses of unburied men / That do corrupt my air: I banish you." (3.3.124–127). Coriolanus's speech is gritty, muscular, and often monosyllabic. Every word he speaks distances him from the citizens, until he seems to tower above them, delivering his words of condemnation as if they were bolts of lightning: "Despising / For you the city, thus I turn my back. / There is a world elsewhere." (3.3.137–139).

No matter how objectionable Coriolanus's words may be, his magnetism is undeniable. Before leaving for exile, he tells his mother, "I shall be loved when I am lacked" (4.1.16), and these words mirror most people's experience of watching the play in

Do the people of Rome control Rome's freedom and independence, or are such notions in the gift only of a strong and decisive leader whose protection may crush the collective will?

performance; the play loses some of its zest whenever he leaves the stage. While the people of Rome believe themselves to be the city's core, Coriolanus asserts the power of the individual, and it is his character that dominates this play, dwarfing the role played by the city's people. Coriolanus is alarmingly self-assured and self-reliant, forever acting "Alone" (5.6.117).

A play for all time

In following Thomas North's translation of *Plutarch's Lives of the Noble Greeks and Romans*, Shakespeare presented a fractious and politically explosive period of Roman history. In recent years, historians have questioned whether Coriolanus ever existed, but certainly Plutarch viewed him as a historical character, whose lineage could be traced back to early kings of Rome.

Shakespeare and his contemporaries were living through a similar era of social and political unrest, in which insurrections and corn riots were similarly a feature of their own world. Shakespeare's choice of subject matter was characteristically full of controversy, contemporary relevance, as well as commercial interest: the play exemplifies Ben Jonson's statement, in the Preface to the First Folio in 1623, that Shakespeare's works are "not of an age, but for all time". ∎

Coriolanus, played here by Toby Stephens in a 1995 RSC production, is covered in blood following the battle at Corioli. He is a man of action, not a man of words.

A German hero?

Shakespeare's Coriolanus is an ambivalent hero, and the audience is never entirely certain whose side to take. This ambivalence has left space over the centuries for *Coriolanus* to be appropriated for political purposes by both right- and left-wing ideologies. This was never more true than in 20th-century Germany, where Shakespeare was the most performed playwright, and all sides sought to claim his legacy.

Under the Nazi regime in the 1930s and 1940s, Coriolanus's position as a powerful leader battling against a failing democratic system was emphasized. Germans were encouraged to see Hitler as a similar figure – with the implication that, to avoid the play's tragedy, it was necessary for the masses to follow him unwaveringly.

In the 1950s, an adaptation by Bertholt Brecht called *Coriolan* stressed the class warfare in the play. It highlighted the attack by the people on their corrupt Roman leaders. Brecht was working in Communist East Germany, and the play was dedicated to the German proletariat.

THOU METST WITH THINGS DYING I WITH THINGS NEW-BORN
THE WINTER'S TALE (1609–1610)

Polixenes, King of Bohemia, has been staying with his boyhood friend Leontes, King of Sicily. When his pregnant wife, Hermione, persuades Polixenes to stay longer, Leontes becomes jealous, convinced of an attraction between Polixenes and his wife. Leontes orders his adviser Camillo to kill Polixenes. Camillo, sure of Hermione's innocence, warns Polixenes, and he and Polixenes escape from Sicily.

Leontes's son Mamillius starts to tell his mother a story when Leontes, taking Polixenes's flight as proof of Hermione's guilt, orders Mamillius to be kept from his mother. He asserts that the baby on the way is Polixenes's and sends Hermione to prison. Messengers are sent to the oracle at Delphi to confirm her guilt. Hermione gives birth in prison, and her friend Paulina takes the baby girl to Leontes hoping to soften his attitude. Instead, he turns on her. Paulina defies him, but he accuses her husband Antigonus of egging her on, and tells Antigonus to take the babe far away and abandon it.

Messengers return from Delphi. Leontes puts Hermione on trial. When the oracle's words proclaim Hermione innocent, Leontes declares the oracle false. Then comes news that Mamillius, pining for his mother, has died. Hermione faints and is carried out. Paulina tells Leontes bitterly that Hermione is now also dead from the shock of losing both her children. Leontes, remorseful, sees this as a sign of the gods' wrath. Meanwhile, Antigonus abandons the babe (whom he calls Perdita) on the shores of Bohemia, where she is found by a Shepherd. Antigonus is killed by a bear. Sixteen years later, Polixenes talks with Camillo of his son Florizel's love for a shepherd girl. They decide to go to a festival incognito. On a country road, the clown Autolycus sings of his way of life. Perdita and Florizel (known to Perdita as Doricles) appear dressed in festival costume. At the festival, Polixenes (in disguise) is charmed by Perdita. But when "Doricles" says that he will wed Perdita, Polixenes threatens to disinherit Florizel. Florizel decides to take a ship, and Camillo tells him to go to Sicily to make peace with Leontes. In Sicily, Leontes, still mourning Hermione, vows never to remarry. Florizel and Perdita arrive, bearing Polixenes's message of forgiveness. Leontes is moved, but then comes news that Polixenes has arrived in Sicily. Autolycus reveals how Leontes has found his long-lost daughter. They all go to a chapel in Paulina's house to see a lifelike statue of Hermione. Paulina orders the statue to descend, and Hermione comes alive miraculously. She embraces Leontes, then finds that Perdita is alive. All is forgiven, and Paulina and Camillo are told to wed. ∎

IN CONTEXT

THEMES
Jealousy, suffering, hope, love, redemption

SETTING
Winter in Sicily, and summer 16 years later in Bohemia and Sicily

SOURCES
1588 Robert Greene's romantic prose tale *Pandosto*.

The Winter's Tale combines the pastoral humour and romance of *As You Like It* with the dark power of *Othello*. Yet the play is something of an enigma. In Shakespeare's day, a winter's tale was something told by old wives at the fireside. It was a fanciful story, typically with a simple salutary lesson. As Leontes's son Mamillius says when he proposes to tell his mother a story, "A sad tale's best for winter" (2.1.27). And in many ways that is what *The Winter's Tale* is: a sad story with a happy ending, a tale of loss and redemption.

Winter and tragedy

The first three acts of the play are not like a fairy tale at all; they are an emotional drama as grim as any classical tragedy. King Leontes of Sicily finds his wife Hermione so successful in persuading his boyhood friend Polixenes to stay longer that he suspects they are having an affair. His mind is eaten up with jealousy, expressed in language so sodden with sexual innuendo that it almost loses sense: "Gone already! / Inch-thick, knee-deep, o'er head and ears a fork'd one!" (1.2.187–188) He is talking about wading deeper into adultery, with the "forked one" the horns of a cuckold, a husband cheated in adultery. But the imagery is phallic and lewd.

As he becomes increasingly obsessed, Leontes behaves erratically, like Othello, but he has no need of an Iago to feed his suspicion; it is all there in his fevered imagination. It is what he memorably calls the spider in the cup – you might swallow it happily in ignorance, but you will throw up if you see it.

His rage escalates, and Leontes proceeds to destroy those closest to him. Separation from his mother kills Mamillius, and the shock of her son's death kills Hermione. Only with the loss of all his family does Leontes come to his senses and realize the horror he has wrought.

The play's first part is almost a full-blown tragedy. And yet the action all takes place in just three short acts, not the conventional five. Leontes's jealousy seems to erupt out of nowhere and takes just a few hundred lines to explode to the point of no return. Some audiences find the abruptness and extremity of his reaction difficult to accept. In barely an hour of stage time, the entire tragedy has been played out. Yet this mini-tragedy's ending is subtly different from the other tragic plays. In the longer tragedies, the extremity of suffering in the protagonist's self-discovery means that the only way out is death. In *The Winter's Tale*, Leontes is utterly distraught – but he is alive, and will go on living with the knowledge of his mistake for a further 16 years.

As he leaves the stage, not to reappear for an hour, Leontes vows to do penance every day – "...tears shed..." he says, "Shall be my recreation" (3.2.238, 239). He will have no pleasure, but the word "recreation" has another meaning – tears will be his re-creation, his rebuilding and redemption.

The tragedy does not end with Leontes's grief. A brief final scene shows Antigonus laying Leontes's baby daughter on the shores of Bohemia, and naming her Perdita, the "lost one". It is the last disaster made »

A production of *The Winter's Tale* at the Deutsches Nationaltheater, Weimar, Germany (2012), presented the Sicilian court as a harsh place reminiscent of an earlier, reactionary Germany.

by Leontes's folly – and yet it seems like the beginning of a fairy tale, with an abandoned princess. In true fairy tale style, the lost babe is discovered by an Old Shepherd – but not before Antigonus meets his end with one of the most famous stage directions of all time, "Exit, pursued by a bear" (Act 3, Scene 3). (In the play's first production, a real bear may have been used – there was a famous bear-pit near the theatre. Now, almost always, however they enact the bear, directors play it for laughs.) With the entry of the Old Shepherd and his son, with their good-natured rustic quirks, the play suddenly shifts from darkest tragedy to romantic comedy.

A pastoral idyll

When the play recommences in Act 4, it is in a different world. Time has moved on 16 years. The scene is the countryside of Bohemia in early summer. The mood is wholeheartedly comic and romantic, as the baby Perdita, now 16 and a shepherdess, is courted by Polixenes's son Florizel at a sheep-shearing festival.

Few plays experience such a dramatic change in genre. Indeed, the shift is so sudden that some critics have labelled *The Winter's Tale* one of Shakespeare's "problem plays". To some extent, it reflects the contemporary vogue for "tragi-comedies" developed by playwrights such as John Marston, but none of the tragi-comedies of the day feature the stark midstream shift of *The Winter's Tale*.

The play is often grouped with *The Tempest*, *Pericles*, and *Cymbeline* as a "late" play. These are sometimes described as "romances" because they have something akin with the poems of the Middle Ages that told stories of courtly love in fantastical settings.

The marked midplay shift in *The Winter's Tale* is quite unique. Even so, the play has the same simple three-part structure as many of Shakespeare plays, including *As You Like It* and *A Midsummer Night's Dream*. These plays begin with a problem in the ordered "real" world of the court. They then move into the fantasy world of nature for the problems to be worked out before returning to the court where everything is resolved. *The Winter's Tale* works in the same way. The key difference is how fully the problem in the real world, the world of Leontes's court, is developed, growing into a full tragedy before the healing journey into nature begins. Indeed, it is a problem so deep that it cannot be solved by Leontes or Polixenes themselves. It can only be solved by their children.

The shift from Sicily to Bohemia is in some ways a re-generation, a reflection of the fact that nature is always renewing itself. After the

| **Winter death** Leontes's jealousy of Polixenes sets in motion a series of disasters. Mamillius and Hermione die. But the tragedy leaves the seed of a resolution – in the form of a banished baby daughter. | **Summer rebirth** The daughter, Perdita, grows up in a happy land of festivals and revelry. She falls in love with Florizel, who is Polixenes's son. They are a new generation unmarked by the sins of the old. | **Renewal, life continues** Perdita and Florizel return to Sicily to heal. As if through the power of youth and love, a statue of Hermione is brought to life. Leontes is forgiven, and harmony is restored. |

The play's distinct parts follow nature's cycle of death, rebirth, and renewal. Winter's tragedy is replaced by summer's rebirth, problems are solved, and life continues.

━━━━━ **Sicily**

━━━━━ **Bohemia**

harshness of winter, spring brings forth new life, and nature is a continuous cycle of death and rebirth. The Old Shepherd who finds the lost baby Perdita sums up this rebirth when he says: "Thou metst with / things dying, I with things new-born" (3.3.110–111).

Summer and rebirth

The Bohemian section of *The Winter's Tale*, then, symbolizes a rebirth. The structure of the play mirrors, intentionally or not, the story of the European rebirth, the Renaissance. The Leontes story is a dark, Greek-style tragedy set in the classical Mediterranean. Perdita and Florizel's story is a romance of the kind developed in Europe, and set in Bohemia. Shakespeare is perhaps showing how the classical flame has been renewed by a new European generation.

In *A Midsummer Night's Dream*, the star-crossed lovers escape into the woods to fulfil their romance. In *The Winter's Tale*, however, when Polixenes forbids his son Florizel from marrying the apparently lowly shepherdess Perdita, the young lovers flee from the summer fantasy world of Bohemia to the wintry Sicilian court. It is this reversal that enables them to be the bearers of redemption, bringing warmth and life back to the chill of Leontes's Sicily. In fact, their return literally restores life, because at the extraordinary climax to the play, a statue of Hermione comes to life.

Statue of limitations

There has been much debate about the statue. Is it a statue that comes miraculously to life, or has Hermione been in hiding for 16 years, waiting for this moment? Hints emerge that she has been hiding, when it is said that Paulina has been visiting the hidden house ever since she died. But this whole moment is unusual in that we, the audience, don't see it coming. Most of Shakespeare's plays employ dramatic irony. We know what some characters in the play don't, and the drama comes as they finally discover the truth. In *Othello*, for instance, we know that Othello has been duped by Iago and we hang on our seats until the moment Othello learns what we already knew. But Hermione's coming to life is a plot twist out of the blue. At the end of Act 3 Paulina tells us that Hermione died, and such is Paulina's forthrightness that we have no reason to doubt her word.

Some critics find this twist so unbelievable that they feel it weakens the play. Yet the surprise of the living statue is deliberately intended by Shakespeare. He acknowledges through Paulina that the resurrection is scarcely believable: "That she is living, / Were it but told you, should be hooted at / Like an old tale" (5.3.117–119). And herein lies an answer. Are we meant to "hoot" at it, provoked to laughter, so that we leave the theatre not lost in gloom but chuckling at the wonderful absurdity? Maybe, then, Paulina's words "You precious winners all" (5.3.132) are addressed to us. Shakespeare has given us hope that even the very worst errors can be redeemed. ∎

HANG THERE LIKE FRUIT MY SOUL TILL THE TREE DIE
CYMBELINE (1610–1611)

King of Britain, Cymbeline banishes Posthumus, his adopted son, who has married his daughter Innogen. Cymbeline's queen wanted her idiot son Cloten to marry Innogen. Posthumus flees to Rome where Giacomo bets him he can seduce Innogen, but when Giacomo arrives in Britain, Innogen resists his efforts. The wicked Queen asks Dr Cornelius for a poison but the doctor gives her a sleeping draft.

Giacomo smuggles himself into Innogen's bedroom in a trunk. He sees her half-naked and steals the bracelet given her by Posthumus. In Rome, Giacomo shows Posthumus the bracelet and describes Innogen's body to prove he has slept with her. Posthumus gives Giacomo Innogen's ring and swears vengeance on her.

Cymbeline refuses the tribute imposed by Rome, so the Roman ambassador Lucius declares that Rome is at war with Britain. In Wales, the exiled Belarius tells tales of the old days to Cymbeline's two sons Guiderius and Arviragus, whom he has stolen. Pisanio receives a letter from Posthumus asking him to kill Innogen, but Pisanio flees with her to Milford Haven, where she hopes to meet Posthumus with the Roman army. The queen has given Pisanio "poison", for Posthumus. In Wales, Pisanio shows Innogen Posthumus's letter. She begs Pisanio to kill her but he persuades her to follow the Roman army in disguise. Cloten pursues Innogen, disguised as Posthumus. Disguised as the youth Fidele, an exhausted Innogen is given shelter by Guiderius and Arviragus.

Innogen takes the "medicine" given her unwittingly by Pisanio. Cloten challenges Guiderius, who returns with Cloten's head. Arviragus finds Innogen, apparently dead, in the cave. Belarius lays her next to Cloten's headless body. Innogen wakes to see the corpse. She thinks it is Posthumus and that she has been betrayed by Pisanio and Cloten.

Lucius, now general of the Roman army, makes Innogen his servant. Posthumus rues that he urged Pisanio to kill Innogen and joins the British disguised as a poor soldier. Thanks to Belarius and his sons, the British beat the Romans. Posthumus dresses as a Roman and offers himself as a prisoner. He dreams of his dead family and the god Jupiter urges justice. Belarius and his sons are rewarded. The queen dies and her wickedness is exposed. The Roman captives are brought before Cymbeline. Innogen, still in disguise, sees Giacomo with Posthumus's ring. Giacomo admits he lied to Posthumus. Posthumus confesses his part in Innogen's "death". Innogen shows she is alive, but Posthumus does not recognize her. Pisanio verifies it is Innogen, and she and Posthumus are reunited. Belarius reveals that the two boys are Cymbeline's lost sons. ■

IN CONTEXT

THEMES
Jealousy, deception, suffering, hope, love, redemption

SETTING
Cymbeline's court in ancient Britain, Rome, a cave, and later, Milford Haven in Wales

SOURCES
1353 The wager plot in Bocaccio's *Decameron*.

1587 Basic historical background is taken from Holinshed's *Chronicles*.

Cymbeline is one of the strangest of Shakespeare's plays. This darkly romantic tale tells the story of the misguided king of ancient Britain, Cymbeline, whose misjudgment loses him two sons and his remarkable daughter Innogen, before, in the end, all is restored. The plot is so convoluted that commentators have ridiculed it as a mess, although now most critics acknowledge that on stage it is a captivating masterpiece.

The play is based, in part, on the historical king Cunobelinus, who ruled over southern England at around the time Jesus was born. Shakespeare found the story of Cunobelinus in Holinshed's famous *Chronicles*, where he is known as Kymbeline. However, the story Shakespeare weaves in his play *Cymbeline* is almost entirely divorced from any historical truth. Indeed, Shakespeare seems completely unconcerned with any historical consistency. When the hero Posthumus is banished from ancient Britain, for instance, he ends up in Rome at the time of the Renaissance. There, Posthumus's companions, who have Italian names like Filario and Giacomo, talk anachronistically of France and England. And when the Roman general Lucius lands with his army in Britain, he lands in Milford Haven, the port in west Wales where Henry Tudor landed in 1485 to claim the throne of England as Henry VII. The British court physician is named Doctor Cornelius, which calls to mind the famous 15th-century German magician Cornelius Agrippa, while the Latin name Posthumus is an odd one for an ancient Briton, or for anyone.

Patchwork of influences

This apparent mishmash is surely not carelessness on the part of Shakespeare but a deliberate act of association to create a play that has both contemporary relevance and mythical power. It is part fairy tale – with a wicked stepmother, lost princes living in a cave, and a sleeping beauty – and part tragedy.

Shakespeare brings in a variety of elements from his earlier plays. When Posthumus, fooled by the lies of Giacomo, becomes disastrously jealous of Innogen, it recalls Othello's murderous jealousy of Desdemona fuelled by Iago. And Innogen's discovery of what seems to be her dead husband when she wakes from her deathlike sleep echoes Juliet waking to the dead Romeo.

The complex plot is not easy to follow, but its three main strands – the story of Innogen and Posthumus; the loss of Cymbeline's two sons; and the conflict between Britain and Rome – all echo earlier plays by Shakespeare, brought together in this work by a fast-moving plot.

A matchless heroine

The story of Innogen and Posthumus is the emotional heart of the play. In Innogen, Shakespeare created one of his most admired heroines – steadfast, loyal, brave, and resourceful. At the beginning of the play, Posthumus is described as a worthy hero, a more than suitable companion for her. Yet as soon as he is away from her in Rome, his nobility drops away and he falls prey, much too easily, to foolish machismo. He not only agrees to Giacomo's bet that he can seduce her, but also readily believes that Giacomo has succeeded. Then, in an act of stomach-churning duplicity and cruelty, he sends two letters, one to Innogen declaring undying love and the other to Pisanio asking him to kill her. Fortunately, Pisanio, perhaps the play's true hero, refuses Posthumus's bidding and helps Innogen escape in disguise, to try to put matters right. No wonder many critics have heaped scorn on Posthumus as an »

The court of Cymbeline

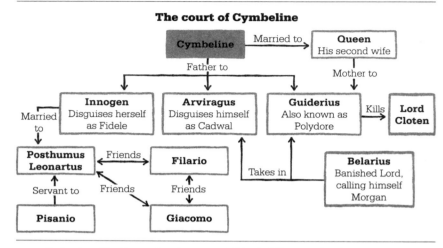

unworthy husband for the peerless Innogen. Feminist critics have highlighted the male stereotyping that portrays women as either virgins or whores, which the wager seems to play out. But perhaps there is another theme here.

A middle ground

The British court is torn between the decadent corruption and false honour of Rome and the rough innocence of wild Wales, where Cymbeline's lost sons Guiderius and Arviragus are brought up in a cave by Belarius. Even the heroic Posthumus's moral compass is set spinning in the competitive world of Rome, where men trade verbal blows over empty ideas of honour – such as whose country's women are the purest. Away from corrupting influences in the natural world, Guiderius and Arviragus grow up honest and true. "Great men / That had a court no bigger than this cave, / …Could not outpeer these twain" (3.6.79–84), exclaims Innogen when she meets them for the first time. She has no idea, of course, they are her lost brothers.

The opposition of the court and the country is a common theme in several of Shakespeare's plays. In *A Midsummer Night's Dream*, *As You Like It*, and *The Winter's Tale*, characters all journey into the wild to learn to see things afresh before they can return to the court with sense restored.

What's different in *Cymbeline* is the third place that lies between civilized Rome and wild Wales – the British court. It is as if Cymbeline, or Britain, must make a choice between the two.

In the end, Cymbeline doesn't have to make a choice. He makes peace with Rome and welcomes his Welsh-raised sons back into the fold. The queen, who fomented the discord by encouraging him to defy Rome and trying to set up her son Cloten in place of the lost twins, is dead. Reconciliation may be the message of the play. Its relevance would not have been lost on audiences when the king says: "Let / A Roman and a British ensign wave / Friendly together… Never was a war did cease, / Ere bloody hands were washed, with such a peace." (5.6.480–486).

Contemporary resonances

The purpose of the play may become clearer if it is seen in its historical context. The battle for the soul of Britain was still fierce. The Protestant Reformation had the upper hand, but Catholicism still had an immense presence, and there was a real threat of a Catholic comeback, as the Gunpowder Plot of 1605 had demonstrated. In Rome, Posthumus is played upon by a Frenchman, a Spaniard, and an Italian (Giacomo) – one man from each of the major Catholic countries – and the

Dutchman, from the largely Protestant Netherlands then fighting for independence from Catholic Spain, remains silent.

There is every chance that *Cymbeline* would have been performed in front of King James I of England (James VI of Scotland), and the resonances would surely not have passed him by. James, like Cymbeline in the play, was king of all Britain, uniting England, Scotland, Wales, and Ireland for the first time under a single monarch. He also, like Cymbeline, had two sons and a daughter. And James, at that very moment was, like Cymbeline at the close of the play, entering into negotiations with Rome to find peace.

Contemporary audiences would not have missed the point that the crucial intervention in Cymbeline comes from Wales, the home of the Tudor dynasty that had ruled England until James's accession on the death of Elizabeth I in 1603. The focal point of the action is Milford Haven in west Wales. This town had nothing whatsoever to do with ancient Roman or ancient British history, but as the place where Henry Tudor landed to start the Tudor dynasty, finally ending the Wars of the Roses, it was a name that still resonated strongly in Shakespeare's England.

History and myths

Of course, Rome is not just the contemporary city that Posthumus finds, but it also signifies ancient, classical Rome, the Rome of Augustus when much of Europe, including Britain, was united in the comparative peace of the Roman Empire, the *Pax Romana*. It was also the time of the classical gods – and it is the Roman god Jupiter who appears to Posthumus and promises justice and the return of Innogen. In fact, Innogen's deliverance comes from a Wales steeped in Celtic myth. At the end, Cymbeline promises to march through Lud's town – London, named after the Celtic king of Britain and mythical god Lud – to the temple of the classical god Jupiter.

The final scene, in which all the convoluted knots of the plot untangle, was once scorned for its improbability, though now critics agree that it works dazzlingly well on stage. It is almost impossible not to be moved by Giacomo's confession and Posthumus's howls of anguish as he lashes out at Innogen – before all is revealed, the lovers are reunited, Cymbeline finds his lost sons, and everyone is reconciled, but for the wicked queen who, conveniently, is dead. The message seems to be that, however improbable it seems, peace and forgiveness is possible if it is looked for. ∎

Giacomo and Innogen

Giacomo's soliloquy as he creeps around Innogen's chamber has a tenderness that seduces the ear— and, some critics argue,

makes the audience complicit in the act.

Having emerged from a trunk in her room, he describes the sleeping Innogen in memorably exquisite poetic language: "Tis her breathing that / Perfumes the chamber thus: the flame o' the taper / Bows toward her, and would under-peep her lids, /To see the enclosed lights, now canopied / Under these windows, white and azure laced / With blue of heaven's own tinct" (2.2.18–23).

The distinguishing mark on her breast, the evidence for his claim to

have seduced her, "the crimson drops / I' the bottom of a cowslip"—is an image of such natural purity that it is easy to forget the intrusion he is making.

Giacomo, with his seductive language, tries to twist even rape into something beautiful. He likens his deed to the ancient Roman king Tarquin's brutal rape of the noblewoman Lucrece in such a way that it sounds like an act of tenderness. This poetic pornography makes for a deeply disturbing speech.

WE ARE SUCH STUFF AS DREAMS ARE MADE ON
THE TEMPEST (1610–1611)

The ship carrying Alonso and Antonio is caught in a storm and wrecked on a strange island. From the shore, the wizard Prospero assures his worried daughter Miranda that the storm was conjured by his own magic and that all aboard are safe. Prospero then tells her how he was once Duke of Milan, until his usurping brother Antonio drove him to sea in a storm 12 years ago, when Miranda was an infant. Washed up on the island, Prospero used his knowledge to make servants of the island's magical spirit Ariel and the monster Caliban, son of the witch Sycorax, who is being punished for trying to rape Miranda.

Alonso's son Ferdinand meets Miranda and they fall in love, despite Prospero's feigned disapproval. Fearing that Ferdinand drowned, Alonso and most of his company are lulled to sleep by Ariel. Antonio and Sebastian plot to murder Alonso and the good courtier Gonzalo, who dreams of a commonwealth where all might be happy. But Ariel wakes up the company before Antonio and Sebastian can do any harm. Elsewhere, Caliban meets the drunken Stefano and Trinculo and believes they are gods.

Prospero enslaves Ferdinand and makes him carry logs, which he does willingly out of love for Miranda. Ferdinand and Miranda pledge to marry. Caliban tells Stefano and Trinculo how he is Prospero's slave, but will be theirs, and Stefano may have Miranda, if they help him kill Prospero. Ariel gets them all to argue by impersonating each. He conjures up a magical banquet for Alonso and company to the sound of music, but before they can eat, he condemns Antonio for usurping his brother.

Prospero admits he was merely testing Ferdinand, and gives his blessing to the marriage. He conjures a magical masque to celebrate with song and dancing nymphs. Suddenly remembering that Stefano, Trinculo, and Caliban are plotting to kill him, Prospero halts the masque and orders Ferdinand and Miranda to hide. Stefano and Trinculo are lured by Prospero's magical robes, then chased off in terror by spirits transformed into dogs. As Prospero dons his magic regalia, Ariel tells him that Alonso and his court are full of remorse. Moved by Ariel's gentleness, Prospero decides to forgive. He traps them all in a magic circle, explains his true identity, and then reveals, to their amazement, Miranda and Ferdinand playing chess. Stefano, Trinculo, and Caliban are forgiven, too. As they all take ship to Naples for the wedding, Prospero frees Ariel and renounces his magic, and then asks the audience to set him free by clapping their hands. ■

IN CONTEXT

THEMES
Loyalty, servitude, freedom, love, magic

SETTING
A magic island, probably in the Mediterranean

SOURCES
8 CE The play is original, but draws inspiration from Ovid's *Metamorphoses*.

1603 Michel de Montaigne's essay "Of the Cannibals."

1610 News of the shipwreck of the *Sea Venture*.

S et on an enchanted island ruled by the wizard-like Prospero, *The Tempest* is a play of magic and wonder, beautiful poetry and fantastical imagery. It has the most spectacular opening of any of Shakespeare's plays – in the form of the mighty storm of the play's title. Yet it is one of the hardest plays to fathom, a mystery that has absorbed countless hours of debate, and inspired radically different interpretations. It is perhaps this very mystery that is key to the play's power.

The Tempest was probably the last play Shakespeare wrote by himself, and some interpretations have hung on this biographical detail. Critics a century ago began to describe it as a "late" play, arguing that it was the culmination of the Bard's work, his swansong to the theatre. Prospero, they believed, was a portrait of Shakespeare himself, creating the storm and the island's magic out of the air just as Shakespeare creates his magic on the stage. Prospero's evocative speech, which ends the magical wedding masque, was read as Shakespeare's own rueful farewell:"Our revels now are ended. These our actors, / As I foretold you, were all spirits, and / Are melted into air, into thin air; / And like the baseless fabric of this vision, / The cloud-capped towers, the gorgeous palaces, / The solemn temples, the great globe itself, / Yea, all which it inherit, shall dissolve; / And, like this insubstantial pageant faded, / Leave not a rack behind."(4.1.148–156).

This does indeed sound like a poetic goodbye for a great magician of the theatre. But this is not actually the end of the play. Prospero's words here are a conjuring trick to lull Ferdinand and Miranda into sleep while he deals with another plot against him. Neither Prospero nor Shakespeare are quite yet done. And if Prospero really is Shakespeare, then he has painted an unflattering portrait of himself. It is not »

Tempestuous relationships

until his magic spirit Ariel shows Prospero the value of kindness at the end of the play that he learns the wisdom of forgiveness. Up until then he is proud, vengeful, and something of a tyrant. When Prospero conjures the tempest to trap Alonso and Antonio on the island, he is bent on revenge, not reconciliation, and uses his magic to enslave Ariel and Caliban, not to liberate them.

Art or nature?

Few critics today would argue that Prospero is a direct portrayal of Shakespeare, or that *The Tempest* is autobiographical. Nonetheless, there are parallels between Prospero's role and the work of a dramatist. The key word is "art". Just as it is Prospero's "art" to control Ariel and Caliban through magic and bring his abusers to the island, so it is the dramatist's "art" to create an enchanted island on a simple wooden stage.

The play asks what it means to be human – and art, according to the humanist philosophers of the age, was the highest expression of humanity. Art is what lifts humanity above "base" nature – what separates Prospero from the raw, unprocessed beast Caliban.

Shakespeare puns on the two meanings of "art" – art as a noun meaning skill, and art as a verb meaning "be". "Thee," Prospero tells Miranda, "...who / Art ignorant of what thou art." (1.2.18–19). Then a few lines later he says, "Lie there, my art" (1.2.25) to his magic robe as she helps him remove it. The question of which forms the essence of humanity – the magic arts of a master scholar like Prospero, or art as simply "being" – is at the heart of the play.

Liberal and occult arts

Since classical times, students had learned the liberal arts, the skills needed to play an active role in civic life, and Prospero was, as Duke of Milan before his exile, "for the liberal arts / Without a parallel." But he became so absorbed in study that he delved into deeper arts, and neglected the real world. This is, in some ways, an echo of Doctor Faustus in the famous play of that name by Christopher Marlowe, written in the 1590s. Faustus, whose name, like Prospero's means

A 2009 production by the Baxter Theatre Centre of Cape Town, with Antony Sher as Prospero and Atandwa Kani as Ariel, mixed racial politics with playful African mythology.

"fortunate", is also a brilliant scholar who, becoming bored with the liberal arts, plunges into hidden, secret methods, until finally selling his soul to the devil in exchange for ultimate knowledge and power.

Even the most serious philosophers of the age believed that there was another realm beyond Nature, an occult realm of the spirit, and that its discovery was the goal of philosophy. The word "Magic" was used to describe the knowledge and mastery of this hidden dimension. Shakespeare's contemporary Francis Bacon was the great pioneer of modern scientific method based on physical evidence, yet even he believed that magic was "sublime wisdom", while the brilliant 16th-century mathematician and alchemist John Dee, perhaps another inspiration for Prospero, spent much of his life trying to communicate with angels.

The loss of human feeling

Yet the problems with Prospero's absorption in this other world are apparent from the start. As the ship founders in the storm he has conjured, and the sailors cry in terror, only Miranda has the humanity to empathize: "I have sufferèd / With those that I saw suffer!" (1.2.5–6). Prospero's blithe reassurance that there's "No harm" (1.2.16) done seems barely adequate in the face of such anguish, and brings Miranda's all-too-human response: "O, woe the day!" (1.2.15). It is with a shock that Prospero at last learns human feeling and sympathy from the inhuman Ariel: "Hast thou, which art but air, a touch, a feeling / Of their afflictions, and shall not myself, / One of their kind, that relish all as sharply / Passion as they, be kindlier moved than thou art?" (5.1.21–24).

Prospero's treatment of Ariel and Caliban is even more dubious. He tells the story of how he freed Ariel from the tree in which he was trapped by the witch Sycorax, but he keeps Ariel in servitude. His treatment of Caliban is worse. Caliban, the product of his mother Sycorax's night with the devil, is enslaved by Prospero, and turned from an innocent child of Nature, who willingly showed his visitors the wonders of the island, into a resentful beast. As Caliban retorts, schooling has brought him no benefits: "You taught me language, and my profit on't / Is I know how to curse." (1.2.365–366).

One of Shakespeare's sources for *The Tempest* was Michel de Montaigne's essay "Of the Cannibals", which is quoted almost word for word in Gonzalo's plea for a commonwealth based on humanity. In the essay, Montaigne describes the "noble savage" of the New World, untouched by the corruption of the old, and Caliban, it seems, was once such a creature. Caliban retains traces of a sensitivity to the island's natural spirit that he expresses more poetically than Prospero; it is Prospero whose schooling turns Caliban to a "piece of filth".

For all Prospero's knowledge, he has learned only mastery. He is, then, not so different from Antonio who usurps his rule, or Sebastian who plots with Antonio to kill Alonso. More tellingly, mastery is the lesson he teaches Caliban, who plots to kill Prospero.

Prospero the colonial

Over the last half century, more and more critics have focused on Prospero as a forerunner of a European colonist and have seen in his enslavement of the island's original inhabitants, Ariel and Caliban, an exploitation of native people by European masters. This resonance in the play may be no accident. Explorer Sir Walter Raleigh had tried to establish a colony at Roanoke, Virginia, in the 1590s, and Shakespeare was in contact with the Virginia Company that founded the first successful English settlement at Jamestown in 1607.

Letting go

In the end, though, Prospero learns the folly of his attempts to control everything. He breaks his staff to end his magic power, "drowns" his books, forgives his foes, and at last sets Caliban and Ariel free.

As Prospero admits in the Epilogue, with all his magic gone, he has only his own faint human strength to rely on. But he, like Shakespeare the playwright, acknowledges that the real power lies not with him but with the audience, who can either approve or disapprove of the play. Their applause will set him free from the bondage of expectation. ∎

An American play?

In September 1610, a sensational story reached London of a storm that had engulfed the *Sea Venture*, a ship carrying settlers to Jamestown, Virginia. All 150 aboard were washed onto a reef off Bermuda, and there found an exotic island, seas teeming with fish, and skies filled with gorgeous birds. Helped by the natives, the survivors lived on the island while they built a new ship. That Shakespeare was partly inspired by this story is clear, and *The Tempest* has been called the "American" play, even though Prospero's island was in the Mediterranean.

There was a Spanish empire in the Americas at the time that, in the 15th century, had enslaved the indigenous people with the godlike power of its technology. Whether Shakespeare intended it or not, the play has found such a resonance with the colonial past that this has become a key thread in many interpretations. Caliban, not Prospero, is often the focus. Black actors have been cast to emphasize the way European colonials enslaved native populations.

FAREWELL, A LONG FAREWELL TO ALL MY GREATNESS!
HENRY VIII (1613)

Buckingham vents his anger at Cardinal Wolsey's pride and ambition, displayed in his extravagant celebration of a hollow peace treaty with France. But before he can denounce Wolsey to the king, the cardinal lays false accusations against him. The duke is arrested. At the same time we hear of the impending fall of queen Katherine who, a few scenes earlier, had successfully intervened with the king against harsh taxes secretly imposed by Wolsey. The crafty cardinal gives out that he is responsible for this reprieve.

Katherine loses status when Henry falls in love with Anne Boleyn. Brought before a court whose judges, especially Wolsey, she denounces as biased, the queen defends her marriage. In a private meeting with Wolsey, she continues her spirited defence, but finally accepts defeat. Katherine's hostility towards Wolsey, however, persists until her final hour, in exile at Kimbolton. Having been told of the cardinal's death she gives a scathing verdict of his character, yet allows her gentleman usher to enumerate his virtues.

As Katherine falls, Anne rises. Soon after meeting the king at Wolsey's banquet, she is awarded the title Marchioness of Pembroke. The cardinal, however, favours a marriage with the French king's sister and fears Anne's Lutheran faith. Publicly he pretends to advance the divorce, thus securing the king's favour. Secretly, he asks the pope to delay the proceedings as long as possible. When Henry learns of this double-dealing, Wolsey loses power, and shortly after dies. The dukes of Norfolk and Suffolk, who supported Katherine over the unfair taxes, quickly adapt to the new power balance, welcome Henry's secret marriage to Anne, and appear newly raised to the titles of Earl Marshal and High Steward at Anne's subsequent coronation.

Henry becomes his own man with Wolsey's fall. He replaces the cardinal's men with councillors of his own choice. The christening of Henry and Anne's daughter Elizabeth closes the play, with the archbishop predicting that her golden reign will justify Henry's dubious dynastic dealings. ∎

> 66 Love thyself last.
> Cherish those hearts
> that hate thee.
> Corruption wins not
> more than honesty.
> **Wolsey**
> **Act 3, Scene 2** 99

IN CONTEXT

THEMES
Integrity, royal marriage, political ambition

SETTING
Court of King Henry VIII; York Place, Cardinal Wolsey's London home; Westminster Abbey; Kimbolton Castle

SOURCES
1548 Edward Halle's *The Union of the Two Noble and Illustre Families of Lancaster and York*.

1563 John Foxe's *Acts and Monuments*.

1587 Holinshed's *Chronicles of England, Scotland, and Ireland*.

Herbert Beerbohm Tree played Wolsey in a lavish 1910 London production that boasted a huge cast. The play went on to have a long and successful run on Broadway, New York.

C o-written by Shakespeare with John Fletcher, *Henry VIII*, or *All is True*, explores a decisive period of the king's long and famous reign: his divorce from Katherine of Aragon, his marriage to Anne Boleyn, and the birth of the future Elizabeth I. Against a background of ceremony and spectacle, the action maps the rise and fall of some of Henry's closest courtiers and, as the play's alternative title suggests, casts an ironic light on the motivation of all concerned.

Wolsey's power
Henry is presented as the source of greatness. Like the sun, his royal beams gild life by granting status and power to those he favours. When this light is with held for whatever reason, the individual withers and declines. For the first part of the play, the king's favour is strongly influenced by Wolsey. By carefully controlling access to the king, he is able to mediate what Henry sees and hears, and so selectively shape what he believes to be the truth. It is a privileged position that allows Wolsey to replace courtiers he distrusts with those who will do his bidding. He even acts on the king's behalf without his knowledge, as when he initiates the harsh taxes against which Katherine appeals. As custodian of

the king's great seal (the stamp of royal authority), Wolsey thinks he has Henry in his pocket. These gatekeeping powers make him a dangerous enemy, as the Lord Chamberlain points out: "If you cannot / Bar his access to th' king, never attempt / Anything on him" (3.2.16–18).

Fall from favour
Buckingham is the first to fall from grace. Furious at Wolsey's abuse of power, he wants to denounce him to Henry. But Wolsey blocks his move with lies, priming the duke's surveyor to give false testimony so that, before Buckingham can speak out, he is arrested as a traitor and executed. Katherine seems secure in Henry's favour when, kneeling, she petitions him against Wolsey's taxes, and he raises her to sit beside him as he rescinds that law. But when she next appears, Henry fails to repeat the gesture, leaving her on her knees before the court of the divorce hearing. It seems that Wolsey's carefully sown doubts about Henry's divorce now trouble the royal conscience.

Wolsey has risen from a humble butcher's son to become Lord Chancellor of England; and his fall from greatness, when it comes, is just as far. Proud and arrogant, he is detested by those who know of his double-dealing. But as long as he has the king's ear, his position is secure. It is ironically appropriate that, unwittingly, Wolsey himself betrays his deception to Henry. An incriminating letter asking the pope to delay the divorce as long as possible, **»** along with an inventory of his personal wealth, get mixed up in some state papers sent by the cardinal to the king. Wolsey's own hand undoes him. With Anne rising in the king's favour, Wolsey had feared that her Lutheran faith would work against his ambition to become pope. He needed more time to persuade the king away from her and towards a possible French marriage. It is a satisfying twist that such a concealer of truths and manipulator of events should be brought low by this momentary failure to control either. Only when his glories are gone does Wolsey recognize that Henry has outwitted him: "The King has gone beyond me" (3.2.409). This is a turning point in the play, for after Wolsey's fall Henry exerts his will with far greater authority.

Variable truths

Henry VIII presents historical truth as relative, and dependent on more than a single point of view. This is evident in the way the audience is positioned to read the drama's state ceremonies. It is made clear that each one conveys a message that only partly fits the truth. Wolsey's Field of the Cloth of Gold (a lavish peace conference near Calais), we learn, celebrates a short-lived treaty. The trial of Katherine can't afford her the "right and justice" (2.4.11) its ceremony promises because, as is evident from her position on her knees before the court, Henry intends a specific outcome. And her refusal to continue the charade makes this plain. Even in the elaborate closing ceremony celebrating the christening of Elizabeth, a noticeable, ominous absence is that of the new Queen Anne.

Shakespeare and Fletcher convey these shifting perspectives by altering historical chronology to create a moral pattern of rise and fall, which they set alongside a secular pattern of political stratagem masked by theatrical show. Thus, as the Prologue admits, their play is as much a "chosen truth" (Prologue: 18) as the history it portrays. ■

A 2009 production in Ashland, Oregon stayed true to the play's original stage directions, with elaborate, crowd-pleasing ceremonies and pageants.

IS THERE RECORD OF ANY TWO THAT LOVED BETTER THAN WE DO, ARCITE?

THE TWO NOBLE KINSMEN (1613)

The wedding of Theseus, Duke of Athens, and Hippolyta, Queen of the Amazons, is disrupted by three grieving queens who plead with Theseus to attack Thebes and its evil ruler Creon, who has killed their husbands in battle and denied them burial. In Thebes, cousins Arcite and Palamon are disgusted by their corrupt uncle Creon and contemplate fleeing the city when news comes of Theseus's imminent attack. Despite their anxieties, they remain and fight, but are captured, taken to Athens, and imprisoned.

While in jail, Palamon and Arcite surprise their captors by consoling one another with their close friendship. However, their relationship is tested when Palamon looks out of the prison window and sees the Amazonian princess Emilia gathering flowers. He proclaims instant love for her, as does Arcite, and the two friends argue over a woman they do not know, nor seemingly have any hope of attaining.

Arcite is suddenly released from prison and banished to Thebes, but disguises himself, determined to get close to Emilia. Palamon becomes the object of affection for the jailer's daughter, who plans and executes his escape in hope of winning his love.

Arcite enters a sporting contest hosted by Theseus in which he wins a wrestling match and is rewarded by being made Emilia's servant and "master of the horse". On a May Day outing in the Athenian woods, Arcite encounters Palamon; an argument ensues over Emilia, and the kinsmen decide to duel

for her. Their duel is interrupted by Theseus who condemns them both to death. Pleading for their banishment rather than death, Emilia is forced by Theseus to choose one of the cousins as her suitor. When Emilia is unable to choose, Theseus agrees to organize one final fight between the cousins – the winner will receive Emilia's hand, the loser will be executed.

Meanwhile, the jailer's daughter goes mad searching for Palamon in the woods and is treated by a doctor, whose cure is to have a would-be-suitor pretend to be Palamon and bed her. Emilia cannot bring herself to attend the contest between Palamon and Arcite and the progress of the fight is reported back to her. She prays to the Goddess Diana that whoever loves her best should win. Arcite is the winner and claims Emilia for his own, regretful that his friend must die.

News arrives, just as Palamon is about to be executed, that Arcite has fallen from his horse and is fatally wounded. The kinsmen are momentarily reunited in friendship, and with his last breath Arcite bestows Emilia to Palamon. ∎

Dear Palamon, dearer in love than blood
Arcite
Act 1, Scene 2

The *Two Noble Kinsmen* is a collaborative work by William Shakespeare and John Fletcher, who also collaborated on *Henry VIII* and *Cardenio* (now lost). Shakespeare is believed to have written the following scenes: Act 1 / 2.1 / 3.1 / 3.2 / 5.1 / 5.3 / 5.4, although he may not have been responsible for all the writing in some of these scenes.

Scholars believe that Fletcher was entirely responsible for the character of the jailer's daughter, who in her madness echoes Shakespeare's Ophelia. *The Two Noble Kinsmen* was not among the plays included in the First Folio of 1623, and was unpublished until 1634. The play is notable for its use of theatrical effects and spectacle, common features in plays written for indoor theatres such as Blackfriars.

Friendship tested

Trials of friendship feature throughout Shakespeare's works. In charting the deterioration of the relationship between friends, Shakespeare dramatized a rich range of emotional responses: resentment, disappointment, frustration, and anger. From a dramatic perspective, it is far more interesting (and entertaining) to present conflict between friends than contentment. Major obstacles must be overcome if feuding friends are to be reconciled. Little wonder then that Shakespeare's career opened and closed with tales in which friends momentarily transform into rivals.

A highly physical production by the iconoclastic Cherub Company at the Young Vic, London, in 1979, had an all-male cast. Anthony Rothe and Daniel Foley played the dueling kinsmen.

Though 20 or more years passed between his writing of *The Two Gentlemen of Verona* and *The Two Noble Kinsmen*, Shakespeare's belief that tests of friendship made for good drama remained firm. He and Fletcher went to some lengths to emphasize the bond of friendship between Palamon and Arcite, a bond that would be broken with the entry of Emilia into their lives. When imprisoned, the two men take comfort from the fact that they will be locked up together, shut away from the world, "enjoying of our griefs together" (2.2.60). Rather than revolting against their captivity, the cousins embrace the opportunity to enjoy one another's company; the jailer's daughter is surprised to see that "they eat well, look merrily, discourse of many things, but nothing of their own restraint and disasters" (2.1.37–39). The chivalrous men look upon their prison as a "holy sanctuary" (2.2.71) that will help preserve them from worldly vice and corruption: "We are young, and yet desire the ways of honour / That liberty and common conversation, / The poison of pure spirits, might, like women, / Woo us to wander from." (2.2.73–76).

In Chaucer's *The Knight's Tale*, Arcite and Palamon joust in chivalric fashion to win the hand of Emelye. Arcite wins but then is fatally injured. Before he dies he tells Emelye to marry Palamon.

Friendship broken

Given occasion to reflect upon his relationship with Arcite, Palamon is moved to utter "I do not think it possible our friendship / Shall ever leave us" (2.2.114–115). Palamon's confident assertion is filled with dramatic irony. The heightened language of devotion will soon turn into exclamations of contempt: "Why should a friend be treacherous? If that / Get him a wife so noble and so fair, / Let honest man ne'er love again." (2.2.233–235). Having established the bond between the men, the dramatists overturn their courtly gentility within a few lines:

"**Palamon**: You love her then?
Arcite: Who would not?
Palamon: And desire her?
Arcite: Before my liberty.
Palamon: I saw her first."
(2.2.159–163)

Palamon's closing line, "I saw her first", which can be amusing in performance, marks the beginning of the rift between the two men. Before the cousins part,

Arcite reprimands his rival for dealing "so cunningly, / So strangely, so unlike a noble kinsman" (2.2.193–194).

Though they become rivals for Emilia's affections, the men's respect for one another remains. Their conflict is enacted in a courtly fashion throughout, providing great comic potential on stage. As the cousins arm one another for combat, their conversation befits their gallant refinement:
"**Arcite**: Will you fight bare-armed?
Palamon: We shall be the nimbler.
Arcite: But use your gauntlets, though – those are o'th' least. Prithee take mine, good cousin." (3.6.63–65).
Arcite's dying words express his love for Palamon, which rivals, if not supersedes his love for Emilia: "Take Emilia, / And with her all the world's joy." (5.6.90–91).

Bonds between maids

While Palamon and Arcite doubt that there is a record of "any two that loved" (2.2.113) more than they, audiences may disagree. Emilia's love for her childhood friend Flavina rivals the intimate bond enjoyed between the two noble kinsmen. Remembering her dead friend, Emilia speaks with a passion and tenderness that she cannot muster to describe her feelings for Palamon or Arcite: "That the true love 'tween maid and maid may be / More than sex in sex dividual." (1.3.81–82).

At the close of the play, Emilia and Palamon are bonded by the fact that they have both endured the "loss of dear love" (5.6.112). The couple are thrown together leaving Theseus to ruminate upon this surprising turn of events: "O you heavenly charmers, / What things you make of us!" (5.6.131–132). ∎

INDEX

Numbers in **bold** refer to main entries, those in *italics* refer to the captions to illustrations.

ACKNOWLEDGEMENTS

Dorling Kindersley and Tall Tree would like to thank Helen Peters for the index. Special thanks also to Dr Romana Beyenburg-Restori for her help with the text.

PICTURE CREDITS

The publisher would like to thank the following for their kind permission to reproduce their photographs:

(Key: a-above; b-below/bottom; c-centre; f-far; l-left; r-right; t-top)

17 Alamy Images: epa european pressphoto agency b.v. (b). **20 Alamy Images:** AF archive (b). **21 Getty Images:** Universal History Archive / UIG via Getty Images (tr). **24 Alamy Images:** ark 2013 (tl). **Getty Images** (tr). **26 Alamy Images:** Geraint Lewis (b). **27 Getty Images:** E+ (bl). **29 Alamy Images:** Lebrecht Music and Arts Photo Library (tr). **30 Corbis:** Leemage (b). **32 Alamy Images:** Lebrecht Music and Arts Photo Library (b). **33 Corbis:** Bettmann (tr). **37 Dreamstime. com:** Georgios Kollidas (t). **39 Corbis:** Angelo Hornak (br). **40 Getty Images:** UniversalImagesGroup (bl). **43 Getty Images:** Werner Forman / Universal Images Group (tr). **45 Corbis** (t). **46 Corbis:** Ken Welsh / Design Pics (tl). **47 Alamy Images:** Peter Coombs (bl). **49 Corbis:** Robbie Jack (t). **50 Alamy Images:** Heritage Image Partnership Ltd (b). **51 Getty Images:** Alinari Archives, Florence (tr). **55 Alamy Images:** AF archive (bl). **56 Corbis:** Clive Nichols / Arcaid (b). **59 Getty Images:** Time Life Pictures / Mansell / The LIFE Picture Collection (l). **61 Corbis:** Historical Picture Archive (br). **63 Corbis:** Hulton-Deutsch Collection (b); **64 Corbis:** Leemage (bl). **66 Alamy Images:** Mary Evans Picture Library (bl). **67 Alamy Images:** AF archive (tr). **70 Dreamstime.com:** Honourableandbold (tl). **73 Dreamstime.com:** Barnschop (b). **74 Corbis:** Robbie Jack (tl). **76 Alamy Images:** Lebrecht Music and Arts Photo Library (br). **77 Alamy Images:** Alastair Muir (tr). **78 Alamy Images** (bl). **79 Alamy Images:** The Print Collector (bl). **83 Robbie Jack** (tr). **86 Alamy Images:** Geraint Lewis (t). **88 Corbis:** Robbie Jack (br). **90 Alamy Images:** Geraint Lewis (t). **91 Dreamstime.com:** Jorge Salcedo (bl). **93 Alamy Images:** AF archive (bl). **95 Alamy Images:** Geraint Lewis (tr). **97 Corbis:** Michael Nicholson (br). **98 Corbis:** Lebrecht Music & Arts (tr). **101 Corbis:** Metro-Goldwyn-Mayer Pictures / Sunset Boulevard (br). **105 Corbis:** (bl). **Alamy Images:** Lebrecht Music and Arts Photo Library (tr). **106 Getty Images:** Daniel Zuchnik / FilmMagic (bl). **107 Dreamstime.com:** Dirk De Keyser (tr). **Getty images:** Leemage / UIG (bl).

108 Dreamstime.com: Dml5050 (tr); Hámor Szabolcs (cra/lover); Ia64 (cra); Markobradich (tc); Meinzahn (cla); Vetkit (ca); Simonkr (cla/justice). **109 Corbis:** Fine Art Photographic Library (bl); Hulton-Deutsch Collection (tr). **111 Alamy Images** (br). **112 Dreamstime.com:** Zaretskaya (tl); **113 Corbis:** Robbie Jack (tr). **Corbis:** Facundo Arrizabalaga / epa (bl). **114 Corbis:** Bettmann (bl). **115 Getty Images:** Leemage (bl). **119 Corbis:** Historical Picture Archive (tr). **121 Corbis:** Robbie Jack (tr). **123 Corbis:** epa / Facundo Arrizabalaga (b). **125 Corbis:** Michael Nicholson (tr). **127 Corbis:** Neil Farrin / Robert Harding World Imagery (t). **128 Alamy Images:** Paul Springett 02 (tl). **129 Corbis:** Tim Brakemeier / epa (b). **130 Corbis** (bl). **131 Dreamstime.com:** Georgios Kollidas (tr). **135 Corbis:** (tr). **139 Corbis:** Hulton-Deutsch Collection (bl). **Alamy Images:** Prisma Archivo (tr). **140 Getty Images:** Hulton Archive / Culture Club (tl). **141 Alamy Images:** Geraint Lewis (tr). **143 Corbis:** Christie's Images (br). **144 Corbis:** Smithsonian Institution (tr). **Corbis:** Robbie Jack (bl) **145 Corbis:** Hulton-Deutsch Collection (tr). **146 John Springer Collection** (bl). **149 Corbis:** dpa / Uwe Zucchi (b). **150 Getty Images:** National Galleries Of Scotland (t). **151 Alamy Images:** Moviestore collection Ltd (tr). **Corbis:** Robbie Jack (bl). **154 Corbis:** Reuters / Heinz-Peter Bader (bl). **Getty Images:** AFP / Anne-Christine Poujoulat (tr). **157 Alamy Images:** Geraint Lewis (tr). **159 Corbis:** Bettmann (tr); Leemage (bl). **160 Corbis:** The Print Collector (tl). **162 Corbis:** San Francisco Chronicle / Katy Raddatz (t). **163 Corbis:** The LIFE Picture Collection / William Sumits (tr). **165 Corbis:** Bettmann (br). **166 Corbis:** Bettmann (bl). **167 Dreamstime.com:** Csaba Peterdi (br). **169 Corbis:** Christie's Images (tr). **171 Alamy Images:** Geraint Lewis (br). **172 Alamy Images:** Geraint Lewis (tl). **173 Getty Images:** Universal History Archive / UIG via Getty Images (tr). **175 Alamy Images:** The Art Archive (bc). **176 Alamy Images:** Geraint Lewis (t). **178 Dreamstime.com:** Dennis Dolkens (tr). **179 Corbis:** Stapleton Collection (b). **181 Alamy Images:** INTERFOTO (tr). **Corbis:** Robbie Jack (bl). **183 Alamy Images:** dpa picture alliance archive (tr). **184 Getty Images:** DEA / M. SEEMULLER (bl). **189 Getty Images:** Universal History Archive / UIG via Getty Images (bl). **192 Alamy Images:** Geraint Lewis (tr). **193 Dreamstime.com:** Yakov Stavchansky (tr). **195 Corbis:** Lebrecht Music & Arts (tc). **196 Corbis:** Nik Wheeler (b). **198 Corbis** (b). **199 Alamy Images:** Mary Evans Picture Library (tc).

All other images © Dorling Kindersley.
For more information see:
www.dkimages.com